The Last Civil War Scout
The Diaries and Letters of Colonel Given Campbell, CSA

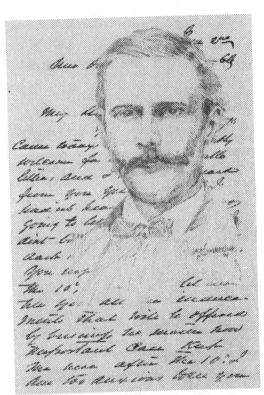

Wayne Wolf

Jack Simmerling

Paul Faeh
South Suburban College

McGraw-Hill, Inc.
College Custom Series

*New York St. Louis San Francisco Auckland Bogotá
Caracas Lisbon London Madrid Mexico Milan Montreal
New Delhi Paris San Juan Singapore Sydney Tokyo Toronto*

LENOIR-RHYNE COLLEGE

McGraw-Hill's College Custom Series consists of products that are produced from camera-ready copy. Peer review, class testing, and accuracy are primarily the responsibility of the author(s).

The Last Civil War Scout
The Diaries and Letters of Colonel Given Campbell, CSA

1 2 3 4 5 6 7 8 9 0 HAM HAM 9 0 9 8 7 6 5 4

ISBN 0-07-071524-6

Editor: Reaney Dorsey
Cover Illustration: Jack Simmerling
Cover Designer: Maggie Lytle
Printer/Binder: HAMCO Corporation

SOLDIER-LAWYER OF RENOWN
STRICKEN AFTER RETIREMENT

The original photograph of Given Campbell which accompanied his obituaries in the papers of St. Louis on November 21, 1906. His testimonial reads in part, "Mr. Campbell was in charge of the escort for Mr. Davis and was with the head of the 'lost cause' nearly up to the time of the capture of Davis. . . . About twelve hours before the capture President Davis requested Mr. Campbell, as head of the escort, to leave him."

Dedication

To the unsung heroes who have made it possible for me to complete this project: my wife, Lynn, my parents Joseph and Vivian Wolf, and two stalwarts Smiley and Doodle

Wayne L. Wolf

Acknowledgments

The authors would like to extend a special thank you to the following students of history that helped in the endless hours of transcription necessary to produce this book: Leeann Atwood-Sanders, Diane Augustyniak, Bobby Burton, Patricia Childers, Judy Fields, Barbara Goeske, Jacqueline Guillan, Dennis Hancock, Judith Nebel and Madge Russell. Our sincere appreciation for your time and efforts.

Introduction

Over two decades ago Jack Simmerling and Donald O'Toole discovered several caches of family letters and documents in an old house on Prairie and Indiana Avenues in Chicago, Illinois. This discovery began the long trek of transcribing and organizing the hundreds of these letters of the Bryson, Woods, Wilkerson and Campbell families. This book is a culmination of a portion of that research as it chronicles the life and letters of Col. Given Campbell, and his wife Elizabeth (sue) Bettie Woods, stalwarts in the cause of the Confederate States of America.

Very few original diaries of Civil War date exist. Yet, the authors were privileged to have two complete ones to include in this book. The first was Given Campbell's kept from Dec. 1860 - Dec. 1861. This extensive diary provides a fascinating account of Mr. Campbell's early law practice, the political events of Kentucky and Missouri as the inevitable war crept ever closer, and Given's account of his ardent courting of Miss Elizabeth (sue Bettie) Woods, the daughter of a prominent St. Louis merchant. The colorful descriptions, local events, and personal glimpses create for the reader a sense of being in ante-bellum Missouri, going through the daily trials & tribulations, and pursuing young love in the chivalrous South. The second diary was kept by both Sue Bettie and Given from January to June 1866. It chronicles the hard months immediately after the South surrendered, the burden of Southern Reconstruction, Sue Bettie's illness, and their long separation while she is convalescing. It too transports the reader to the heyday of New Orleans' French Quarter and Garden District, the strange medicinal cures of the day, the relaxed Southern life style among the magnolias and oleanders, and romantic love in the Southern tradition.

Between these two diaries is the amazing war correspondence of the Campbells and their families. The rigors of Civil War camp life, the loneliness of a soldier's existence, personal glimpses of Generals Hood, Wheeler, Morgan, Forrest and Blair, and the emotions of a young, betrothed couple separated by four long years of genocide provide a romantic love story told by the couple themselves through their original letters, containing all of the unedited grammatical errors, punctuation eccentricities, and misspellings. Several of the original letters and diary entries have been reproduced in the book so that the reader can gain a personal insight of, and acquaintance with, this young Southern couple. And finally, we must extend to the unnamed relatives over the last century that preserved these letters so that a previously untold piece of the Civil War could be related our sincere thanks and historical appreciation.

Wayne L. Wolf
Paul Feah
Jack Simmerling

Given Campbell: A Short Biography

Given Campbell was born December 1st, 1835 at Salem, Livingston County, Kentucky of James and Mary (Given) Campbell, both of whom resided for many years at Paducah, Kentucky. Given spent the years of his boyhood and early youth in Paducah. His grandfather, James Campbell, was a native of the Parish of Breadalbane, Perthshire, Scotland and one of the Ardkinglas branch of the Campbell family who emigrated to Petersburg, Virginia and fought in the wars of the revolution and 1812. His paternal grandmother, Marie Jeane Victoire de la Porte (daughter of General De la Porte) was a refugee from France during the "Reign of Terror," who also settled in Virginia. On the maternal side Mr. Campbell sprang from the Givens of South Carolina, descendants of one of Marion's gallant band, and the Davis family of Kentucky.

Given Campbell received his college education at Center College, Danville, Kentucky and went to the University of Virginia during the years 1855-1857, where he graduated in law, receiving his B.L. Degree there. He came to St. Louis in 1857, was examined and admitted to the bar by Judge James R. Lackland. He practiced law with success until 1861 when he became Captain of Co. G. "Dixie Guards," in the Second Regiment of Missouri Infantry commanded by Colonel John S. Bowen. He was with his company at Camp Jackson when the troops under General Frost surrendered to General Lyon. He was later unconditionally released by General Frank P. Blair (his second cousin), and then entered the army under General Sterling Price, continuing in the Confederate service until the close of the war. He served in the cavalry under Generals Morgan and Forrest and later under General Wheeler, leaving the army with the rank of Colonel. After the war he talked little of his army record but his fellow soldiers referred to him as a gallant and distinguished officer who saw a great many hard campaigns and fought in numerous battles throughout Missouri, Tennessee, Kentucky and Georgia. He was in command of the cavalry escort of Jefferson Davis until a few hours before the President's capture. Jefferson Davis, in his memoirs, speaks of the readiness of "Captain Campbell" and his entire command to render any service needed in behalf of himself or the cause he represented.

A brief leave of absence granted him by General Wheeler enabled him, on January 26th, 1865, to marry Susan Elizabeth (Sue Bettie) Woods who he had been engaged to since before the war. They were married at Tuscaloosa, Alabama while

Sue Bettie was visiting relatives. Miss Woods was the daughter of Robert K. and Susan Woods of St. Louis. This connection prompted Given to return to St. Louis shortly after his parole on June 8th, 1865 with the intention of resuming his legal practice. He found this impossible however because of the rigid enforcement of the "Test Oath," and set out for New Orleans where he quickly resumed practicing law and took a leading position at the bar and an active part in public affairs, including being a delegate to the Democratic Convention of 1872.

Given returned to St. Louis in the fall of 1873 and resumed a thriving and lucrative law practice which saw him try numerous cases and rise to the position of Vice-President of the St. Louis Bar Association. He continued to practice law until November 13, 1905 when the Bar Association hosted a farewell retirement dinner for him at Southern Hotel. From there he moved to his retirement home near Paducah, Kentucky. His retirement however was to be brief. After a short illness, he died at the home of his son, Dr. Given Campbell of 3429 Morgan Street, St. Louis, on Tuesday, November 20, 1906. He was buried in Bellefontaine Cemetery on Thursday, November 22, 1906.

Given Campbell's last will and testament, executed July 1, 1885, instructed his wife, Susan Elizabeth, to invest $100 in a watch for each of his children. The balance of his estate was left to his wife as he stated, "I bestow my blessing upon my children and wish them at all times to love, cherish and honor their dear mother and each other, and to look to their mother, in whom I have implicit faith and confidence, for counsel and advice in every contingency of life." Given was survived by his wife and three children: Dr. Given Campbell, James C. Campbell, a member of the St. Louis Bar, and Mrs. Albert D. Evans.

Mr. Thompson, a member of the St. Louis Bar, in a speech given shortly after his death, tried to sum up the community's feelings toward Given Campbell in the following lines:

> "His life was gentle and the elements
> So mix'd in him that Nature might stand up
> And say to the world, 'This was a man....' "

Part One

The Private Journal of
Given Campbell, Capt.
20th Kentucky Regiment
of Volunteers, C.S.A.

PRIVATE

Brief Journal from Dec. 1st, 1860 to Dec. 1st, 1861
Given Campbell
Paducah, Kentucky

An ambrotype of Sue Bettie Woods taken when she was 20 years old in a palmetto cap

A wonderful early photograph of Given Campbell Jr. and Susie Campbell when they were aged 12 and 7 respectively. The photo was taken by F.W. Guerin of No. 627 Olive St., St. Louis, Mo.

Dec. 1st, 1860

To-day I was 25 years of age, Saturday December 1st, 1860. It was predicted by a stuttering mountebank several years ago, that this year would be the most eventful of my life, and from the indications it seems that the prediction will prove true. A great contest is on the eve of breaking out in this fair land whose end and effects no human kind can forsee. There will be a rapid dissatisfaction among all classes and sections, which the ensuing Congress will only face with open discord. The whole country North and South East and West is suffering the evil contest on this *political* panic, for there is no cause for *financial* panic. This day I paid a visit to a beautiful and refined young lady Miss Sue: Betty Woods. She is a lady of most lovely person and character, amiable *almost to a fault*.

2d Sunday.

To-day spent the morning with Dr. George T. Harrison in his office, on Locust near Eighth, in the afternoon went to Mr. Hutchinsons to dinner. At night paid up a few visits to my lady friends viz. Mrs. Bruce, Miss Churchill, Mr. McKinley.

Dec. 3d. 60 Monday.

Went to the Court House and had a cause continued, looked over a few papers in cases, came to my room (office) and read several passages in Herodotus in Euterpe, it is entertaining to compare ancient institutions with the modern ones of the same state, and the mind can find no better employment than studying the future from the *past*, nothing unusual today.

4th. Tuesday.

Remained in my office the most of the day and brought several suits for the Feb. S. of Circuit Court at night by special invitation went to the club party the "Saint Louis Social Club." There were, Mr. Smith at whose house it was given, Miss Mary Mitchell, Miss Churchill, Mr. Dangen, the beautiful widow, Miss Schaumburg, Miss Chambers, Misses Coleman, (grand daughters of Mr. L. Crittendon) and many others I was very much pleased with the party and made myself appreciable to Miss Mitchell. Many of my old friends were there.

5th Wednesday.

Nothing of interest transpired to day.

1860   1

Dec

1st To-day I was 25 years of age — Saturday
December 1st 1860. It was predicted by a
strolling mountebank several years ago
that this year would be the most
eventful of my life. And from
the indication it seems that
the prediction will prove true —
a great contest is on the eve of
breaking out in this fair land
where end & effect no human ken
can foresee. There will be a rapid
dissatisfaction among all classes &
section, which the ensuing congress
will only fan into open discord.
The whole country north & south east
& west is suffering the evils consequent on
this political panic, for there
is no cause for financial panic
This day I paid a visit to a beautiful & refined young lady Miss
Sue; Betty Woods. She is a lady of
most lovely person & character —
amiable almost to a fault

2d Sunday. To-day spend the morning
with Dr. George Y. Harrison in his
office on Second near Eighth, in
the afternoon wrote to Mr. Hutcheson
to Virnice at night paid up a few
visits to my lady friends viz.,
Mrs. Bruce, Miss Churchie, M. McKaity

3ᵈ

Dec. .60 Monday. Went to the court House &
had a cause continued. Looked
over a few papers in cases
Came to my room (office) and
read several passages in Herodotus
in Euterpe. It is interesting to
Compare ancient institutions with
the modern ones of the same state.
The mind Can feed no better on
Employment than Studying the future
from the past. Nothing unusual
to day,

4ᵗ Tuesday. Remained in my office the
most of the day & brought several
Suits for the Feb T. of circuit Court.
At night by special invitation went
to ~~the~~ Club party the "Saint Louis So-
=cial Club". There were, Mrs Smith at
Whose house it was given, Miss Mary
Mitchell. Miss Churchill, Mrs Dwyer
the beautiful Widow, Miss Schaumburg,
Miss Chambers. Misses Coleman, (grand daugh
ters of Jno. L. Crittenden) and many others
I was very much pleased with the
party truine very self especially to
Miss Mitchell. Many of my old friends
were there —

5ᵗ Wednesday — Nothing of interest trans-
=pired to day,

6th Thursday.

Came to office at 9 A.M. & read the papers, the Republican & Bulletin and Democrat, read the Pr. Buchanans Message to Senate & House, his views about voluntary secession being an unquestioned right of a state, I mean his denial of that right is correctly stated but his reasoning to prove the fact that a state has no right to decide I do not agree with. He involves himself in a difficulty when he comes to the question of coercion. His place for the compromise as set out in his message is as good as I should desire for the South, but my opinion is that the North will not agree to his terms—last night I went to see Miss Sue Betty—and found out that she had been told about my having given Anne Patterson a lock of my hair. This circumstance annoyed me very much, and it also learned me a lesson, i.e. never to allow a woman, other than a wife or near and dear relative, to have the power to wound your sensibilities. Now this lock of my hair was repeatedly requested from me by this Miss Patterson, and was repeatedly refused, and when I asked her what she wanted with it, she said that it was because she really wanted it. And because she, she wanted it she asked for it. I told her I thought it was to make fun of & to add to her collection of such things. She swore it was not her motive &c. It needs not this to remind me that treachery often lurks beneath a fair exterior. Went to Restaurant de Paris, cor. of Walnut and 5th & ate dinner in company with our regular mess., Dr. Michel, Mayrant, Pollard, Dr. Hawes, Dr. Harrison, politics the theme of conversation, all of us are strong States Rights & Secessionists as for me I believe in a demand of redress of grievances & additional guaranties for the South and unless these are conceded by the North then Secession. At night went to see Miss Mary Mitchell, returned about 10 ½.

7th. Friday.

Nothing new to-day. Had a long talk with Proventicia Gustave and in the afternoon got right tight on Rhine Wine, unintentionally, went home & at night went to see Miss Molly Martin from Nashville, Tennessee at Samuel Kirkmans.

8th.

To-day had a bad headache and neuralgic eye ache.

Dec. 60

Transacted very little business. Was sad & despondent. In the afternoon went to see Miss Sue Betty Woods and took a walk. It was a glorious afternoon. The weather was very balmy & pleasant. Explained to her about that "lock of hair" satisfactorily. Had a very pleasant walk & visit and came away at 6½ P.M. At night paid a visit to Miss Nisbet.

9th. Sunday.

To day went to hear Mr. Brooks preach his farewell sermon previous to his departure for Europe for his throat he was so unwell he could not preach, and his place was filled by another, who delivered a good Sermon on the resurrection. At church saw Miss Bettiw W. with a lovely dress (Southern manufacture). At night went to the German opera.

13th. Thursday.

Nothing transpired today.

14th. Friday.

Last night went by invitation to reception of the Laclede Club & had a pleasant time.

15th. Saturday.

This passed till evening then attended a caucus to organize a basis of action for a States Rights Party, and to organize "Minute Men."

16th. Sunday.

The soldiers came back today from the Southwest. They looked soiled & travel-stained like veterans. Went to Mr. Brooks church to hear Dr. Plumer. He is a fine preacher & is great on *illustration.* After church walked home with Miss Sue Betty— a lovely girl—after noon took a walk with her, was charmed.

17th. Monday.

To day, South Carolina calls her convention to determine whether she will go out or remain in the Federal Union, a great day in the destinies of this Republic. The times are very dull. No trade and Exchange ruling from 10 to 15 percent on the East—None on the South, the country is fast drifting to her crisis. For several days till 21st I have not much to note, except that I increased my attentions to Miss Sue Bettie.

Dec. 21.

Started to Ky. to day and rem$\underline{d}$. there till Dec. 31. Was at home on Christmas. Florence was sick but was convalescent when I left.

January 1, 1861

To-day I went to see the following persons—
Mr. Dr. Smith. Miss Mitchell staying there,
Mr. L. D. Coalter. F.A. Dick,
Mr. N. Valli, L.A. Buwish,
Miss Shaw, M.A. Pallen, Dr.
Ringbiess (Miss Puss Hunt)
Mr. Charles Belcher, Mr. N.B. Taylor
Mr. Andrew Woods (Misses Irwin and Martin)
Dr. Hutchinson, McKinley, J.B. Alexanders,
Dr. Kennard, E.M. Bruces
Tom Days (Miss Helen), Miss Hunton
Logan Hunton, Miss Nisbet,
J. Sturgeon, Mr. T. Page
Sonlards, Rudolph, Tompkins
Patterson, Pope, Dean's, Mr. R.K. Woods,
R. Campbell, Mr. W. Wills, Jno. Wickham, Hugh Campbell, D.A. January, F.P. Blairs, and after having finished I then went to Samuel Kirkmans, and sent in my card for Miss Sue Betty W, who was not receiving calls and she came into the parlor and then I stayed for supper—or rather dinner—and after tea went with her to Mr. Andy Woods, and then went to Mr. N.B. Taylors to a party and had a delightful time with Miss Mary Mitchell.

Jan. 2d.

Came to office with some letters and then went out paying bills. (For list of Bills paid see last page of this book). Went to see Dr. Hawes. He was sick with erysipelas. After tea went to Mr. Andy Wood's to bid Miss Martin and Miss Moore goodbye. Miss Mollie Martin is one of the most brilliant women I know of. I enjoyed myself very much and had a pleasant visit.

While there saw Miss S.B.W. and asked her to go to concert with me. She agreed to do so, as I bade Miss Charlotte Irwin goodbye she asked me when she was "to have me for a nephew." Came home and retired. Last evening had a severe touch of Rheumatism.

Author's Note: The list of bills referred to on January 2nd has been reproduced on the following page.

Jan'y 1st 1860 —

Paid for overcoat to Mullin &
wood —   13.00

Pd Lewis & Graham clerk a
receipt Hal bill for 1860 17.00

Mr Hoard bill & receipt for it 8.50

Pd Dr Hammon ʃ on acct — 5.00

Pd Gardins bill & receipt for it 23.50

Sundries   3.00
                                 ———————
                                  70.00

Over went 106.00, Jan 3rd 2 45 — Bal 31.
Oct. Lory   8.00 $3—

Our Mother 5.00
" Florence 3.00 — Pd

Gilson   10.00

Paul   8.00 Pd — Jan 3d —
Walter   3.00 Pd watson 2,
Lewis   17.00 " — 15

              153.00
              148.00
Balance —   20.00
                8.00
              10.00
              20.00
             $15.00

Jan. 3d.

To-day nothing of interest transpired except that in the evening I went to the Opera Concert at St. Louis Opera House with Miss S.B.W. to hear Madame Fabri in her diff.^t *Roles*. I had a delightful time and was very well pleased with the young lady.

Jan. 4th.

To day nothing new transpired at night went to bid two of my friends Misses Coleman goodbye, and afterwards went to see Miss Mary Mitchell. There met Col. Hay. Had a pleasant visit and was invited to take tea next evening. The weather clear and delightful. At night clouded but cleared off again.

Jan. 5th.

Saturday. To day was beautiful and warm. Nothing new transpired. Went to Miss Mary Mitchell and at tea learned that Eugene Longenmane had forged largely and had absconded—After left went in company with two gentlemen to see Danl. R. Russell, the Commissioner of the States of Mississippi to Missouri. He is a sensible man & a strong Southern Rights man. He argues plausibly for separate secession—in afternoon went up to see Miss S.B.W. & made up my mind to play on the slake-a-heart and was if I can win it.

Jan'y 6. Sunday.

To day rose late. Ate breakfast at the Restaurant de Paris and came to Planters House. Saw several friends after twelve went out into the country and there saw Miss Mitchell and Miss Berry and Col. Mitchell and was very delightfully entertained by Mr. & Mrs. Goode. Came home. The weather was pleasant and warm in the morning but sloppy & disagreeable at noon & in the afternoon—

Jan'y 7th.

News today from Washington is very dark & ominous. The B. Republicans of the North agree to no agreement which would operate as a compromise of the principles on the slavery question. The Devil seems to have taken possession of the people & the decree seems to have gone. Birth Ephriam is joined to his idols while alone—for a little Brotherly Love & a little concession to the injured South would heal this sad breach, but alas the future holds out no lamp to light our path to peace & happiness. The weather is damp & cloudy. Mr. B. Gough, The Great Temperance orator, lectured to-night at there Lila's Hall. Court commenced to-day, after a vacation of two weeks. Geo. W. Goode told me to-day that he had cause to believe that T.A. Davis his agent had left here & absconded with many belonging to him (Goode).

Nothing of interest transpired till night when after having gone to the Laclede Club I attended a meeting of "Minute Men." The purpose of the meeting was to organize. Col. McClanen was elected President. The way that the matters were conducted was not satisfactory to me. These officers did not have weight and influence enough. After that went to Dr. Michels Room & he made some French coffee. Mayrant my Roommate was there & pretty drunk, & very funny. Several speeches were made by M.R. Cullen, Wm. M. Cooke, Jas. George, B.W. Duke &c.

Jan. 8th, 61.

Nothing of interest today. The weather uncertain and cloudy & sunny by bits. Brought suit to-day against Wm. A. Barksdale & Co. for $10,000 for Bk. of Louisville. No news of any interest from the Capitol. Discussion reluctant fast gaining ground. I have had a fair vision to flit before me several times today in the shape of an ideal Lady. S.B.W. will go & see her tonight. After dinner I left the Restaurant de Paris & went to the Laclede Club. After tea went to see Miss Bettie, found her at home. She came down & we had a very pleasant evening, till Mr. Memford came in and I left the Parlor went up to the Library to see Mr. Kirkman. Had a short conversation & after a few minutes returned to the Parlor. Miss Bettie had told Mr. M that she did not wish him to visit her & that she did not think his remarks about her "that she loved me and I did not love her" was gentlemanly &c. I came down. He was still there sitting up in an embarrassed attitude. He left in a few minutes & I had a delightful time till 11 P.M. and left. I came very near courting her but the fear of a refusal deterred me. I was told by her that she would never marry a man who had been refused by another and in the next breath she indicated that she had been informed that I had been rejected by Miss Anne Patterson. I made an engagement with her to go to church on Sunday night.

Jan. 9th.

Today mild and clear & cloudy by turns. Came to office & found that T.A. dawes had forged Mr. Goode's name on several papers (notes) & had absconded. Garland requested me to help him try a case in court. Agreed to do so but case deferred the next day. At night went with Miss Mary Mitchell to J. T. Leveringere and took tea. Had a pleasant time. R.R. Hutchinson took Miss Berry.

Jan. 10.

Nothing new today except news of the firing into the "Star of the West" by the Charlestown forts. Kirkman came & told me that he had a sister & cousins, a Miss Polk from *Tennessee* staying at his house & asked me up. I went up & had a pleasant visit. Miss K. is pleasant & aprecable but not handsome. Miss P. is very pretty & quite entertaining.

Jan. 11th.

Weather beautiful. Today U.S. troops took possession of the Caston House hence excitement among the people. No further matters of interest.

Jan. 12.

Weather beautiful & mild. Nothing new today with the exception of a monster Mass Union Meeting. The meeting was called under Black Republican auspices and the other parties hostile to Black Republicans took possession of the meeting and passed Resolutions indorsing the Crittendon Resolutions, an anti-coercion Resolution & a Convention Resolution. The Resolutions were unanimously adopted. Anticipations of a riot existed, but the meeting was very quick and orderly. The Black Republicans took no part in it. At night went to Geo. T. Harrisons room & drank punch with J.B. Cates, J.M. Brown, C.N. Hawes, D.C. Woods, H.A. Garland, and Dr. J.C. Bragg. Came home at 12. M. and retired.

Jan. 14. Sunday.

To. rose very unwell. Had my bowels very much deranged from the effects of something I had eaten the night before—rose at 9. Dressed myself, went to breakfast, was unwell all day. Went (9th and Chest.) to Rev. Mr. Brooks church. Heard a good sermon and walked home with Miss S.B. Woods to Samuel Kirkmans. Was asked in to dine by Mr. K. and as I was standing on the steps of her door I noticed the look which Miss S.B.W. gave me there was so much kindness & gentleness in it that, I felt that my cause was not hopeless. Declined to go, while on my way up home with her she told me she would start for Nashville, at the command of her mother, as soon as she could get an escort. (Her Father was sick there) & that she had an escort on Tuesday. I made up my mind to bring matters to a Crisis for it had been my intuition to address her for some time past. I went up to see her after tea and when her boy came to the door, I asked him if Miss Bettie was ready to go to church. He went in and told her and she said she would go.

Though it was damp under foot & threatened rain, we started & as we got outside of the door, the small rain drops began to fall. We went in to the parlor. No one was there, and sat down to wait for the rain to cease—Till it was too late to go to church. I remained and had a pleasant and delightful conversation, all the time endeavoring to bring the conversation into the right channel & get the proper feeling between us favorable to a declaration. I did not exercise my insecurity in vain, for after speaking of the influences of women on men for good, I said that if I was ever sure it wd. be through the instrumentality of a woman. I then related to her a dream which I had heard my father tell of himself, when living in Hopkinsville, the turning point of which was that as he was about to give up & be destroyed he was rescued by a ladies hand. I thought it not wrong to substitute myself in his place, and then I said to her that I thought the time had come when that helping hand should be stretched forth to meet me, and asked her in a meaning tone if she would do so. She said yes if she could be of any service to me in the way of saving me from impending ruin. I paused an instant, and then told her that I now took advantage of the opportunity to make a formal declaration of what my attentions for some time past must have indicated, that I loved her deeply & devotedly, that I had long loved her, that it was not a matter of a day or an hour that I had weighed the matter in my mind, and now I offered her my hand and heart. She was very much confused & looked down, saying no word. I asked her if they were accepted. She still passed, and the silence began to be very uncomfortable to me. I told her that I would like to hear my fate, she said that I had taken her by surprise, that she had heard all persons say that I was in love with Miss Anne Patterson. I told her that if that was the only obstacle in the way I could soon remove it, for that I had not a spark of love for Anne P—and I knew myself that far. She told me that all persons had told her so, and that she had not looked upon me as an admirer. I then told her that I knew I was not fully worthy of her but that if the Lord spared my health, it should not be many years till the time would come where she would not be ashamed to have her name connected with mine. She replied in a blushing modest manner, that she "never would be ashamed of such a connection." I thought the voice and the name were the sweetest I had ever heard. I asked her then if she would accept me. She gave me her hand. I was blinded & deep sense of satisfaction crept over me. We then went on the talk as young people would be supposed to do with like circumstances. She told me that she did not think she was the kind of woman to make me happy, that she had not the cultivation necessary, that I ought to marry a girl of a different mind. I told her that I was perfectly satisfied with her and that there was no need for her to be finding fault with herself. But before this matter was consummated she told me that she had heard me say that I would court a lady I did not love upon a consideration of honor & that if that had any operating influence on this matter she wanted to know it. I told her that I had never considered the question of honor, but only my inclinations (which was true). She also told me that if I ever felt any return of the old feeling, I should tell her. I told her I would. I remained about half an hour longer & when I parted she permitted me to seal the engagement with a kiss on her fair forehead. I was unwell when I went & when I left was well & light hearted. In all the whole affair she displayed great delicacy and consideration of herself and for me and in her suggestion, that she was not suited to make me happy. I could discover the self sacrificing spirit of a devoted Christian & a true woman. The brightest day, the day *marked with* a white pebble.

Jan. 15.

To-day was the darkest day of the winter. I went to Dr. Harrisons office and confided to him my engagement & he was very glad, thought I was in luck. I went to A & M Gardner & ordered $150 ring for the engagement ring. After tea went up to Kirkmans, went into the parlor, saw Miss Polk & Miss Kirkman & also my own *fiancee.* Had no opportunity of speaking to her apart. She told me she would leave for Nashville on Wednesday, bid them good night & left.

To-day gloomy & rainy. No news from the Seat of Govt. Telegraph wires down or not working. At 12.M. went up to see Bettie, remained there an hour and ½. Had a delightful morning call. She goes on evening of the 17th to Nashville in company with a Mr. She promised me her daguerrotype. I had a deep satisfaction in my position & before I left she promised me that she would read everyday some in a history, told her goodbye and left. Came to office, transacted some business & then went to dinner. Went to my room and retired at 10½.

Jan. 16. Wednesday.

Waked this morning and snow on the ground. Weather cloudy and damp. Came to office. Did a little business. At 2. PM went to Gardner and got the Engagement Ring, paid him $60.00 on it in Mo. money, got my ambrotype taken and at 3. PM went to Mr. Kirkmans to see her. Remained there a short time and had a delightful conversation, gave her the ring & daguerrotype & also returned to her the daguerrotype of her cousin Miss Hamilton. She gave me her picture, taken some two years ago; not a good one, and at my departure she permitted me to kiss her fair bright brow. I went over the River with her in the omnibus and remained in the cars till they left. Bid her goodbye. Came home, with a prayer on my lips for her safe journey & health to him and hers. At night went to my room, read several letters & then went to sleep.

Jan' y 17.

Weather warm & cloudy. No news today of consequences except increasing tariffs of the anticompromise spirit of the Black Republicans, commenced my course of studies again & have determined to read every day at least 30 pages of law. In evening gave an old lady a dollar on the ground of her being a Kentuckian & being in distress, and went security for two dollars for her baggage. At night went to see Miss Kirkman & Miss Polk. Took Mayrant up with me, remained a short time. When we came out the snow had whitened the ground, came home & retired to rest.

Jan. 18.

Rose earlier than usual. Took some medicine prepared by Dr. G.T. Harrison, came to my office, and went to the Restaurant de Paris to breakfast as the Club dining is discontinued. The weather is clear and warm, though snow has clothed the earth in a mantle of white. Paid 4 visits tonight, Miss Churchill, Miss Hunton (at McKinleys), Miss Nisbet, Miss Mitchell.

Jan'y 19.

Saturday. Weather delightful & warm. Nothing new today-but I wrote for the first time to my *fiancee, my little Bettie*, at Nashville, Tenn. Care of *Mr. James Woods*.

Jan. 20.

Today was Sunday. Went to hear Revd. Dr. Gundy at Mr. Brooks Church, corn. of 5th & Walnut. He preached a fine sermon. Walked home from church with Miss Kirkman. Ate dinner at Restaurant de Paris & at 3. started to Mr. Goode's. The day was delightful and the ride agreeable. I went with Dr. Harrison. We went also to Col. Churchills near Goodes, and remained about half hour. Took tea ot Goode's. No news to-day. My mind has settled down into the profound conviction that there may be a temporary fix up of the troubles in the States, but no permanent reestablishment of good feeling among the States & that within the years a dissolution of the Union is inevitable, for Brotherly Love, which is in the great land of our union, has long died out.

Jan. 21. Monday.

Day was beautiful and mild. Attended to a good deal of business to-day, and read law and general literatures. I am beiginning now, once again, to get back into the close & studious habits of my past life, no incident occurred of any interest. At night went to the meeting of the "National Guards," an Engineer Corps. for the first time & took a drill. Came to Dr. Harrisons Room & then went home and retired.

Jan. 22.

This morning the weather was beautiful & clear. D.G. Fowler at Planters House arrived yesterday from Paducah. Dr. Boreland also came down from Lincoln yesterday. Commenced reading Abbot on Shipping and to-day looked anxiously for a letter from *Bettie W. my all-* was invited to Mr. Clarks on Pine Street to meet some young ladies, and went up, and saw Miss Porter of St. Charles, Misses Alexander, daughters of J.B. Alexander, and others. Mr. J.H. Terrell was here to-day. The night was beautiful & the morn shone beautifully, but the wind shifted to the East, which in this climate nearly always brings bad weather. I was disappointed in not having a letter from home today and also from Nashville.

Jan'y 23. Wednesday.

This morning broke upon us cloudy and damp weather, looked like rain. The political skies are more cloudy. Georgia seceded on last Saturday. Ky. Legislature passed on 22nd Resolutions pledging the State to resist invasion of the Southern States, by the North. At all hazards & to the East Extremity. A.R. McNain comes into my office every day & seems to be riding a hobby, he has, so he says, discovered hydraulic power which he says will do away with steam. He says that if he can get capital he can make a machine of immense power to act only by water. Still water, he talks a great deal about it. Invited to go up to Dr. Mr. & Mrs. Pallens to a masque party, a small one. Election of Captain and 3d. Lieutenants to-night in National Guards. Drizzling rain this evening-wind from the East. At night went to Dr. Mr. & Mrs. Pallens to masque party. Had a very pleasant time with my lady acquaintances & among the rest A.L.P. Have never ceased to congratulate myself that I did not marry her. She is a woman of bad heart & contemptible character.

Jan'y 24th.

Last night about 11 oclock the snow commenced to fall and it was a heavy fall for about 2. hours or three hours, about 4. inches. This morning was clear & cold. Philharmonic Concert to night.

Jan'y 25.

Nothing strange transpired to-day. At night went to drill of National Guards.

Jan'y 26th.

To-day at 10. PM Louisiana Convention passed ordinance of Secession. Nothing of remark today.

Jan'y 27.

Today was beautiful but cold and at 11. o'clock went out in Mr. G.W. Goode's carriage with Miss Mitchell (Mary) and Miss Berry and Dr. Harrison. Had a very pleasant day. Came in Mr. G's Buggy. The ladies remained in the country. At night Dr. H. and myself paid several calls, and found only one young lady at home—Miss Camelia Dean.

Jan'y 28. Monday.

The day dawned clear and warm, but about 12. it clouded. The thaw to-day was the source of a great deal of mud.

Political indications are yet very dark & ominous for the peace & entirety of this govt. As yet I have had no letter from Miss Bettie. It has now been nearly 10 days since I wrote & no reply. I am hardly inclined to believe that it can be negligence & carelessness. There must be some good reason for her silence. Her father as I am informed is very much worse and the whisper is current that he may never arise from his bed, but this his dissolution is imminent. God forbid! For the society of this city can't afford to lose such members as R.K. Woods. It would be hard to extinguish the few honorable lights at this time. Went at night to drill at Natnl. Guards, 1st Company, Captain Hazeltine. No letter from Bettie yet.

Jan'y 29.

Day was beautiful and warm and air balmy and mild. No political news of any consequence. A split in the Democratic Party in this state is widening. The Pure States Rights Democrats held a caucus at Jeff. City on Saturday night & nominated Jas. L. Green for Senator of Mo. in Congress. The Douglass democracy bolted the caucus & will not vote further. Parsons, in the Senate of Mo., takes strong Southern ground. He is for secession & advocates the cause totally. I went to night to see Miss Polk & Miss Sallie Kirkman. Left at 11. PM.

Jan'y 30.

Day dawned clear & beautiful but very cold. Came to office at 7 ¾ & went to breakfast at 8. at Rest. de Paris. Came to office. Nothing of interest transpired. Heard last night that Mr. Woods was better. Am reading Abbot on Shipping, & Clarendons Hist. of the Rebellion—no letter today.

Jan'y 31.

Dies infaustus commence. This morning I received a letter from Miss S.B. Woods, Nashville, Tenn. I was rejoiced when I saw the superscription "Nashville"—but when I opened it and read it, my heart sunk within me, and bitterness overflowed my heart. I feel stunned. The blow came like a Thunderbolt in a clear sky. She went on to say that she loved me, but that she, in obedience to her fathers wish (who was very ill), felt it to be her duty to ask me to release her from her promise. I read this letter with care & pain and answered it, telling her I could not do so under the circumstances but I left the whole matter to her. She could do it but I would not, as the reason was that her father did not desire her to be engaged to any one. I am surprised to hear this.

1861

Jan'y 28 10 days since I wrote — no reply, I am
hardly inclined to believe that it
can be negligence & carelessness there
must be some good reason for his
silence. The father as I am informed is
very much worse & the whisper is current
that he may never arise from his bed but that
his dissolution is imminent. God forbid it
for the society of this city could ill afford
to lose such members as R. K. Woods, It
would be hard to extinguish the few
honorable lights at this time —
went at night to drill at Nat'nl Guards,
1st Company, Captain Hazeltines —
no letter from Bettie, yet.

Jan'y 29 Day was beautiful, warm &
air balmy & mild. No Political news
of any consequence — a split in the
democracies party in this State is widening
the Pure States Rights Democrats held a
caucus at Jeff City on Saturday night &
nominated Jas. S. Green for Senator of
Mo. in Congress. The Douglas democracy
bolted the Caucus since not vote for him
Parsons, in the Senate of Mo. takes strong Southern
ground. he is for secession & advocates
— the Course with.
I went to night to see Miss Polk &
Miss Sallie Kirkman, left at
11. PM

1861

Jan'y 30. Day dawned clear & beautiful
but very cold — came to office
at 7¾ & went to breakfast at
8. at Rest— Dr Paris — came to office
Nothing of interest transpired,
heard last night that M— Woods
was better, am reading Abbott
on Shipping. & Clarendons Hist
of the Rebellion — no letter today—

Jan'y 31. Dies nefastá commence — this morning
I received a letter from Miss S. B
Woods, Nashville Tenn. I was re-
=joiced when I saw the super-
=scription "Nashville" — but when
I opened it & read it, my heart sunk
within me. and bitterness overflowed
my heart. I felt stunned, the
blow came like a thunderbolt
in a clear sky, she went on to
say that she loved me, but that
she in obedience to her father's
wish (who was very ill) felt it
to be her duty to ask me to
release her from her promise,
I read this letter with care & pain
+ answered it, telling her I could
not do so, under the circumstan-
=ces but I left the whole matter

1861

Feb 1 when the large centre stone fell upon
the floor, and the floor was cov⁻ with
sawdust, I looked for it in vain &
could not find it. I was troubled in
my dream, on acct of the omen, &
waked to find it a dream, which fore-
-told to me the deed which was to
be attempted that day, to withdraw
the Centre gear from me — I expect a
letter from her,

I have commenced the day with a new
stock of resolution — and now I feel the
stimulating influences of my recovering
will & its encouraging & cheering words
have made me, myself again. —
she loves me. If this is so, I will marry
her if I live & she lives also. —
I endeavored to draw my mind
from its own distress by the un-
=usual immersion in business
& partially succeeded, at night
went to Armory of N. G. & drilled, —
after went to my room & opened my
trunk read her letter & looked at
her picture & my heart was again
sad, retired at 11.

Feb 2 Rose at 8. came to my office & read
the papers, the weather is slushy &
rainy,

1861

Feb 2d — Nothing new today. At night the States
Rights Democracy held a meeting
to appt delegates to a convention
to nominate Officers Candidates —
to the Convention which is to
be held on the 28th at Jeff City
They passed a resolution that
they instructed their delegates
from (5th ward) to vote for no
man who would not pledge
himself to secession, in case
a compromise on the basis of
Crittendens Resolutions was
granted by the north. —
I did not attend this meeting —
as I do not desire to do anything which will damage me
politically, & the part of a wise man
is to seize the Golden opportunity
as it passes — this one has not
yet born in sight & at night
paid a visit to Miss Polk &
Miss Kirkman & afterwds
went to Mr N. H. Taylors with
Maynard, had a nice time
tho Miss Miller was particularly
unconvincing. —

Miss W. is old enough to be married, and the only way in which I can acct. for it (his objection) is a sick man's whine, or a profound selfishness, which would hazard his childs happiness, rather than see her love another more than him. He has no objection to me so he says. I admire the high and generous nature of the girl & her devotion & obedience to her parents, but the scripture is "obey your parents in the Lord" and I believe that the love she bears to me is the voice of God, which should not be choked. She says that in future when we meet if I choose to claim the fulfillment of her promise she will be prepared to do so, if her father is then willing. The balance of the day was wretchedly & miserably passed by me. Weather cloudy & cold in agreement with my feelings, so sad & cloudy.

Feb. 1, 1861.

Last night I read three chapters in the Bible & retired, sending up a short prayer for her I love. I am benefitted by these things. They stimulate the spirit of child-like reliance on a great supporting power—God— I had not prayed & read as much in the Bible, for many months. We know not the value of our Jwels, until we are about to lose them & I did not know the depth of my love for her until I am in danger of losing her. This matter was singularly foretold to me by a dream a few nights ago, the very night before that the letter was written by her to me. I dreamed that I had procured a Diamond ring with three diamonds in it, one large one in the middle, & a smaller one on each side, and that the ring was for her. In the same connection I dreamed of her father & mother. I thought I had the ring in my hand, examining it when the larger centre stone fell upon the floor, and the floor was covd. with sawdust. I looked for it in vain & could not find it. I was troubled in my dream, on *acct. of the omen*, & waked to find it a dream, which foretold to me the deed which was to be attempted that day, to withdraw the centre from me. I expect a letter from her. I have commenced the day with a new stock of resolution—and now I feel the stimulating influences of my recovering will and its encouraging & cheering words have made me myself again. She loves me, if this is so, I *will marry her if I live & she lives also*. I endeavored to drive my mind from its own distress by the unusual immersion in business & partially succeeded. At night went to Armory of N.G. & drilled. After went to my room and opened my trunk. Read her letters and looked at her pictures and my heart was again sad. Retired at 11.

Feb. 2.

Rose at 8. Came to my office & read the papers. The weather is sloppy & rain. Nothing new today. At night the States Rights Democracy held a meeting to appt. delegates to a convention to nominate candidates to the Convention which is to be held on the 28th at Jeff. City. They passed a resolution that they instructed there delegates from (5th Ward) to vote for no man who would not pledge precisely to secession, in case a compromise on the basis of Crittendon's Resolutions was granted by the North. I did not attend this meeting as I do not desire to do anything which will damage me politically and the part of a wise man is to seize the Golden Opportunity *as it passes*—this one has not yet "Love in sight." At night paid a visit to Miss Polk & Miss Kirkman & afterwards went to Mr. N.B. Taylors with Margaret. Had a dull time for Miss Miller was peculiarly uninteresting.

Feb. 3rd. Sunday.

I went with Dr. Harrison on a long walk. Went into and examined the Catholic Church which (has just been completed) is situated on 7th Street near Chonteau Ave. Had an engagement to go with Miss Kirkman to church but she went off & did not wait for me as I was not punctual. Nothing transpired today. Day was beautiful but rather cold.

Feb. 4.

Day was beautiful & mild. Nothing new today—my mind is not so much troubled about the letter I had from Miss Bettie, as I have in a manner settled down to the belief that I will marry her any how. To-day Circuit Court commenced. Nothing of consequence done. Weather delightful.

Feb. 5.

Weather delightful. Nothing new transpired to day. At night went with J. B. Cates to see Misses Polk and Kirkman (at Samuel Kirkmans). I had a long conversation with Miss K & she seemed to indicate that she knew all about my affair with Miss S.B.W. & the objections by her father. She said that a struggle between contending emotions was going on in my bosom—I endeavored to find out & she said that she would not tell me what she knew. My inference was that R.K.W. had written to his sister Mrs. K. & she had told Miss K. I left unsatisfied & not in good spirits.

Feb. 6th.

Weather was spring-like. It was so mild & pleasant. Nothing transpired of interest to-day. I thought much about Bettie & was pained to learn from Mr. Lapsley that he (Lapsley) thought Mr. Woods had the consumption and that the reason why his abscess was not healed was because if it healed he would die of Lung disease. Dr. Michel who attended him here said he thought not, that he did not believe that he had consumption. No letter to-day. At night went to see Mr. Blair & Frank said that the

Unconditional Union Ticket headed by Gamble How &c. would be elected to the Convention from 7 to 10,000 majority. Frank says that if the State Secedes from the Union Mo: St. Louis will secede from Mo! & he says he will hang out & maintain the breach of the Union against the State & that St. Louis can resist and defy all the rest of the State. He is for combining the States who have seceded & says that the ticket before spoken of was nominated to knock in the head the fusion ticket & to break up the little league to fight the B. Republicans in the April Elections.

Feb. 7.

Last night it turned cold and to day was clear and cold. No news of consequence, except additional troops were sent here about 300, and Maj. Bell removed from the Arsenal and Capt. Levy put in his place. Maj. B. was favorable to the South and he was removed. No letter from Bettie yet. At night went to a masquerade party at Dr. M.A. Pallen's. I went about 12 M. in citizens dress, had a delightful time. While there I met Miss Polk dressed beautifully. She was by all odds la reine de bat masque. Miss Patterson was also there as a Dutch woman & also as a tambourine player. She was very gracious and polite, but the pill, though coated, was of poison still. Miss Bettie Thurston was there and many others. Retired at 3½.

Feb. 8th. Friday.

The weather spring like and beautiful. Nothing of interest transpired to-day. At night I paid a visit to Miss Polk and found some fools & remd. only a few minutes.

Feb. 9.

Weather mild & beautiful. Has the appearance of rain. Nothing of interest transpired today up to noon. I have compared them all to Miss S.B.W. & she reigns supreme *facile princeps*. At night I went with Dr. Harrison to some places of amusement.

Feb. 10. Sunday.

To day arose & took some coffee in my room and after that went to Post Office. Had 3 letters & among them one from Miss Bettie. I read it & it was short but to the point. She broke off the engagement, "for the present at any rate." The news very much distressed me. The reason she gave for it was because she was opposed to long engagements & because her father was opposed to long engagements, and the letter was written in a cool & strong style. I am certain that she has heard that I am attentive to Miss Polk & her exacting & jealous nature has made her write thus, under the influence of pique. I am not however discouraged, for if she really loves me, the breaking off of the engagement for the present while she is absent, is not so serious after all, for I feel certain that if she continues to love me, I will certainly marry her. She is Miss Woods *now* but before the end of the year 1861 she will be Mrs. Campbell, unless some great calamity over which I have no control intervenes. It is a short lived thing this thing of human happiness. It was 4 weeks today since we were engaged, and now it is broken off. I wrote to her a little to day, asking leave to come over to Nashville & see her. On yesterday the Southern Convention nominated & elected Jefferson Davis President of the provisional govt. and Alex.[d] H. Stevens of Geor, Vice Pr. Weather today was oppressively warm for the season. It rained last night & to night also. I did not go to church to-day. I had the blues horribly.

Feb. 11.

Day dawned beautifully. Weather clear and mild, but windy. Nothing of interest transpired in our local affairs. To-day I had a settled sadness that the weather could not drive away. At night went with Dr. Michel to see Mr. Andrew Woods. Did not find her at home. Miss Sweringen (from Ill.) and Miss Julia Barret we found at Jas. T. Sweringens. Also called to see Mr. Pope.

Feb. 12.

Day clear and mild. Nothing new to-day. Still have the blues. Went to drill at night.

Feb. 13.

Weather still warm but cloudy & sprinkling rain. J. B. Cates told me to-day that E.V. Bryan, alias "Red," had gone to Nashville to see Miss S.B.W. To-day I dismissed the case of Mr. J. Anderson &c. v. William D. Griswold at the plaintiffs cost and at his request. J.J.A. told me to-day that he would certainly settle up the _____Bills. Staid with that.

Feb. 14.

To-day I came to my office at 8½, rather later than usual on acct. of the dreary weather. At 1 PM I went to Mr. Deans on Locust between 11 and 12th Streets, to call upon James F. Casey & his bride who was Miss Emma Dent from this county. Remained there about one hour. Had a pleasant time talking to the Bridesmaids, Miss Mitchell, Miss Emily O'Fallon, Miss Dean &c. At night I went to St. Louis theatre to see Barney Williams & his wife who are great in comedy (Irish). Political events thicken. Day before yesterday, Lincoln the Pr. Elect made a short speech at Indianapolis, which though foolish and unworthy of the man whom the people should have to rule over them yet shadowed forth a spirit of stern determination not to compromise or yield the rights of the B. Republican Party & to coerce the Seceding States. The affairs of our distracted country are growing more desperate every day. A day or two since there were 56 heavy failures in N.Y. City which shows the effect of the Southern Secession on the arrogant & dictatorial North.

Feb. 15th.

Day was dark and snowy but it melted as it fell. Nothing new to-day.

Feb. 16th.

Day same as yesterday. Was in Circt. Court nearly all day waiting on Law Docket. It is high time for me to have an answer to my last letter to Bettie & if she does not answer it, I shall feel bound to resent it, in a way becoming a gentleman altogether her equal in station and birth, as one who loves her but will not lose his self respect to administer to his physical & spiritual weakness. I have done my best to please her and now I have almost run the length of my forbearance and humility. Before this I did not know how pride *could* stoop when the heart commands—at night went up to Kirkmans, saw Miss Sally Kirkman and heard that R.K.W. was much better & could be here in about 3 weeks.

Feb. 17. Sunday.

Went to Dr. Hutchinsons Sermon in church, cor. of 17 and Olive. Saw Mr. Churchill & sat in same pew. After dinner went to see Miss Polk at Mr. Deans after tea. Aunt Caroline Watts died in No. La. a short time since & was buried to day at Paducah. Disease of the Heart. Went to see Miss Mary Mitchell & had a very pleasant visit.

Feb. 18. Monday.

Election day for the Election of Delegates to the State Convention. Was a fine day cool & dry. Was quite busy to-day.

Feb. 19.

Weather fine. Nothing new today. The majority of the Citizens Ticket over the Union Constitutional Ticket was about 4700, a Black Rep. victory.

Feb. 20th.

To day got a letter from my *dearest*. She said she would be at home in about 2 weeks, but the letter still said the Engagement must be broken off as it must necessarily be very long one. I intend to bring the power of an almost unconquerable will to bear towards a consummation of my wishes to make her my wife. Weather is beautiful. At dinner I indulged rather too fully in wine. MO. from the returns has probably gone for the "Union as it is."

Feb. 21.

To day was a beautiful day. Mr. Hughes has been in the city for a few days trying to fix up with the Directors of the Bk. of Louisville, with rather bad prospects. I have analyzed my feelings & find that I love Miss S.B.W. more than I have ever loved any other. Today I went in company of Genl. Frost & Capt. Hazeltine to the Armory of N.G. & heard the band, noise was very loud but good music. At night went up to Dr. Kennards to see his sisters, the eldest about 32 or 36 is the picture of an old maid red hair of the sulky hue, reddish complexion, large & straight mouth, blue eyes, and satisfaction writ on her face. The younger about 22 or 24 is a sweet looking girl but rather homely, the main characteristics of the family as to hair eyes & complexion— remained there till 9 and then went to see Miss Sally M. Polk. Had a very pleasant visit. She told me that Miss S.B.W. had tried to persuade the Doctor to advise her father to stay 3 weeks longer. She was having such a delightful time that she did not wish to leave. This was told for my edification.

Feb. 22.

The day was beautiful & too warm for fire. The military was out on a grand parade to-day, the National Guards Mo's 1 and 2 came in fine condition. Nothing new to-day. Dr. G.T.H. says he has made up his mind to leave her unless his father forbids him. He says he has wasted his time & money & resents it. He is in love with Miss Mary Mitchell, but has a faint heart. At night went to the theatre to see Barney Williams & wife in Comedy. About 1 o'clock at night there was a very light wind accompanied by very heavy rain & much sheet lightning.

Feb. 23rd.

Day dawned cloudy and windy but by 8 AM it had cleared off beautifully and the streets were washed off by the hard rain last night. Yesterday at Phila: Pa. A. Lincoln raised a flag of 34 stars, an index to his intention not to regard the separation of the Cotton States. Day passed off quickly.

Feb. 24. Sunday.

Did not go to church this morning. The day was clear & cool & dry under foot. In the afternoon about 2. o'clock Mr. Geo. W. Goode sent for me to come out to his House for dinner. Dr. Harrison & self went out and met Col. D.D. Mitchell & his daughter, and passed a very pleasant afternoon. Came in town & after supper called at Mr. Andrew woods—not at home—Mr. Kirkmans not at home. At Mr. Glasgows to see Miss Julie Clark and she was not there. I then went to the 2d Presbyterian Church & heard a sermon from Dr. Porter.

Feb. 25. Monday.

The telegraphter announced the departure of A. Lincoln Pr. Elect from Harrisburg Pa. in disguise. This movement being prompted by a fear of assassination on his way to Baltimore or in that city, and his friends to save his valuable life, induced him to sneak away in disguise. A most noble & heroic action there that the Pr. of the Great Confederacy has done. Today got into the trial of the case of Given Watts & c. vs. Lemoine—case lasted all day & begins again tomorrow. At night went to drill & after went to the Philharmonic Concert.

Feb. 26th.

Day was very beautiful & mild. Cause of G.W. &c. vs. J.B.S. Lemoine was contd. & the testimony closed about 1 ½. The court adjourned the case for argument on the instructions till a Law day, as the instructions would decide the case. Today went to the Laclede Club to board at $20 per month. Day passed off quickly. At night went to see Miss Sally W. Polk, and she gave me a beautiful scarlet cap which she had worn at Bat Masque at Dr. Mont. Pallens, which I had asked her for & she promised to give to me. She said that she would give it to me if she thought I would appreciate it, and asked me if I would prefer it from her to any lady *in St. Louis.* I told her "yes" & it was true for I do like her better than any lady in *St. Louis.* This might be truly sd. as my dearest Miss Sue Bettie is *now* in Nashville.

Feb. 27.

The weather warm & hazy, looks like rain. I received an invitation to a party in Nashville from the one I love, to day, and this slight indication of remembrance touched me. The political skies are brightening & the shadow of the coming events indicate that the Peace Policy of Wm. H. Seward will direct the administration of A. Lincoln who seems to be a weak & indifferent president. Genl. Twiggs has given up the posts &c. in Texas to the State and is severely criticized by the B.R. papers. At night went to see Miss Mary Mitchell.

This morning was beautiful & at most too warm. About 3 PM it became cloudy & looks like rain. I am informed that RKW and family will return on tomorrow Friday on the Runyan. News came to-day that the Peace Congress had reported. The terms not yet known. Our State Convention met to-day, but I do not expect them to do much. At night Geo. E. Harding & played a little game of "Draw" with Price, Len$^{\underline{d}}$, Rozier & McKnight and Harding, lost $8.00, came home at 11. found Mayrant a little intoxicated. He had been drinking with Sonlard & Johnson, went out again & took 4 or 5 more drinks and then took a long walk & went to bed.

March 1.

The day was charming in the afternoon. I went out to walk with Miss Sallie Kirkman. She asked me to tell her who I was in love with & she would give me some advice. I told her, and she said she thought if I desired to I could marry her that she thought she wd. suit me Exactly, & that she believed that the young lady liked me best of all her acquaintances.

March 2.

Nothing of interest to-day.

March 3rd. Sunday.

Arose this morning. It had rained hard last night. Went to the 2d. Church & Dr. Wines was preacher. Did not go in. Came home and found Dr. G.T.H. We took a walk towards the River to see if the S.B. Hillman on where the Woods family were to return had come. Came back & went into Rudwriters wine Saloon and took two shopfen of Rhine wine "Foster T. Anima." Then went to Rest. de Paris & took dinner. When I arrived at my room Boemstein G.P. was there. He wanted me to be one of the witnesses of his wedding. We went to the house and at 8½ the ceremony was performed by Mr. Krebs the pastor of the Lutheran Church, cor. of 8th and Walnut or 9th and Walnut. They had no attendants, i.e. Bridesmaids & groomsman. But the bride was attended into the room by Mad. Schiller & Mad. Berrays & her sister & Mad. Pfieffer, and 4. Girls had bouquets which they held in the hands. The Bride & Groom took their position on the floor in the room back of the parlor, in which the supper was set, which was the bedroom. She was dressed plainly, had on a neat ashes of Rose Colored silk dress & she wore a little hat. Dr. Krebs addressed them in German for about 5 minutes explaining to them the duties of man and wife its responsibilities & then shortly & briefly asked them if they would take each other for better or worse, & they assented. He told the man to take the woman's hand. He pronounced them man and wife. There was no benediction & by request it was left out, Boemstein being an infidel. the groom then kissed the bride & then the congratulations taking place, the gentlemen advancing and handing to the ladies each a bouquet, then supper came and each ones name was in the plate. It was a good supper and they had plenty of wine, Claret and Rhine wine and Champagne. The Guests were the Ladies already included & Dr. Hermanes, Hiligartner, Smith and Dr. _____ and Dr. Berrays, the brother of the Editor Sigmund Boemstein, Dr. Krebs & one or two others. I left at 10½.

1861
March 4. Monday.

On this day fruits in a great degree depends the future weal or woe of this Continent. The inaugural address was delivd. & Mr. L. was only sworn in as Pr. of U.S.A. The document in my opinion is one of the weakest state papers & the worst expressed I have ever read. He is for coercion i.e. non-recognition of the Southn. Confederacy. We must look out for war. To-day the convention met here. This morning a secession flag was hung out of the Berthold Mansion the headquarters of the Mo. Minute Men. It caused much excitement any many threats were uttered about tearing it down, by Germans & Republicans. Sevl. fights occurred, but the minute men were in the House arrived & well prepared for any attack. None was made.

March 5.

This was an ill stand day for me. Miss Sue Bettie got home this morning on the Runyan. At night I went to see her. When she came in the room, I took her hand & welcomed her. I could hardly speak. After remaining a short time, Mr. Albert Tennant & Hugh Kirkman came in. They remained till 102 & left. I saw that all was wrong. She had not on my ring and the gleam of her eyes towards me were cold. There was not the cordiality that I had expected. As soon as they left I told her that I would take the present opportunity of coming to an understanding & then recapitulated what had occurred since she left & our letters. I told her that in all my intercourse & conversations with her I had been perfectly open & honourable, that I had confessed my love for her & time & absence gave me no reason to retract it, and that I thought it was due from her to me to be fair & open, and that I wished her to tell me if her feelings toward me had changed. She told me that she thought she said so in her last letter to me & that they had. That she no longer loved me, that she was mistaken in her feeling for me. That she had the highest respect & admiration for me & liked me better than any gentleman in St. Louis, & that she mistook this for love. That she met a young gentleman in Nashville in whom she took an interest which led her to know her heart. That she did not love me. She told me that she had an "understanding" with this man, but not an engagement and that unless she changed her mind and wrote him not to do so, he wd. be here in about 3 weeks. As he had told her he could not let matters rest as they were. I asked her if she loved him well enough to marry him. She said she did not know & seemed to bear some doubt in her mind. She told me she would not engage herself to him, unless she did love him. She said that she was not the kind of woman to make me happy, and that I would tell her so in less than a month, to which I replied, that I held it a privilege to love her & one of right, & that I should continue to do so, & to come and see her. I asked her if there was any hope in the future, she said not, that she thought there was no possibility of ever loving me. I told her I intended to continue & if by harder work & nobler exertions I could improve myself I would do so. (Here a great struggle took place in my bosom between Pride & Love). I told her in my subsequent attentions she should never see anything sinister or humble or unbecoming a proud & high nature. I told her that I felt in myself that she was intended for me & that she must excuse me when I told her that I felt that though she was Miss Woods now the day wd. come when she would be Mrs. Campbell. She said that she did not think she wd. ever love me. I told her she had told me so before, that I knew she had held out no ray of encouragement, but I would go on & she also promised me that I contd. to love her she would let me know by one way or another if she ever felt a return of the lost love for me. She told me that when she told her mother of the engagement she objected so seriously, and then she said she thought she loved me, but time & changes & another young man had taught her better. She said her mother had no objection to me whatever—She told her she wd. send me the ring I gave her and the daguerrotype as soon as she unpacked her trunk. I told her I did not care what she did with them, she might *throw them in the fire*.

(Author's Note: Written on the side of the journal was the following, "She told me that if he came and she engaged herself, and I asked her if she had she would tell me.")

Conclusions

My object in waiving my pride (which prompted me to rise in haughty disdain & throw myself on the sustaining prop of my heart my pride) was to secure my love. I have profited by experience, and in the battles of this world we must sometimes stoop to conquer. I love her, and I feel that my cause is not hopeless. I know that she had many difficulties to contend with in preserving me in her mind, her family objections, the taunts & influence of Anna Irwin, the agreeable young man, & many extraneous circumstances all brought to bear against me, and she not being of a determined nature gave way & then the engagement was hardly concluded before she left me & went away & the absent is ever wrong. The reason why I pursued the course I did was because, I felt that if she admired & respected me and liked me & loved no one else that I might make many corrections in my conduct towards her & might please her and woo her, for heretofore I have never taken the trouble to woo her, now I will do so, and I felt that unless there is a strong & active countervalling will, at work to thwart me—That I will succeed. I will proceed cautiously & skillfully & if there is any trouble in magnetic influence of a superior will I will not despair. I have great advantages in understanding her position. These things complied with what Miss Sallie Kirkman told me about her, and with what I believe the nature of the prize & with the experience of my friends, who have won on the second trial induce me to try again. If I succeed I will esteem myself the most fortunate.

March 6th.

I slept very little last night & for the first time in my life had the heartache the real heartache. I could not sleep for thinking of her, and the more I thought the more satisfied was I that it was my true cause with a view to her character, & I am yet more and more resolved to try it again. The day dawned beautifully and mild. I am more and more determined to pursue my wills commands. I went to see Dr. Harrison and told him all and he commended my cause. I also related the whole to J.B. Cates and he told me I had done right, and that under the present state of affairs he wd. not give up. He told me I had done as I ought in all my conversation with her, that I had not sacrificed too much. I also wrote to mother & told her the circumstances but not the reasons & requested her advice. After tea went to the club & played wuchre till 10 ½. Slept well last night.

March 7.

Today was pleasant & moderately clear. No news today of consequence. I get encouragement on all sides to proceed in my affair with Miss Sue Bettie. Miss Polk who I strongly suspect knows something told me to go on & not turn back in all things, also J.B. Cates. Went to night to a reception given to the Mo: Convention at the house of D.A. January, cor. of Washington Ave. & 12th Street.

March 8.

To night went to see Miss Sue Bettie. was invited into the Library. Found Cornelius Tompkins there, sat down and was on my good behavior for some time. T. left & then I spoke to the purpose & flatter myself that I did not altogether leave her with the same impression as when I left the last time. She did not say anything about the picture or the ring, but as I was leaving she told me that Miss Sally Polk wished to see me to invite me to go somewhere. She seemed a little confused. I told her I would go and see her.

March 9.

Today at 12. M. went to see Miss Polk and we went to see "The Heart of the Andes," a painting on Exhibition here painted by "Church." She told me she wished me to go to Hannibal with her and Miss Bettie Woods & Samuel Kirkman. This was the message Miss W. spoke to me of. I told her I would go if she wished it and she told me she would be very happy if I would go, so at 4. O'clock P.M. I went to the S.B. Hannibal City, the Keokuk packet, & remained there a little while & the carriage of R.K. Woods came down & in it Miss Polk, Miss Bettie K. Castleman (age 14) & Miss S.B.W. I escorted Miss Bettie on the boat & had a very pleasant trip up. I divided my attentions equally between Miss P. and Miss W. I went to church with them in Hannibal, the 1st Presbyterian.

March 10.

New School & heard a sermon on the 20th verse of the 3d. Chapter of Revelations. I did not gain any point during this part of the trip. After dinner we walked up on top of one of the high hills and looked at the scenery. Remained there about one hour and returned just as we got to the Hotel about 3 ½ the Du' Vernon, the packet, we were to return on, came down and we went on board. The time passed away during the evening rather unnaturally but not unpleasantly. I did not have an opportunity of speaking much alone to Miss Bettie, but divided my time almost equally. I did not lose much by this trip, but do not know that I have gained much either. I do not despair of winning yet. Miss Polk says significantly "try try again and you will win."

March 11.

Arrived here about 5. A.M. Got off the Boat about 7. A.M. & walked to the carriage with the Ladies. I with Miss Bettie to the carriage & put her in & then bade her good bye. She told me she hoped to see me very soon. Nothing new to day. The new Law Record made its first appearance today. I became a subscriber, the Daily Evening Journal also, I subscribed for 1. mo.

March 12.

At night went to R.K.W's. No new developments. Met about 8 or 9 Men there.

1861.

March 14 Nothing new today — I tried three
cases today in Com Pleas &
Cont'd one — at night got a letter
from Mother giving me advice
as to my conduct with S. B. W.
It was the kind that I would
naturally look for in such a
matter of proud high nature.

March 15 This was a most disagreeable dis-
= tly day. at night I went to U. K. W.
with J. B. Calis. I stopped in the
parlour to see Mr W. & he greeted me
cordially & kindly but — yet I did not
see in the old Lady's conduct the
same free measure of heartiness
as I had seen before. I remained
awhile & went up stairs & found
the three young ladies Miss W.
Miss Polk & Miss Kinkman & a
room full of "whipper snapper's
little insignificancies. I saw no-
= thing particularly to discourage
me nor anything to particular
= ly encourage me; I remained
tonight —

1861

March 16 This Day passed off quietly. Nothing done, Day clear & cool — nothing of interest eat done today —

March 17 Sunday. was St Patricks day. had an engagement to go to Church with Miss Bettie W. started up rather late & met her & her brother on the way they having waited for me & left as it was getting too late, went to church with her, and heard a Sermon in 2d Pres. Church cor of 5th & Walnut, on the way home she seemed Kinder & more satisfied with me than at any time since she had returned, and complie =mented me on my improvement in being more charitable, I told her that I was owned by Athenic society & She told me she was tired of it too I remarked that she liked Nashville but & asked her when she expected her Nashville friend over, she told me that he "was not coming at all" on my way up I asked her if she would allow me to come & see her in the day, as it was impossible to speak to her much in Eve =ings where so many were there & She told me yes she wd be glad to have me come, as we left I saw any kindly dance of kindness —

1861.

March 18 To-day is the day for Dr Geo: T. Har=
=rison to leave for Va. I have known
him long & intimately (over the period
of near seven years) and during all
that time I can truly say I never knew
him do an ungentlemanly or dishon=
ourable act to to entertain a mean
or ungenerous idea, he is magnan=
=imous, & generous almost to a
fault. I saw him about 12. M & asked
him to walk over to Goebel's
Flora Garden as I wished to order
a bouquet for Miss Bettie W. we
went & on the way he related to me
his last interview with Miss Wn & showed
me a small locket with a lock of
hair which he avowed he an meant
to his heart — I ordered the bouquet &
we returned at 4. O'clock all of
"Our crowd" Brown Calm Haws Meaff
&c were at the cars to bid him good
bye. he hated to leave & I was
almost unnerved I never hated
to give up any one as much since
I left Sandy Baldwin — after
tea went to Drill & left at 9,
& with R.R. Hutchinson paid a
visit to Miss Polk to bid her
Goodbye also. we went about
9 1/2 dine & meeting people there

1861

March 18 among others were Miss S.B.W. & Miss
Kutman — I remained till 12. O'Clk
& had in the meantime a delightful
talk with her, she said she hated
to leave & that she was sorry to part
from me — that I had done more
than any one else to make her
time pass pleasantly while here &
that she would ____ forget me & so
that I had introduced to her her most
pleasant acquaintances. and
then she told me that she pre—
—dicted for me in this world all
the success I ____ wish & told
her to go on & ____ in all my
____ & looked significantly to
Miss S.B.W. & said ____ to ____ up any
thing for I ____ succeed in the
end. I bade her good Bye ____ a
heavy heart for ____. I have gone
into Society I have met but one
lady in whose character I find more
to admire & love — she is beautiful
but a fragile flower, small about
5 feet 2 or 2½. and symmetrically formed
has beautiful eyes large & dark blue,
a fine complexion, pretty hand &
feet & a face of much expression —
& a mouth of sweetness filled with
beautiful teeth. she has no brother &

March 13th.

Took a long walk with Miss Kirkman who was stayg. at R.K.W.'s. I told her all about our affair & she told me that Bettie cared as much for me now as she ever did. She approved of my conduct & said she did not love that Nashville man. That she was miffed at my conduct & that was the ground of it all. She told me not to discontinue my visits, but to go on as if nothing had ever happened and she thought all wd. be right again. I am much encouraged by several things & think that if I manage rightly she may yet return. She advised me to seek an interview & have a plain talk with her that the more plainly these things were managed the better they were. Dr. H. told me about his affair with Miss Mary Mitchell. She rejected him but he thinks & so do I that she loved him. As she was nettled to bitter tears, & in her agony told him she wd. *not* say "no," but he told her she had decided in her cool judgment and he wd. not bind her under all excitement. Tonight I was present at a dinner given by several of us friends of Dr. G. T. Harrison, complimentary to him before his departure to old Va. He leaves us for his old house. It is hard to give up a fine a man & as true a friend. The dinner passed off pleasantly, with almost too much wine. There were present, Catis Browne, J.M. Hawes, Bragg, J.J.O'Fallen, Snead T.L., Jno. Wickham, Lee Wickham, R.R. Hutchinson, Mayrant, Dr. Michel, H.A. Garland, J.H. Carlisle, Dr. M.A. Pallen & Dr. Papin, W.C.P. Carrington and myself and two others I don't now remember—the dinner was a very fine one & was given at the House built by D.D. Mitchell on Paul Street. We left at 12½ at night. This was the first time I was ever drunk in St. Louis. All but Bragg got the same way.

March 14.

Nothing new today. I tried three cases today in Common Pleas & Cont. one. At night got a letter from Mother giving me advice as to my conduct with S.B.W. It was the kind that I would naturally look for in such a mother of proud high nature.

March 15.

This was a most disagreeable and dusty day. At night I went to RKW's with J.B. Cates. I stopped in the parlour to see Mr. W. & he greeted me cordially & kindly but yet I did not see in the old Lady's conduct the same full measure of heartiness as I had seen before. I remained a while & went up stairs and found the three young ladies Miss W., Miss Polk and Miss Kirkman & a room full of "whipper snappers" little insignificances. I said nothing particularly to discourage nor anything to particularly encourage her. It rained tonight.

March 17. Sunday.

Was St. Patricks day. Had an engagement to go to church with Miss Bettie W. Started up rather late & met her & her mother on the way, they having waited for me & left as it was getting too late. Went to church with her, and heard a sermon in 2d. Pres. Church, cor. of 5th & Walnut, on the way home she seemed kinder & more satisfied with me than at anytime since she had returned, and complimented me on my improvement in being more charitable. I told her that I was soured by St. Louis society & she told me that she was tired of it too. I remarked that she liked Nashville best & asked her when she expected her Nashville friend over. She told me that he "was not coming at all." On my way up I asked her if she would allow me to come & see her in the day, as it was impossible to speak to her much in evenings when so many were there & she told me yes she wd. be glad to have me come. As we left I saw a kindling glance of kindness.

March 18.

To-day is the day for Dr. Geo. T. Harrison to leave for Va. I have known him long & intimately (for the piece of near seven years) and during all that time I can truly say I never knew him do an ungentlemanly or dishonourable act to entertain a mean or ungenerous idea. He is magnanimous & generous almost to a fault. I saw him about 12.M. and asked him to walk down to Goebel's Floral Garden as I wished to order a bouquet for Miss Bettie W. We went. On the way he related to me his last interview with Miss M. & showed me a small locket with a lock of hair which he would wear nearest to his heart. I ordered the bouquet and we returned at 4. O'clock. All of "our crowd" Brown, Cates, Hawes, Bragg &c. were at the cars to bid him good bye. He hated to leave & I was almost unmanned. I never hated to give up anyone as much since I left Sandy Baldwin. After tea went to Drill and left at 9. & with R.R. Hutchinson on paid a visit to Miss Polk to bid her goodbye also. We went at about 9½ & met many people there, among others were Miss S.B.W. & Miss Kirkman. I remained till 12. O'clock & had in the meantime a delightful talk with her. She said she hated to leave & that she was sorry to part from me. That I had done more than anyone else to make her time pass pleasantly while here and that she would never forget me &c. That I had introduced to her the most pleasant acquaintances, and then she told me that she predicted for me in this world all the success I could wish and told her to go on & persevere in all my aims & looked significantly to Miss S.B.W. & said not to give up anything for I would succeed in the end. I bade her goodbye with a heavy heart, for since I have gone with society I have met but one lady in whose character I find more to admire & love. She is beautiful but a fragile flower, small about 5. feet 2 or 2½, and symmetrically formed, has beautiful eyes, large & dark blue, a fine complexion, pretty hands and feet and a face of much ex-pression & a mouth of sweetness filled with beautiful teeth. She has no brother & no sister and no father. She told me once that in many particulars she would like to have me for a brother. I feel almost as warmly to her as such one may, and if any one should lift a straw against her in harm or speak a word too rude to her I would resent the offender, by a right, the right of the love I bear her, not such as I bear to Miss Bettie, but a deep fraternal love. I promised her I would write to her a long letter full of news, and will do so. A Senator was elected by the Legislature today. Waldo P. Johnson a States Rights Calhoun Va. Democrat. He fills Green's place. I have confi-dence in him & hope that he will not disappoint my hopes, that he will be a staunch champion of the South.

March 19.

This afternoon I went at 4 P.M. to see Miss W. found her at home & had a very pleasant talk with her for nearly 2 hours, & when I got up to leave she told me to wait that she had something for me, that she wd. go and get. I knew what it was. It was my daguerrotype & our engagement ring—I was much agitated & thought in my mind what I must do. I feel that she acted right in giving them to me under the circum-stances. When she came in she gave them to me. I said not a word for a minute or two and then told her I was sorry to see them, that I had hoped she had destroyed them &c. She then said that she did not think she was the kind of woman to make me happy. I told her that I did not think she was just to me in this professing that I knew her nature & my own and that I was satisfied that she was, and went on to try & convince her so. She said that she knew she did not come up to my standard and was not enough intelligent &c. I told her that she was my equal in all but age and prayed her not to wreck my happiness on such grounds. She told me that she did not love me enough to engage herself. I told her all of my love for her in words of my hearts prompting. I was much affected. I told her that I did not despair of yet winning her & that when the future did become a dreary blanket to me, & I did despair that. I then should be an altered man, my destiny would be changed. I should never love again. She said she did not doubt that I now thought that I loved her, but she thought I could in time see some one I loved more, & she hoped I would get over this love for her. I asked her if my cause was hopeless regardless she told me that she would not be acting right to tell me that she thought she wd. ever love me, that she did not think she would, but that she would not say that there was no *possibility*. That all things were possible. That she did not think it probable. She told me that she, at the time she engaged herself to me thought she loved me, but was mistaken. She told me that she did not love the Nashville man. That she loved no one and never had loved anyone, but that she liked & admired & esteemed me more than anyone else, and that there was more probability that she would love me than another because she liked me better than any other. The result of it was that she did not put me off hopeless. She told me that *whenever* I felt inclined to come to see her she would be glad to see me no matter when I called nor how often. I looked at the daguerrotype of myself that I had given her and bitterness overflowed my heart. I put it on the floor with the face up and placed my heel on it and crushed it. She told me not to do it in a pained & suffering tone. I took it up & looked at and placed it on the floor again & again crushed on it with the heel. She again implored me not to do so & told me if I was going to treat it so to give it to her. I gave it to her & requested her to burn it. I took the ring in my teeth to break it & she told me as I cared anything for her not to do so. I did desist but I told her no one else shd. ever wear it. That I would destroy the circle that had girdled her finger. She told me not to do so it was wrong. She asked me to bring her daguerrotype to her. I asked her to let me keep it a little while, after I had urged my request she said she did not think it would be right for her to give it to me— and that under the circumstances she did not think it would be right, that she would rather I would have it than any one else but she had given her picture to no one. She said she wd. rather not give it to me, but that she would not command me to bring it back, but still she would rather I would. I bade her goodnight & she asked me to meet her at the party at Mr. Givens. That night, I told her I was sad & did not feel like a party. She said she hoped I would meet her & be as gay as ever. This was the first day of the 3d. week after her return & in that period I have made some progress. She has discarded her Nashville beau. This was more than at first I hoped in so short a time. She has lost her resentment apt. me & tells me she likes me best of all, & she also says that there is a possibility of her loving me & she at that time told me that there was hardly a possibility. No she says that there would be more room to hope she wd. love me as she liked me best of all. Besides I have not sufficiently wooed her, & I ought not to suppose that a womans pride would permit her to come to terms so soon. This thing of the return of the daguerrotype & ring was a think of restraint & it is best it is over. I am now on an easier footing & will endeavor to win by all the arts and graces, which love & thought can induce to further an honourable affection. I met her at three and she looked a little sad. I went over to her & spoke to her & persuaded with her & told her that if I had done anything wrong or hasty or had hurt her feelings in what I had said she must forgive me, as it was not often I let my feelings get the better of my judgment but that I could not help it & that in the matter of the gaguerrotype she must overlook it. She said yes she would exercise charity & forgive all. I made an engagement to go to see the Heart of the Andes with her after supper some evening, & bade her good night & left for home. I was sad & heavy of heart all night & waked to a brighter hope.

March 20.

Nothing new to day.

March 21.

To-day I was engaged in the trial of the cause of Given v. Lemines in the Court of Common Pleas. The case was finished all but the argument some days ago, & today it was argued by defts. After their close the Court signified that all that remained to be done wd. be to settle the instructions & render judgment for plffs. in the afternoon. I went to see Miss Kirkman & stated to her what occurred Tuesday afternoon, and she told me she thought I had received as much encouragement as most gentlemen wd. wish, & she said that she thought Bettie cared more for me than she would like to admit. That I ought to go on, and she told me to have a talk with her & to ask her to reconsider, & fix a time when she will give this a decisive answer. I went up to see Miss W. after tea to get her to go to see the Heart of the Andes but she had the headache & declined going. I asked her to go to see the Campbell's Minstrels & she said she would go with me on tomorrow night. I remd. till near 9. & then Edwd. Bridle came in and I left and went to see Miss Mitchell and met Miss Churchill there. Remd. till 10.

March 22.

At night went with Miss W. to the Minstrels. Had a very pleasant time. On my way back I told her I had her daguerrotype & she sd. "give it to me." I tried to induce her to let me keep it, but she wd. not, & told me that she would not be actg. right if she did that. It wd. do me no good to keep it always & much less for a while. I made an engagement to meet her on Sunday afternoon at 3. O'clock.

March 23.

To-day I went up to bid Miss Sallie Kirkman goodbye. I told her that I was getting more & more discouraged, that I was now satisfied that Miss W. did not love me, and she told me that she believed & was satisfied that Bettie loved me, but that she did not think was acting right, in not telling me that she loved me. She also told me enough to convince me that Mr. Woods is the *real cause* of the breaking off of our engagement. She told me to go on and not be discouraged too easily. I bade her goodbye, and handed her into the carriage with Miss Bettie Woods, and came home. It does seem as if misfortunes never come singly, all of my stays & supports in my troubles are leaving me. Dr. H. has gone & so has Miss K. I am desolate indeed _____

March 24.

To day Charles Mayrant, who is & has been my roommate for some moths, went on an invitation over to Mr. Geo. W. Goode's to dinner, about 4. miles out on St. Charles Rock Road. We had a delightful drive and when there we met Col. Mitchell & Miss Mary, and Mr. Goode & his family. We had an excellent dinner & true Virginia hospitality. Left at 4½ and came to town at 5. I stopped on Lucas Place to fill my engagement at Mr. Woods, went in and found Miss Bettie at home. Remained about 1 ½ hours, and just before leaving I told her that I wished to make a request of her, and then went on to tell her my troubled & unhappy state of mind, and finished by asking her to fix a time when she would give me a definite answer, when I would have no hope or much joy, that if my hopes had to meet an end I should prefer that they should go by the headsmans axe & not by slow torture. She told me that she thought she had made that all plain at our last conversation about it, and that she could answer as well now as then. I told her not to answer now I did not desire to hear it now, for I know what she would say, and then asked her to ponder all these things in her mind & not to consult anything but her own heart. She said she would do so & that she would not prejudge me but that she thought that the answer then would be the same as it wd. be now. I told her I would prefer to hear it then and until then I should hope. She told me to fix the time & I did, the last Sunday in April. The 28th. day, when I will get her answer. I told her of the gloom of my soul & she then told me not to give up my all dreams of happiness. I bid her goodbye & left. After that I passed a miserable night. I am satisfied that she will say "no," and yet I shall leave no stone unturned in the meantime, but will marshall all of my acquirements to bring this to bear in my favor. If she says no in a decided & positive manner then it will be for me to quit for *a while & wait*, but I have not made up my mind to forgo all hope & will not do so. I shall array again my shattered forces, and with more warmness & more skill I will endeavor to circumvent & then storm this fair fortress.

March 25.

This day is Monday, and as I lay in bed this morning I thought over all of my affair, and was gloomy indeed, but after having taken a cup of coffee I came to my office and had been there but a few minutes when a boy came in & told me that Lucas Watson was dying. I went over to see him, and showed him the charges for $120 which he had drawn & he said he wished that go to his wife. He appeared rational but very low. He told me that he wished all of his property to go to his wife. I went to get paper &c. to write his will when, but when I came back, it was questionable if he was in his right mind. I thought he was and Dr. Mingar also thought so, but when I began to talk with him he said wait for an hour until he was rested & then he would do so.

In about five minutes after that he died easily & without any apparent pain. He was a genteel and faithful servant & faithfully attached to his superiors. He died without any priest or confession. He had so it was said married his wife on the night before he died. They having been separated. Circuit Court commences today "our convention" having finished its labours. I saw Miss W's. carriage to day and it almost made me sick, for I could not help but think that her brief experience in the monde had changed her much. I am now satisfied that fashionable society together with an ambitious & wordly mother who wishes to make a display, have dimmed the radiance of as pure a gem as the dark laboratory of the earth's deep heart has ever produced. That young lady loved *me* dearly once, but her mother spoiled the purity of the stream and diverted its course. How much of misery & unhappiness does she stand responsible for.

March 26th.

Nothing new to day. At night I went upon an invitation to Mr. N.B. Taylors on Pine at 14 and 15. to take supper. Met Miss Hawes, Duke, Hutchinson, Scott & Bryan & Dickerson, and Misses Eliza & Cornelia Dean, Miss Mattie Churchill, Miss Burke of N.Y.; Mrs. Scott and Mrs. Pratt. Supper at 10. Had a passable time. Left at 12.

March 27.

Day clear & cool. Arose at 8. Took my coffee with Mayrant. Came to office feeling very badly. Nothing transpired worth noting today. Went to see Miss W. Did not find her at home.

March 28.

Was in Ct. House all day. Had 4 cases, tried one & got a judgment, rest not reached. There was a storm with rain about 1 O'clock P.M. At night went to see Miss Woods & did not find her well enough to see visitors. Did not leave a card, and made up my mind not to go to see her till next week.

March 29.

Today in Ct. all day waiting for case of Throop v. Bk. of Louisville not reached. At night went with R.R. Hutchinson to see Miss Ellen Alexr. but did not find her at home, and then we went to see Mr. Bryan & Mr. N.B. Taylor.

Mar. 30th.

In Ct. nearly all day. Cause not yet reached. At night stayed with M.

March 31. Sunday.

There was a very heavy storm with thunder & hail to day. It rained all day & all night till bedtime.

April 1.

The election for Mayor & city offices came off today. The "unconditional Union" ticket was headed by Mr. How for Mayor & the Union anti-Black Republican Ticket was headed by Capt. Danl. G. Taylor for Mayor. The election was a very warm one on the part of the anti-Black Republican Party, and went all one way. Taylor and his ticket were elected by about 2600. majority a complete defeat of the B.R. Party. This is not regarded so much by us as a secession triumph as it is a good sign & will strength _____ in the state.

April 2d.

I was busy this morning in U.S. Circuit Court & in State Court also. In afternoon went to see Miss Woods, and found her just going out, in her carriage. She asked me to come again soon. I was invited in but declined, and when she asked me up again soon answd. cool by "I thank you." She will not suit me if she allows such "insignificancies" as Tennent & Bredill & Bryan &c. to be her admirers & favoured Beaux. I will decline any further advances if I see that she continues to like this set of damned fools. At night went to Mr. Dr. Smiths on an invitation to a single supper. Met Miss Mitchell & also Miss Burke from N.Y. City.

April 3rd.

This day was dark & rainy and continued so till night. Nothing new today.

April 4th.

At night went to see Miss Woods & remd. there a short time when Mr. Albert Tennent came in. I held a high head, and had a smart little controversy with Miss W. and made her a little mad, but smoothed it all over, and left in company with Mr. T. Went to Pine Street to see the large procession of the men in honor of the Taylor triumph, and passed by the window of Mr. N.B. Taylor. Saw Miss Mattie Churchill and Mr. Bryan. He invited me in and I went in & remained till 12. & saw the procession.

April 5.

The news from washington & the South looks warlike. At 12. went to Dr. McKellops and he plugged a tooth for me, which has been aching ever since. At night went to the club.

April 6. Rien de Nouvelle.

April 7th.
Today went to 2d. P. Church in morning and after dinner went with Dr. Michel to see Miss Puss Hunt & was caught in the rain.

April 8th.
Came to my office before 7. & was busy writing out a confirmation of judgment of Mr. J. Anderson in favor of the Bk. of Louisville for $23,549.10 2/3/100. Mr. & Mrs. T.F. Terrell are in the city from Paducah. At night went to Natal. Guards to drill.

April 9th.
Day clear & beautiful. Went in the norning to Planter House, and called for Mr. and Mrs. Terrell, and went with them to Mercantile Library. Afternoon went at 4 ½ to see Miss Bettie and we walked to Mercantile Library, to get out a book she wished to read called "Frank Farleigh" and called at Mr. Sin's to pay a party call. At six O'clock I in company with R.R. Hutchinson went to Col. Churchills to supper to meet Govr. Claib. Jackson & Col. Hough. Met Basil W. Duke then came in at about 10.

April 10.
Clear & mild. Today at 11 A.M. J.L.D. Morrison of Belleville Ill. was married to Miss Adele Sarpy. I was invited to their reception but didn't go; at night went to R.K. Woods to meet Miss Julia Clark, and when I went in saw Miss Bettie talking to a Dr. Alexander (in the Army). She appeared to be highly entertained with his talk. I asked for Miss Clark & presently she came in. I had a very pleasant conversation with her till several others some 7 came in & I left. Met McDowell (A) & had a long talk with him. He told me that Mrs. Woods was a "Yankee School Mistress" when R.K. married her, & that she was born in Massachusetts near the line of Connecticut, & that she was older than R.K.

April 15.
The papers have A. Lincolns proclamation calling for 75000 troops & Congress to July 4, 1861.

April 16.
Great excitement throughout the country and the present indications are that the Northern States will back up the President & the Slave States will resist him. It looks like the beginning of a fierce civil war. Mr. T. Paps little daughter Eliza was

buried today. Afternoon at 5. went to see Miss Bettie W. remd. till near 7. O'Clock, and left her. I think I am gaining ground, but will pursue my way carefully. Day clear and cool.

April 17.

Clear & pleasant. Stunning news to-day from Va.

April 18.

Va. has seceded & the troops at Harpers Ferry have, as it is reported, burned the Armory there.

April 19.

There was a riot in Baltimore on the passage of troops.

April 20.

Saturday. I began today to raise a company. R.R. Hutchinson & Wm. Maginnis are 1st and 2nd Lieutenants, the 2d. Regiment.

April 21. Sunday.

To-day was fair & warm and at night went to church with Miss Sue Bettie. She gave me new reason to hope from her treatment of me than she has done since her rapture. I think I can, if I act prudently, now claim my triumph. At night stood guard at N.G. Armory.

April 22.

Busy all day Saturday going about with J.H. Tamle buying arms for Ky. but to day (Moday) I have been building up recruits.

April 23.

Commenced getting up a Military Co. which goes by the name of the "Dixie Guards." R.R. Hutchinson & Wm. Maginnis are also engaged in the same with me.

April 24.

Tonight an election of Officers of "D.G." was held in Wolfs Hall 3d Street between Vine and W. Av. where I was unanimously elected Captain & Hutchinson 1st Lieut. Maginnis 2nd & Howe AJ. 3d.

April 25th.

Busy today about military affairs. During the last few days I have been to see Miss S.B.W. often and her treatment to me was very kind indeed.

April 26.

Took a morning walk with her and at 9. & she treated me very kindly indeed in^t.

April 27.

Went to see her in afternoon and noticed the same conduct as before. She is so religiously kind that I will ask her decision on tomorrow & I am hopeful of a favourable answer.

April 28.

Went to see her and after remaining for an hour I then noticed that she tried to drive off any approach to the subject, but I told her that this was the day I had appointed for her decision. That no change had come over me only I loved her more & did not think I could love any woman so well. I asked to hear from her, and she seemed to be much agitated, put her hand to her face and remained silent and agitated for some minutes. I then told her all the trouble that was in me, if there was any obstacle to tell me & if human energy could repair it I would do so if she was requiring of anything that I would accomplish it. I then told her of the sacrifices I had made for her, the love I bore her, and of my willingness again to make them over for her. She told me when I asked her for her hand that she did not love me well enough to engage herself to me. I told that I knew she did love me & for Gods sake not to deny it. She said nothing in reply but after awhile said that she did not love me. To my mind she seemed in doubt as to the state of her feelings. She told me that she liked me better than she did anyone in St. Louis & she liked no one any where better than she liked me. That she liked me better now than she did a month ago & that it gave her great pain to refuse me. That she said this before to others to whom she was indifferent & that it did not pain her but that she was not indifferent to me. It seemed that she felt as if she hated to refuse me yet was not satisfied of her love to me . I asked if she did not love me some. She hesitated a little & told me no. I asked her to let there be an understanding between us, but she declined and said that she did not think that love ought to be cultivated that it ought to be spontaneous, that she liked me best of all in St. Louis & no one anywhere else did she like better than me that she loved no one. That she preferred my company to others & had shown me so. I then told her that I understood her to say that she did not love me & did not think she would as long as the Green earth revolved. She said with disheartness yes. I then told her that

I was almost glad that we were about to have a long and bloody war & if in the front of the battle I could find a soldiers grave I should be happy. The bell for supper rang and she invited me to stay. I declined & as I went out I pulled off me & gave it to her. She said not a word but remained behind. I went down & left. I was not made depressed, but was as philosophical as I could be & was so much _____ as before, for I felt that my chances were brighter, if I followed them up than before. I am beginning again to resume my sway over her mind and she said a few days ago that "love was founded on respect and friendship" & the experience of the world is that "friendship is akin to love." I am certain that she does love me to a certain extent and that she would tell me so if her family did not oppose her, and if I continue they will be holding the losing hands all the time. I intend to marry her if I can and I shall bring all of my intellect & auspices to bear on that purpose. I told Michel all and he told me not to stop but to go on & that I would win. He and Cates are the only live men I have told anything about it, & he is the only one who knows the last part of it. He tells me not to give up my advantage by neglect but to go on to see her & that the old people will hold the losing cards all the time. I went home and went to bed early & slept well. I am very little depressed, but am more & more determined not to give up on this my first refused & the reason is that her treatment of me in the last few days is like it was just previous to our first engagement & I can improve it into love & will do so. I was wrong in fixing a day & now she is in the dark as to my intentions & I have room for the strategy of love.

July 1, 1861. Monday.

After writing the last page in this book I paid cautious & not very close attentions to Miss S.B.W. till about the 17th of May. Then I went South and remained till the 8th of June, when I returned I found that she had gone to the country. I went to see her and continued to visit her once a week, each visit inspired new hopes in me when with her but when away & I cooly dwelt on her character & nature my heart wd. sink. On last night I came to town with her having previously had an engagement to go to church with her & to come in Saturday evening. I had gone out Saturday but the rain prevented us from coming in on that day. So we came in on the Sunday evening train. I tried to get a hint from her that she would accept me or a sign to go on but she gave none treating me with the utmost kindness & attention. Whilst on our way up to Mr. Woods house I told her that there was one thing that could induce me to return to St. Louis & only one (I had already told her of my intended departure) & that she was the person I asked her if there would be any use for me to come back to St. Louis, & then told her my particular reasons. She said that she with all of my friends wd. be glad to see me. I then told her if in going away I could claim a reasonable hope of ever in some future time possessing her hand that I would leave happy, & took her hand. She permitted me to hold it, & then I want tell her my feelings. By that time we had reached the gate. She started to say something about "unjust to me" &c. when I went in & we took a seat on the steps. We remained there but a short time when we went into the parlor. After a few interruptions &c. I again took her hand & spoke to her earnestly. She told me at first that she liked me better than any man she had ever seen greatly better than any she had ever saw, & went on to say she could live happily with me & how much she admired me & respected me, & that she wished she could love me well enough to marry me. That she had never loved any one, & that she did not think she loved me that her feeling for me was too calm &c. That she did not feel towards me as she thought a woman must feel towards the man she ought to marry. I told her that she was wronging me & herself by telling me this & the only reason was because she had not yet an imaginary feeling which she would probably never have. She said she could live happily with me, but then she had not this feeling which she thought necessary to true love that she would never marry until she did have it. (Except that she married some one to prevent being an old maid). I talked to her plainly & told her that I had not asked her for her friendship & that I thought entertaining the feelings that she did for me she was unjust to me & herself. She said that she wished she was dead & in heaven. She promised me that when I went away, she would think of me many times,& when I told her that she might find out that she really did love me & had been mistaken in her own mind after I was gone away forever, & that regret might come, & asked her to let me know if she ever so felt she told me that, her message might find me changed. I told her that I would send back to her the locket she gave to me when my feelings for her changed, and that this would relieve her from any such an embarrassment. She then promised me that if after I had gone away, she found out that she loved me she would write to me & tell me to come over to St. Louis, and she then said that she would not make such a promise to any other man in the world. She wished that I would feel towards her as she did towards me, and when I told her that it was impossible for my love to degenerate into an active friendship she was sorry. She told me that since I had returned from the South she had treated me with the unreasoned confidence a sister uses towards a brother (this was what I mistook for a returned affection). It gave her great pain. She told me that she had a warmer feeling for me now than she had when she first engaged to marry me. She told me that she was strangely mistaken, that her feelings were too calm and mild *for true love*. I do not know what to think of her. I believe that she loves me for she expresses the indications of love. She is waiting for a feeling which will never come attaining her imaginary wants. Both my happiness & possibly hers and ours are satisfied. I will go away to the wars & endeavor to cover up the deep wound she has made in my heart and by the exercise of a strong will endeavor to accelerate the healing of it, and in leaving St. Louis which I expect to do in a short time I can write on it. That the *happiest* (Jan'y 14th &c.) days of my life & the most miserably unhappy have been spent here, and she has earned both. She is about 5 feet 4" in height, of rather slender frame of graceful carriage with light hair, a pretty head, a beautiful forehead but quite intellectual enough, with bright intelligent eyes the color of a grape, not quite so purple with regular features & a handsome mouth beautiful face & fine complexion, pretty little dimple & a beautiful neck, bust & arm but an ugly little hand, a beautiful little foot, small waist, and a lively charming silvery laugh, sweet voice & an easy flow of chaste & elegant language, & dressed in taste. I know that she loves me & I know she will find it out some day.

July 5.

I went to Glencoe tonight to bid her goodbye. She told me many things in relation to herself, & we had an unreserved conversation for near three hours. I told her the deep love I felt for her and it seemed to have its effect. She told me that she cd. not write to me to tell me to come again, but I talked long & casually to her and showed her that there cd. be no indelicacy & she renewed the promise. I bid her an casual goodbye.

July 8.

I went to see her in town to acqt. her with my intention to deliver myself up at the Arsenal on to day as a prisoner of war & get rid of the Camp Jackson *parole*. She seemed indifferent. I bid her goodbye.

July 23rd.

I got off from the arsenal 21st having been released unconditionally. I saw her tonight & was remarkably well treated. Her manner was so kind. I made an engagement to walk with her on Friday evening 25th.

July 25th, 1861.

I went up to take the walk & found several gentlemen there & her reception of me was not so cordial as before. She kept me waiting for nearly two hours. In the meantime I left her & went to Mr. N.B. Taylors and played euchre till near 10. then went back and we started to walk. My heart was sunk lower than before for I felt that hope had almost been extinct. We had a few slight passes at each other. She had previously asked me to tell her my plans. I asked her if she wished only to know *as a friend*. She said yes. I then told her. She said she expected to see me again soon. I told her that it depended on the happening of a contingency. (She knew what I meant the message). We had arrived at her house & she asked me to take a seat on her steps. I did so. When she informed me that she could not write to me as she had promised, that she thought it wd. make me think less of her & her own respect wd. be lessened. I had to persuade her not to retract it, but she told me that she had dreamed that I had gone away & that she felt that she loved me & had written to me & that it made her perfectly miserable to think of what she had done & that she wd. have given anything to have had the letter back & that when she awaked she was so happy that it was a dream. I told her that I did not think as she did & told her that what I promised was a pendg. proposition & until I returned the locket she was at liberty to accept me & many other things were said. She said that I would soon send the locket to her. I told her perhaps never for death might soon cut me off and that if she married any other man I wd. do so for it would be wrong for me to love another mans wife. She looked at me & sweetly said that I would never love her as another man's wife. I did not know actly. what she meant & asked her if she meant that she wd. never marry any other man than me. She said yes. I then sd. that if I thought there wd. be any use I would ask her to marry me again. She said nothing & then I asked her to correspond with me & if she felt that she wished to see me she wd. say so. She agreed to do so. I asked her if her feelings for me had changed since I spoke to her on the 5th. She said they had that they were much warmer now than then. I do not recollect how it was managed but we became engaged, but with the understanding that if when I left she finds that she does not love me well enough she is to tell me so but she says she will take time before she does so. She at first wished a partial engagement or understanding but I persuaded her to the former an absolute one. I bid her good night.

July 26-27-28-29-31.

On these days I saw her & was delighted with my *fiancee*. She is the woman for me. On the Eveng. of the 31. I went in the country with her & in the company was Miss Sarah Clark & Ellen Kearney, Geo. T. Pitman & Sandsdale. I spent a very pleasant evening and at night took a walk with her in the garden & sat on a bench there and talked over the future. She said she had not mentioned our engagement to her Ma & Pa. I asked if she thought they wd. be willing. She said she knew her Ma w. be, & that she thought her father wd. be as he'd have no reasonable objection to her. We took an affectionate goodbye.

63

July 25. We had then arrived at her house
& she asked me to take a seat on
her steps. I did so. When she inform
-ed me that she could not write to
me as she had promised that she
thought it wd make me think less of her
& her own respect wd be lessened —
I tried to persuade her not to rehall
it. but she told me that she had dream
-ed that I had gone away & that
she felt that she loved me & that she
written to me & that it made
her perfectly miserable to think of what
she had done & that she wd have
given anything to have had the
letter back. & that when she awoke she
was so happy that it was a dream —
I told her that I did not think as she
did & told her that What I promised
was a proceed? proposition & until I re-
-turned the locket she was at liberty to
accept me & many other things were
said, she said that I would soon discard
the locket to her — I told her perhaps
soon for death might soon cut me off
& that if she married any other man I
wd do so for it would be wrong for
her to be another mans wife
she looked at me & sweetly said
that I would never love her as
another mans wife, I did not know

July 25 actly what she meant & asked her if she meant that they wd never marry any other than me - she said yes. I then asked if I thought there wd be any use I would ask her to marry me again she said nothing. & then I asked her to correspond with me so if she felt that she wished to see me she wd say so. she agreed to do so. I asked her if her feelings for me have changed since I spoke to her on the 5th she said they had that they were warmer now than then

I do not recollect how it was made - but we became engaged. but with the understanding there if when I left she finds that she does not love me well enough she is to tell me so but she says she will tell him before she does so. she at first wished any partial engagement or understanding but I persuaded her to the former an absolute one. I bid her goodnight

July 26 - 27 - 28 - 29 - 31 -
On these days I saw her & am delight= =ed with my fiancée. she is the woman for me - On the evening of the 31. I went in the country with her in the company when Miss Sarah Clark X

August 1.

I did not go in to day. The day was excessively warm. Went riding with Miss Bettie & Miss Kearney & Mr. Geo. T. Pitman in the carriage. Was a warm ride. Came home & tried to keep cool in the evening. After sun set I and my damsel took a ride on horseback. She had a very severe headache but the ride did much good for it & it was well when we quit. I bid her a long & sweet farewell, got home & her headache returned. She retired after a while. In the morning she was not at breakfast still sick with the headache. I ate breakfast at six A.M. & then bid all the rest goodbye. During the visit Mr. W. was particularly kind & Mrs. W. very polite. I sent a farewell to my dear invalid & suffering one by her mother & came to town to prepare for leaving St. Louis on the 2nd.

Part Two

The War Years:
1854 – 1866

Paducah, February 10, (18)54

Dear Given,

Carrie and sister have written and its my time now. Sister has gone to saint Louis and carried Mother, Father and Jimmy with her. Us children are here by ourselves. Moses McClure and Joe Campbell stay here at night; we get on finely. Miss Gifford keeps house. All we are afraid of is that we will starve while Father is gone; this morning Sophy went to market and there wasn't a single butcher or peace of meat there. We have to live on meat (I mean bacon) and bread I suppose.

It has rained every day this week. This is the tenth day of March and there have only been three pretty days. I think that if it keeps on as it has begun we will have a delightful spring.

Given since you've been gone we have all come to the conclusion that you are Father's favorite of all his children; before he left for Saint Louis he went to the post office two or three times every day to see if he could get any letters from you. We got a letter from you to day but it was directed to Mother and as I dont know but it has a secret in it I wont open it; you must write to me and let me know how you like Danville and the College. Jim Singleton has come home and set up as a doctor. I saw his card in the paper to day; Henry Jones came with him. He is to be a lawyer. I suppose the next thing we hear of will be his and Medora Small's marriage. Mr. Sheppard has opened his new hotel. It is named the Campbell House, in honor of Father. I saw Miss Sheppard yesterday. She looked as pretty as ever. I never thought she was very pretty. I suppose after you have been in Danville a little while you will forget all about her. I believe I've told you all the news and now I must say good bye. Carrie and Betty join me in love to you. You must answer this letter soon. Florence Campbell.

P.S.

You know I sent a valentine to Elvira Enders. Well last Saturday Miss Gifford and I staid out there all night. Mrs. Enders said that she had got a letter from Elvira, and that she had got a beautiful one from Paducah, and that I must find out who sent it. I promised I would try. She never once suspected it was me. I think she believes you wrote it.

Florence

Joe says you must write to him.

F

Paducah March 28, 1854

Dear Given,

I was very glad to hear from you and I hope you like the place better since you have some of your old school mates with you. Sister has been taken sick and Mother went over there. She had just come home from a visit to Sister and she had been at home two days when she started for there again but Sister is better and she said in one of her letters that she expected to be home in a week or ten days. Mrs. Ann Cooks child is dead. She had a little baby and it is dead. Aunt Caroline is better and I think will soon be about. I dont know whether I have told you before or not but Aunt Clara is going to call her boy Joe. Joe Campbell has been a little sick but I believe he is well now. He has gone in the country and I suppose he will stay there until he gets over all disposition to chills. O Given we have a little pet chicken here and we are petting it the old hen would not let it stay with her without picking it and we took it to try our hand on it. I suppose she took a sconner to it and she thought she would pick it. Next Saturday is April fool day and I expect to have a great deal of fun. I hope you will come on well with your studies for I want you to come home. Cousin Laura has a baby. I believe it is a girl. Miss Gifford was invited to a party. I suppose it was one this evening to Mr. Enders'es but she did not go. I suppose it was given to Miss Jenny Jonson and Miss Fanny Smith. Dont you get very lonesome some times and home sick. I can sympathize with you for I have felt so my self. I know how bad it is to want to be home and cant get there. Jimmie is on the subject of geography and it seems as if he never tires. We plague Florence and Miss Gifford about young Doctor Singleton. This evening Florence went down there and he gave her some candy and she gave some to Miss Gifford and said that she sent them to her. Miss Gifford took them and ate some. Last night there was a fire in town. Do you receleckt that carpenters shed near the Presbyterian Church. It burned up the church caught on fire and it was put out but it burned a little. Now Given this is a long letter and you must answer a long one. I was reported that Uncle Louis was drowned in the back water but it was not the truth. It is past 9 oclock and I will end my letter. So good bye and believe me your affectionate sister.

Carrie C.

P.S. Please excuse all mistakes. You know I cannot spell good.

Good Night
Carrie Campbell

Paducah April 20, 1854

My Dear Given,

I received your letter a few days ago and I have commenced to write an answer to it. There is a fortune teller in town and several of the old men have gone to have theirs told. She tells the present and the past and the future. Ive herd that Uncle Fowler and Mr. Husband's went to her. She tells fortunes by laying her hands on a person's head and by this means she gets up a communion between their spirits. So she tells them by the help of the spirits I suppose. Would you like to have yours told. Aunt Caroline is better and she getting well very fast. I dont suppose from the way you write that you like Danville much. Cousin George is going to Santa Fe this spring and he is going to come back in the Fall for Sister. He will stay out there sometime I expect. Mother wrote to him trying to persuade him not to take Sister in the Fall. Father wants him to wait until you get through your college studies and for you to go with Sister. Sister is better and she will come over here this Spring and stay with us. Cousin George expects to start in two weeks. The yard is so pretty in some places. The grass look like green velvet and the trees most of them are living out and it begins to look like summer. There has been some very cold weather here. Sunday it snowed nearly all day but it melted right away. So I do not believe any of the fruit was killed by it. There is a very pretty book here named THE LOFTY AND THE LOWLY or good in all and none all good by Miss McIntosh. How do you come on in your studies. I believe Mr. Spence is going to stop teaching and I dont know who will fill his place. Mother says you must not quit writing to her because she doesnt write to you. She says you know she doesnt write much and she wants to hear from you. She Mary never did that way.

There has been a Baptist supper in town and I expect there were a great many persons there. None of us went but I have heard enough about it. Jimmie has commenced a letter but the night is his time to write and his eyes have gotten so week that they hurt him if he writes much. Almost all of the peaches have been killed and I expect that we will have a very few. Are they killed in Danville. There was a concert attached to the Baptist supper and Mr. James Singleton sung Nelly Day. Dont you suppose it was beautifully sung. I would like to hear it very much. Well Given this is "long enough" letter. Excuse all bad writing and mistakes. Write soon and believe me your affectionate sister, Carrie.

My Dear Son,

I have returned from St. Louis and left your Sister about the house. We have bad news from George. His health is so much impaired this Spring he deems it advisable to give up every thing and go to New Mexico to live. It has made me very unhappy. Poor George. After he had worked so hard and was beginning to reap the fruits of his industry (for his business was becoming very profitable) to have to give it all up, home, family, friends, every thing, and go off by himself. His idea is to return in the fall and take Mary with him. But I hope we can dissuade him from that. I think he ought to remain through the Winter and come back the next Spring remain with us through the summer and take Mary the next Fall. I cannot give her up so early as he wishes, to go so far. Your Father says when you are through College you may go out and remain awhile with them if you like it. My dear boy you said something in your last letter of a sore throat. Do take care of yourself and if you can manage it commence with the shower baths. If you cant have that, you can get a sponge and tub, and wet your body all over every morning. And Given don't quit writing to me because I dont answer all your letters. You know I never was in the habit of writing much and it makes me so glad to get one from you.

I am proud to hear of the standing of your class and I know you will do honor to it but I am sorry you are so rushed. I dont want you to confine yourself too much. I am afraid your health will suffer. Your Father leaves sometime next month for Virginia. Brother Charles goes with him and he wishes me to go too. I dont know how it will be. I dont intend going if I can help it. My paper is out and I must stop.

Your Mother

Give my love to Rob and in your next tell me how your throat is. If you need money let your Father know.

Paducah, Nov. 27/(18) 54

My Dear Given,

   I have been intending to write to you for a long time but every time I've commenced Betty or some of the other children would write at the same time. Bettie has written you a letter this time too but I am determined that she shant stop me this time. The reason I wasn't willing to write when any one else did was because I knew that you wouldn't like to get two or three letters with just the same news in them. The weather is extremely cold now and almost all the family have colds. We have had two or three falls of snow. The first snow fell on roses. Everything was as green and fresh. All the roses and flowers were in bloom and the trees were as green as they were in summer and you cant imagine how beautiful it looked. Coal is very scarce and Father is afraid to keep many fires and we have all to crowd around one fire place and you may know we are not very comfortable.

   Paducah is quite gay. Now you have heard of the rag ball. I intended to desctibe it to you but I have such a pain in my head and face that I can hardly write at all. Fanny Woolfolk is going to give a grand fancy and mask ball the twelfth of next month and she cant talk of anything else. She asked me if I intended to send to St. Louis or Louisville for my dress. I told her I hadn't decided yet. I'm not going but if I had intended it I think Madame Roche would have had the honor of making my costume. She is going to dress as a bride. I think its bad taste. Mrs. Rabb gave a party not long ago and I heard she intended giving them once a month all through the winter. I dont suppose theres much truth in the report though storms are quite the rage too. If you come home we wanted to give a small party Christmas but I dont suppose we can now. I haven't seen Rob Alexander for some time but when I do I will tell him to write to you. You must write very often. you ought not to wait for us for you know Mother hardly ever writes and we are all so busy that we cant write often. My face aches very much and I must stop my letter. So good night.

Florence

Home, Dec. 28, 1854

Dear Given,

We continued to look for you up to Christmas Day and I was so disappointed you did not come. You could have returned perfectly well. What kind of a Christmas did you have. I thought of you often that day and I have what I consider a very nice present for you. It was a dreadful day here as far as the weather was concerned. The dampest and most foggy day I ever saw. We had any quantity of presents. I will tell you some of mine. Mother gave me one pair of perfume bottles and Dick gave me another pair, so you see I am well provided in that respect. Floy gave me a little statuette of red riding hood. You remember the story don't you. Bettie and Queen gave me a beautiful little box. Carrie gives me a gold charm to hang to my watch chain. White Fowler gave me a fine book. Aunt Clara a beautiful tumbler of Bohemian glass. Aunt Caroline gave me a jar of preserves and Mrs. Marshall a jar of sweet pickles. Then I have a tortoise shell penknife that cost 2.50. Father says I must wait until New Years for his present.

The other children have a great many handsome ones but they will all write and give an account of theirs. We gave Mother some beautiful ones and have one for you from each one in the family, to send first opportunity. If Dr. Wagoner comes down we send by him. How I do wish you could have come. I would have written to you long ago but I kept hoping you would come. George will not return until Spring. In my last letter he wrote he was improving rapidly. I am determined to pay you a visit in the Spring. Joe Fowler has been here to day. He is to be married the 11th of next month to Martha Lesch. He says she is every thing she ought to be. I suppose we will all be invited to the wedding. If so I will go. Joe is very young to marry only twenty-one. They have been engaged two years. You have heard long ago of Moses McClure being shot. The man was tried the other day and is bailed to stand another trial. His being drunk I think should be no excuse. Dr. Kidd is married to Ellen Lawson. Mrs. Enders has had a real blow up with Mr. Senour and the church about having dancing at her house. Did you see Elvira during the Christmas holidays. I am not half done so I will commence a fresh sheet. It is raining here all the time; and blowing like March. I believe Paducah is going mad about storm parties. They have them some where every night. Last night there were two one at Mrs. Castlemans, the other out at Mr. Reynolds, at the farm you know. I believe there is no news in town at all. Jo and Bob are out at home during the holidays and indeed Given I wish there were not coming back again. I would not like them to know I said so. It would hurt them but it is so unpleasant to live in such a crowd and confusion. Jo is a very pleasant boy but Bob is unbearable. The noise worries Father almost to death. We all dined with Aunt Clara on Christmas and had a splendid dinner. Where did you take yours. Hez is left for Louisville yesterday and Dick will start in a few days for Lexington to bring his baby down. Lucy Berry will come with is- and stay here until Spring. Mr. Rossington did not come Christmas as he promised and is not at all pleased with Hopkinsville. Cousin William has been here and stayed a week. Bob did not go with him. I do not think he wants him to go at all. I must stop. We are all well and all send their love. Mother was very anxious for you to come but did not come get your letter of the 9th until a day or two before Christmas, too late to answer it. Answer this soon. Carrie will write in a day or two.

Yours
Mary

Paducah June 7, 1856

Dear Given,

I write to let you know how Mother is. She thought you would be uneasy and wanted me to write to you to night. She is better than she was the last time I wrote, and is I think getting well. She is almost clear of fever and I believe will be pretty well very soon. When I wrote to you we did not know what was the matter with her, but thought it was dysentery but the Doctor says she has typhoid fever. You must not be uneasy about her for she is a great deal better than she was this day a week ago. We telegraphed to Father but he did not get the telegraphix dispatch. Mother got your letter to day. Sister and Cousin George are with us and I forgot to mention her. The baby she is a very pretty baby with large deep blue eyes a strait nose and resembles cousin Georges family more than the Campbells. Sister looks as well as ever. She nor the baby either are at all hurt by the trip across the plains. I am so glad she is so well. You said in your letter that Father started for home to day and would be here by next Friday. I wish he could be here sooner as Mother and all of us want to see him very badly. Well I will bid you good bye dear Given. Carrie .

Oh I forgot to tell you how proud we all are of your being the orator of the commencement and how it surprised us all. We all spread it very fast. We told it to every one who came to see Mother.

CAC

My Dear Precious Son. I am a great deal better than I have been and I hope am recovering. It would not do to call you home now. I am very proud of you my Son. My blessing and love be with you. Good Bye.

Your Mother

Paducah, Sept. 27, 1858

My Dear Son,

Your letter is to hand & I here inclose your ck. of S.B. Hughes Custodian St. Louis Perpetual MS. CO. for one hundred & fifty dollars. I think your course of study will do. It is a good way to impress what you study on your mind & a good way to digest it. You must not be discouraged. Most young men have to wait a year or two and in most cases it is to their advantage. When you do make a start it will be a good one & you will then have no trouble in pushing yourself along. A young man of talents with industrious application to his books & a determined will to succeed cant be kept in the background. Energy & force of character (strong will & self reliance) will soon bring the possessor to the high of his profession. You might barrister in some fair criminal case & you might make some political speeches to bring yourself before the people & be known, but stick to your profession. It will give you fame & fortune. Brass is one thing, strong self reliance is all other. With your education & the self reliance it ought to inspire, you will soon come into notice, and when you think of the discouragements of the present, dont let it dishearten you. Work all the time laying a good foundation. It will never be a tax on me to render you all the reasonable assistance you may require. Never feel discouraged and never let that feeling depress your confidence & energy. I know how to appreciate your situation. When I began the practice it was about 18 months before I made a start & then I had no trouble. Take every favourable opportunity to bring yourself forward as a debator. One good speech where there is an audience helps much. Dont let anything shake your confidence & be discouraged. This has dampened down the talents of many with me frequently. We are all well. I shall not go to N. York. Cap. G_____ has gone with his wife & will attend to my business. Bro. Charles has gone to the C_____Land. We are all well.

Your affectionate father
J. Campbell

Given Campbell
St. Louis
Mo.

Miss Bettie Woods

I send to you the "Leather Stocking Tales" by Cooper, of which we were speaking last Saturday evening. The set is complete except "Deer Slayer," which has not yet been published. The order in which they were written was Deer Slayer, the Mohicans, Pathfinder, Pioneer & Prairie. I think you will find them very interesting as the principal characters are continued through the whole series. Aug. 6, 1860

> Your friend,
> G. Campbell

Mr. Campbell.

I send the accompanying volume, the only one of the series I have not read, with many thanks for the pleasant moments spent in its perusal. As I leave this evening I will have to defer reading the others until I return; if this delay will occasion you any inconvenience however, let me know & I will send them now & get them when I return.

In haste, your friend

S.B. Woods

Chestnut St. Wednesday

Saint Louis, Jan'y 19, 1861

My Dear Bettie,

Agreeably to my promise & my own desires, I have commenced this letter to you, and as it is the first letter I have ever written under like circumstances. You must excuse any awkwardness of style or expression, and ascribe them to a total inexperience of this kind of literature, and to a lack of time for polish & embellishment. You will find it however to speak plainly the language of my hearts affection, and let that bear all my excuses.

I stood on the platform as the train passed on, bearing away, on rapid wheels, the burden most precious to me, and watched it till it was lost in the distance, and then sent up a silent & deep wish for the safety of the one it bore away. I met with Tom Doanle, who had come over to bid Miss Trisgly good bye, and we rolled up our pantaloons & struck into the unknown depths of the mud. The mud was deep, and we had to foot it all the way to the Lowes Ferry Landing—About half a mile—but in a short time the distance was accomplished & we were again in the dark & gloomy city. The thermometer must have fallen several degrees, just about the time you left, for it began to freeze, and by the next day was frozen hard, and since then we have had clearing weather, cool but perfectly clear & tolerably dry under foot; I am glad that the change took place so opportunely for you know that gloomy weather has a corresponding influence on my spirits, and that evening after you left, I did not feel very mirthful, but I have kept up my spirits by the comforting assurance that you are safe in Nashville, among your friends & relations, in the bosom of your family & happy in the society of your Father & Mother.

After you left it seemed to me as if I had lost something & I had that peculiar feeling of vacuity of occupation, which can hardly ever be dissipated except by finding the thing lost—and even while my mind would be absorbed in the mystical labyrinth of a difficult case, it would be suddenly drawn away from the dry abstractions of the law to contemplate a fleeting vision of loveliness & beauty—whose it was, I need not say—I wish you would have the daguerrotype taken & send it to me. I am not satisfied with what you were two years ago—I want your "Counterfeit Presentment" as you now appear. I will tell you how I have been passing my time since you left—though you may think such volunteer information argues vanity—on my part—well perhaps it does, but I will proceed, briefly—

In general I have been studying, harder & more pointedly than for many months past, for now, I have all aims before me, but as to the incidents—I took Mayrant up to see the ladies at Mr. Kirkman's, and he made himself quite agreeable, and acquitted himself quite creditably, I endeavored to atone for my past misdeeds & appeared to have partially succeeded. I have paid two or three formal duty calls, viz Miss Churchill Miss Nisbet &c. Now as to collateral pursuits, I have studied military tactics a little, but you must not suppose from this that "My voice is for War." No! It was, but circumstances alter cases, and a happy circumstance has changed my mind. I am now for peace an honourable peace, however.

But I have spun this letter out already beyond your patience, and will tell you a few items of news. Miss Cora Anderson is to be married in St. George's Church on Thursday to a Mr. Henry Stiles of Phila. They say, that it has been on the tapis a long time & that she marries well. I am glad to hear it, for I liked her; as to church matters, I have heard the name of the minister we heard last Sunday. It is Dr. Grundy. He preaches again on tomorrow day & night. He is a man of some celebrity & decided talents—the Convention bill has passed both Houses of the Legislature of Mo. & will become a law. But the bill provides that it shall be submitted to the people to pass on the question of secession or no secession. This is a good idea & leaves a chance for the "Sober Second Thought" that we hear so much said about now. Your relations & friends are all well—

When you write tell me all about how you are enjoying yourself & how you spend your time, how your Father & Mother are & any other things which will be of interest to you to impart—for anything which interests you will be interesting to me.

I must now close. Excuse this hurried note & answer very soon.

> With much love yours
> Given

P.S. Don't forget the daguerrotype.

> GC

Nashville, Jan. 27th, 1861

Mr. Campbell.

I received your letter of the 19th several days since & would have been more prompt in replying, but my time has been so fully occupied with various other things that I have not had a leisure moment. We had a very safe & pleasant trip & arrived several hours sooner than we expected. The day after we left instead of being rainy as we anticipated dawned bright & beautiful; just as the sort of day I like & I could but think all the while that it was so emblematic of the type of character I most admire— moderate in all things extreme in neither way, genial & shedding warmth & sunshine over all things. I found Grand Pa's & Uncle James Hamilton's carriages both waiting for me at the depot & it was left to my decision where I would stay while in Nashville. Uncle James ended the matter however by ordering my trunk to his house, so here I am for the present at least. I have had a delightful time thus far, & find dear old Nashville as pleasant as ever. I went to a charming party the night after I reached here, danced all night & came home at daylight. The rest of my time has been spent in comparative quiet so far as seeing numbers of old friends could be called so. I found Father better than I expected, tho' still very weak & miserable. I always go up immediately after breakfast to Grand Pa's, where he is staying, & remain with him until after dinner; for the last day or two, I have been reading Parton, Life of Jackson aloud to him & strange to say have become intensely interested in it myself. He has not been so well for the last few days, & the doctors fear that another abscess is forming; if this is so we will be detained here ten months longer, & so soon as Father is able to travel will probably go with him to the seashore. He dined yesterday with the Bells; the honourable John Sums, Jr.—have survived his defeat remarkably well— the city last night resounded to the echo of a hundred guns fired in honour Louisiana's withdrawal from the states. A bad sign this, I fear, & speaks badly for the patriotic spirit of Tennessee. And now that I have said this much on general subjects I come to the part of my letter that I would fain dispense with—but must not—I was rather troubled when I parted from you, thinking perhaps I had been too rash, & that my feelings did not warrant me in making the engagement that I did. But my absence from you has taught me my own heart, & I no longer doubt my affection for you, & yet I feel that it is my duty to ask you to release me from my promise to you, as it is a source of the greatest trouble to my Father; not that he has any objection to you, but it is painful to him to think of me as engaged to any one, and now that he has so much trouble in beling away from home, prostrated by illness & suffering great pain. I would not for the world add a feather's weight to the care that already oppresses him. If he were in health I should not do this, as I do not think it would be just either to you & to myself—but now that he is sick I feel that I owe my first duty to him & even at the risk of my own happiness I will do as he desires as it is possible. I may not long have him to love & obey. You will of course consider yourself also entirely free, & if when we meet again you are still of the same mind, & my Father is then willing you will find me ready to fulfill the promise I made you on that Sunday night that I so well remember. I hope you will undrstand my motive in asking this, & I feel assured that you are too generous to accuse me of fickleness or inconstancy. I wish you would write as soon as you receive this that I may know it reached you safely and then if you will write again while I am here it will be a source of great pleasure to me to hear from you, tho' of course under the circumstances it will not be proper for me to reply. Please do not criticize this letter. I know it is very faulty, but I trust to your kindness to overlook its defects. Take good care of yourself for my sake & do not get into trouble with the Black Republicans. You see I cannot yet relinquish my right to advise you. Good Bye. I have staid at home from church this morning that I might write this letter quietly. The rest are all coming home, so again, Good Bye.

I am very sincerely yours,

S.B. Woods

St. Louis, Mo. Jan'y 31, 1861

Miss Sue Bettie Woods
Nashville, Tenn.

My Dear Miss Bettie,

Your letter so long & so anxiously expected came to hand this morning; when I read it I felt stunned and bewildered, its contents were so sudden & so unexpected, that it was only after I had read & repeatedly reread it, that I fully understand it. I need not say what my feelings were when I read your generous expressions of affection for me altogether so unworthy of such blessings. And here I may say that letter has only deepened the steady current of my love for you.

I fully appreciate the motives which prompted you to make of me the request you have made, and I honour & admire that filial love which you cherish for your dear Father, so unhappily situated & so distressed & shattered by sickness, for he is worthy of it. But after having critically & with painful care read & pondered over the reasons for your request that I shall release you; in justice to myself I cannot take the responsibility of breaking off our engagement, and I will tell you why. In the first place your lofty candid heart admits that it loves me—you know that I love you—your only reason is "that it is the source of the greatest trouble to your father, because it is painful for him to think of you as engaged to anyone." You say that your father has no objection to me but he cannot bear the idea of your being engaged to anyone. Has he no real, no radical objection to me? If he has, do not injustice to me by withholding these, for I wish to hear all. If he has none, then it must be a "Sick man's fancy." I know that in his precarious & low condition he is nervous & susceptible and that his susceptibilities are easily acted upon, and these things in connection with his fondness and devotion for his oldest daughter, the pride of his house—are naturally calculated to make him jealous of a divided heart. If these things are so his mind may change as his malady is cured, and we would both be spared suffering & pain by letting matters vent as they are. If your father has no objection to me & has confidence in my character, it would seem natural to suppose, that in a condition when he might be called away from his family forever, it would be a satisfaction to know that he would leave behind him an arm which would supply the place of a defence, a breast which would serve as a bulwark against the aggressions of the world.

In view of these things it does seem hard that the cherished hopes of a heart, which feels as deeply as my own, should be dashed with this bitterness when there may be no need for it. I have been a changed man since the event of our engagement.

Before that, I had no destiny of my own shaping. I was satisfied to drift with the tide of human affairs subject to the variable winds of fortune. But now when my mind had recognized its destiny & my heart had almost grasped its treasure to see the bark thrown again on the trackless ocean of life without a helmsman & all sails spread is miserable indeed.

I leave the matter to your own discretion, and to the promptings of your heart & better judgment. You are on the ground, an observant & interested spectator, and if you are satisfied that this matter is a settled & serious grief to your Father, or if you think under all of the attendant circumstances that it is not evanescent fancy or whim, and that it is your duty to break it off I will submit to your decision, but you must be the judge. If this is broken off then let it remain as you in your letter signify. As for myself I shall be satisfied with nothing less than the hopeful knowledge of a renewal.

Answer this letter & write soon. I thank you for your kind interest in me and will take care of myself for your sake—For my own sake, I care little what happens to me now.

> Yours affectionately,
> G. Campbell

St. Louis, Feb. 11, 1861

Dear Miss Sue Bettie Woods,

In my last letter to you I said that under circumstances named in that letter I would submit to your decision. Your letter received yesterday informs me that you have decided "rather against your inclination but in accordance with your better judgement." You are the arbitress and I have no appeal from your judgement; but it was conveyed to me with a commentary against which I feel solemnly called upon to protest. You say that "you hope that I will be satisfied with this and that you know I will not care much." It is bitter & agonizing to receive such a refusal, but under the circumstances I did not look for this unkindness. I know that I have few virtues, but if there is anyone which I may claim to possess it is freedom from hypocrisy and as God sees into my heart your remark is unjust. I think I can trace this idea to its source, the St. Louis letter you spoke of as containing the interesting intelligence concerning me. My eyes are now opened & by a reference to past reports which have been carried to you, to injure me. The authors have withheld at his request I think that I recognize them all as of the same insidious brood, the day may come when I can track one there hence without involving a ladies name.

Oh! let me pray you not to listen to any reports to my discredit until you have asked me about them. Do not condemn me unheard. It is a poor privilege that I ask, to be heard in my own defense. If I were with you I might laugh at their designs but you are away, and the poison for which there may be no antidote may be conveyed under the guise of a friendly letter I need none to inform me that I have secret & treacherous enemies who are "skilled by a touch to deepen slanders tricks with all the kind mendacity of hints." And maybe you have listened to their stories. For the sake of placing myself right, I solemnly assure you that since you left here my heart has never once wavered in its attachment for you, but preserves unswerved its true allegiance. I was sorry to notice the cold tone of your letter & found it difficult to account for.

In conclusion I will say that this letter has been written hastily, out of the fullness of my heart, and if I have said what I should not have said, or left unsaid what I should have said I trust that you will retain enough charity to overlook its defects. I am satisfied that we can never understand each other fully, unless we have an interview, and if you will allow me to come to see you for that purpose, write to me immediately. I am very glad to hear of the improvement in your Fathers condition. Will write no more. I have no reach to tell the news.

Good Bye
G. Campbell

Nashville, Feb. 14th, 1861

Mr. Campbell,

I hasten to reply to your last letter in order to remove from your mind as soon as possible any unjust & entirely unfounded suspicion. I assure you in the first place that I would not allow my mind to be influenced against you in whom I have entire confidence, even if any one were so base as to try and injure you in such a cowardly manner as you have suspected & I hope & trust that in the list of my acquaintances there is no one so mean as to attempt any thing of the sort. Believe me when I tell you as a friend that you will never be happy if you allow your mind to entertain suspicions and unkind thoughts against those who have never injured you nor desired to do so in the most remote way. The past report that you refer to of which this author's name was withheld was from an entirely different person from the one who wrote the letter that I referred to, & I should certainly have not said what I did with regard to the remark in that letter, had I known that you would regard it in any other light than as a jest as it was intended. If there had been any serious charge brought against you I hope you do me the justice to believe that I would take a more open handed way of finding out if it was true. Instead of throwing out insinuations concerning it & proceeding in that way, I should have written to you, stated the charge & asked an explanation. But I have had no need to do this, as there has been nothing said that would in the least prejudice me against you. In the letter I referred to, the writer, after speaking of several of my gentlemen friends wrote that he had spent the evening before at Mr. Kirkman's where he had met you & he merely remarked that you were well. I give you my word of honor as a lady, that that was every word that was said in reference to yourself; and you do the gentleman injustice in thinking he would desire to injure you in my opinion for I have often heard him speak of you in the highest terms. In saying that you did not "care much" I was perhaps wrong, but I said it thoughtlessly, & did not attach so deep a meaning to it as it seemed to imply, forgive me if I have done you injustice. I do not think it would be best nor pleasant for you to come to Nashville now as Father's health is improving so fast that we will be able to leave here much sooner than we anticipated, perhaps in the course of a week or two, and then I can explain all that you do not understand if necessary, which I will endeavor to do now however. You know I told you that my Father seriously objected to long engagements & you are also aware that ours would of necessity be a very long one, so for this reason I think it best that no engagement should exist between us. I was too precipitate in making it, but I do not dissolve because I have any less confidence in you than I had then, but for the reason I stated above. The justice & propriety of which I am sure you will see. Please excuse this letter as I have written hastily & have been going out so much lately that my mind is really quite bewildered. We were at a party at Mrs. Martin's last night, at two wedding parties the night before, at a storm party the night before that & are engaged for another tonight. I am so tired I would not go had I not made an engagement. We have to dine out tomorrow & go out again in the evening but after that I intend to decline all parties for a while. I have said all that is necessary now & hoping you understand me. I am as ever, your friend,

Sue B. Woods

Nashville, Feb. 1861 Thursday

Mr. Campbell,

I have delayed this long, replying to your last letter, that I might have time to think well over the matter that forms the subject of this letter. I have looked at it in all its different lights, with anxious interest & after weighing it well in my own mind I have come to the conclusion rather against my inclinations, but in accordance with my better judgment, that it is best our engagement should be broken off for the present at any rate. I have not spoken to Father on the subject since I last wrote you, but I can honestly assure you that he has no objection whatever to you individually, but seriously disapproves of long engagements, & ours would necessarily be one of that nature; so taking these things into consideration, I think it best that it should not be. I hope you will be satisfied with this and I know you will not care much, but if it would give you any pleasure to know it, I will candidly tell you that if I consulted only my own heart in this matter, I would act differently, but I have chosen the other plan because I consider it the wisest & the one most apt to further both your happiness & my own.

I am happy to report Father is very much improved in health since I wrote you last though it will be two or three months yet before he is able to be up. I am having a delightful time here, much pleasanter than I anticipated, but still would much prefer being in St. Louis. I had a long letter from Mr. Wherry the other day, in which he gave me a very interesting piece of intelligence concerning you. Guess what it was! I was glad to learn today that Virginia had set her sister states the good example of standing by the Union. I hope you will do likewise. I hope you will let me know when you receive this letter as I will be anxious until I know it has reached you.

Good Bye

Do not forget your very true friend,

S.B. Woods

Nashville - Feb- 1861 -
Thursday -

Mr. Campbell -

I have delayed thus long, replying to your last letter, that I might
have time to think well over the
matter that forms the subject
of this letter. I have looked at it-
in all its different lights, with
anxious interest, & after weighing it
well in my own mind, I have
come to the conclusion rather a-
gainst my inclination, but in
accordance with my better judgement, that it is best your engagement should be broken off for
the present at any rate. I have
not spoken to Father on the subject since I last wrote you, but
I can honestly assure you that he
has no objection whatever to you
individually, but seriously disapproves
of long engagements, & ours would
necessarily be one of that nature-;
so taking these things into consideration I think it best that it should
not be. I hope you will be satisfied
with this and I know you will not

care much, but if it will give you any
pleasure to know it, I will candidly
tell you that I am .... satisfied only very
.... this matter, I
.... Frankly, but
I have chosen the other plan, because
I consider it the wisest & the one most
apt to further both your happiness &
my own. I am happy to report Father
very much improved in health since
I wrote you last, though it will be
two or three months yet before he
is able to be up. I am having a
delightful time here, much pleasanter than I anticipated, but
still would much prefer being
in St. Louis. I had a long letter from Mr. Hurry the other day,
in which he gave me a very interesting piece of intelligence concerning you. Guess what it was!
I was gifted to learn to day that Virginia had at her sister states
the good example of standing by
the Union, & hope you will do
likewise. I hope you will let me
know when you receive this letter as I will be anxious until I know
it has reached you —
　　　　Good Bye —
Don't forget your very true
　　　　　　Friend
　　　　　　L. B. Moody —

Paducah March 28/61

My Dear Son,

Your letter is to hand and I have read it with careful attention. I regret very much the account you give of your health and of your growing dislike to St. Louis. In these matters you must be your own judge of what is best for you to do. Health is every thing, without it a person can't succeed in life. It is the source of pleasure. That with me would be the most serious item. As to the people, you will find the world all over pretty much alike. You remember Burns' advice to his young friend "You'll find mankind an uncough square & much be they may grieve you." I believe you could rise in your profession in St. Louis to convenience, but if you believe the climate does not suit your health & you are not satisfied, exercise your own good judgment & seek a new theatre for life. Don't let any little temporary discouragement induce you to action in a matter of so much consequence. We are liable to think things and to the disgusts & prejudices they engender for the time. You are experienced enough my dear son to think & act nicely in the matter, consult your health, and to a great extent your feelings, and whatever may be resolve I will no doubt approve of it. I have great hopes of your doing well in life, and with your fixed steady manly principles all that is needed is time to realize my fondest hopes.

We are all in health, times remarkably dull. What has become of the cases with Troop & Norton, and how are you getting along in business. It will be gratifying to learn from you fully as to your business & etc. With my best love.

Your affectionate Father
J. Campbell

Given Campbell Esq.
Atty. at Law
St. Louis, Mo.

My Dear Son,

If you feel that you can't live happily among those people and particularly if your health suffers don't stay. Can't you come home for a little while.

Paducah March 28/41

My dear Son.

Your letter is to hand and
I have read it with careful attention,
I regret very much the account you give
of your health and of your growing dislike
to St Louis. In these matters you must be your
own Judge of what is best for you to do.
health is every thing, without it a person
cant succeed in life. it is the source of
pleasure. That with me would be the most
serious item. as to the people. you will find
the world all over pretty much alike.
Your worthy Burns advises his young
friend "Yet fare mankind an unconth
squad & muckle they may prieve you,,
I believe you could rise in your profession
in St Louis to eminence. but if you believe
the climate does not suit your health & you
are not satisfied. exercise your own good
Judgement & seek a new theater for life.

dont let any little temporary discouragements induce you to action in a matter of so much consequence. We are liable to these things, and to the disgusts & prejudices they engender for the time. You are experienced enough my dear son to think & act wisely in the matter, consult your health, and to a great extent your feelings, and whatever may be resolve I will no doubt approve of it. I have great hopes of your doing well in life, and with your firm steady manly principles all that is needed is time to realize my fondest hopes.

    We are all in health. times unaccountably dull, what has become of the cases with Troop & Norton, and how are you getting along in business It will be satisfying to learn from you fully as to your business &c
        with my best love
                Your affectionate
                  father
                    Hare gale

Given Campbell Esq
   Atto at Law
     St Louis
       Mo

Paducah May 6, 1861

Dear Given,

I intended writing to you last week, but I was so busy in the close of the week that I thought I would put it off to to-day; thinking a day or two would not make very much difference. And now I have so little to tell you about, except the condition of the family, that you must excuse it, if it is a dull letter. we are all well except Mother. She has a bad cold cold, but is better to-day.

Jimmie is at home now. Father wrote for him to come home, for the school Jim said was doing very little good. It has suspended now. I think he came home in very good time for he was quite unwell for a day or two after he reached here, with a boil on his neck. Dr. Thompson lanced it and it is well now. He came home and wanted to join some military company but Mother is opposed to it. There is a Caded Company being drilled, a company of boys which Dick Watts belongs to. I suppose that you and your company are in camp now.

We are all very sorry that things are so, that you have to fight in Missouri, but Kentucky has acted so slow a part that it seems her sons have to leave her. Father says that if Kentucky continues to act in this way, he will go, old as he is, to Virginia, his native state, and offer his services to the Governor, if she looks like she is hard pushed and needs help.

Mother says that she thinks our state has acted such a cowardly part that she thinks that all Kentuckians will have to redeem their own character. She thinks it is awful that her sons and friends have to fight, but I think she has her mind made up to it. Our regiment I believe expect to go into camp soon. The camp is to be some where near Paducah. Captain Tightman is elected Colonel of the regiment.

We have heard that Frank Blair is made a major in the Northern forces. Is it the fact? Do you know where he has taken his family?

we received a letter from sister last week. She was still undecided as to what they would do about coming to the states. She said it all depended on that gun powder business, and George was looking every day for a letter from Washington. I wish we knew whether to expect them or not. George wrote to Father and sister said so herself that she was very fat indeed and had outgrown her dresses.

Well Given, I will close with much love from Mother. Write often as you can.

Good Bye
Carrie

Carrie has said I was sick or unwell. I write this little post script to show you there is not much the matter. Be of good heart my boy. You are on the right side. I want to see you very much.

Your mother

"St. Louis, Mo. May 11th, 1861."

We the undersigned do pledge our words as gentlemen that we will not take up arms, or serve in any military capacity against the United States during this present Civil War. This parole to be returned at any time upon our surrendering ourselves as prisoners of war. (While we sign this parole with the full intention of observing it—we solemnly protest against the justice of its exaction.)

The part in the brackets was added by Col. Brown.

Author's Note: This parole format, added to the bottom of the enclosed letter, was left unsigned. It is not known whether anyone signed it or under what circumstances it was added to the letter. Likewise, the author (except for the bracketed addition) is unknown.

Paducah, Ky. Aug. 10, 1861

My Dear Bettie,

On the morning that I left Glencoe I was sad at the heart, from the fact that I had to leave the house of her I most loved, while she was sick & suffering. I thought all day & the next that possibly the extreme heat might turn your headache into a spell of sickness, and you have no idea how much it troubled me, and to leave if it was so, I delayed till Saturday, when I left on the Ohio & Mississippi Rail Road for Louisville. I arrived at Louisville on Sunday at seven in the morning having had the dustiest & most disagreeable ride of my life. I found Louisville rather excited in consequence of the election which was to come off on the next day, which would in all probability decide the fate of Ky. From what I learn I felt that it was already decided, and that my native state had already forfeited her birthright of bravery & loyalty, for the loaves & fishes of the administration, and the Election the next day justified the opinion, for Ky. has elected a large majority of Union men to her legislature. The next step will be to run out the States Right men, when she will be sealed with the Covenant of Abolitionism. However, the Southern part of the State has given largely increased majorities for Southern Rights and if the upper part of Ky. adheres to the Union the Southern part will go with Tenn. or form a new state.

I left Louisville at 9 A.M. on Sunday on the Louisville & Nashville Rail Road and when we got to the state line we had to change cars as the Kentuckians will not run their trains into Tenn. I arrived at Clarksville that evening about sun set and went from there to "Camp Boone" the place where "the Ky. Brigade in Service of the Confederate States" is encamped. The Camp is beautifully situated about 8 miles from Clarksville in a magnificent grove of oaks, and is remarkably clean & orderly. They have about 1800 men & new levies are coming in every day.

I was most hospitably entertained by the Officers, and the Colonel of the First Regt. told me that he had held open my place for me, until he could do so no longer, as the necessities of the service required it should be filled, & that he thought I would be held by the United States longer than I was. He warmly pushed me to raise a company to go in as the First Company in the Third Regt. & gave me authority to do so & said that he would aid me in any way he could. I am sorry it turns out so but it cannot be helped and the place he wishes me to take is the highest position among the line officers. I came home, and remained one day & then was written for in one of the counties back of here. I went there and they professed to get up a company for me.

I have also had an offer of a company from Louisville Co. & I will determine what I shall do. I would have written to you sooner but for the reason that I have been absent till to day. I showed the daguerrotype you gave me to my mother &

asked her what she thought of it. She said that it was the picture of a very handsome woman & that your face indicated a great deal of character. I told her that the picture was not a justice that the original was incomparably more beautiful. She asked who it was. I told her & told her all about you. After I finished she said that she was glad to hear it, that from what I told her you must be a very fine woman. She remarked at the same time that I was very much in love, which is all very true. When you gave me the daguerrotype I did not think it good enough, because the picture failed to do you justice, but now away from you I would not lose it for any consideration. I have seen many ladies since I left St. Louis but none that can compare to the peerless one I left behind me. You must remember your promise to me. That you will take plenty of exercise on horseback every day, for I do believe that exercise is the secret spring of health & happiness. Take good care of yourself for my sake & write to me very soon

> Yours, with much love
> Given

P.S. I will seal this letter & if it reaches you without being opened in the St. Louis Post Office I write more freely & fully about my movements in my next. Let me know it has been tampered with in the office.

> Yours, GC

August 19, 1861

My Dear Bettie,

I have an opportunity of sending a line to you today & am delighted to do so. I am very anxious to hear from you & hoped to have ere this been happy in your presence. I saw Florence about 10 days since & she's showed me a letter from you to her in which you said it would be very unsafe to come over. This word "unsafe" has become so familiar to me of late that its import is not so energetic as to others. I would risk anything to see you if only for an hour, but about that time, I saw a gentleman from your city who told me that matters there were more stringent than ever & his information induces me to wait till the draft is completed. I have had no letter from you since the two last letters I wrote to you & am consequently very anxious to hear from you. I do not know what would become of me if you were lost to me. I often think that I would almost be lost to myself for this was like fire on certain liquids, draws out the darker lines & streams trails of mans character & the passions of the heart are dispersed for freedom. I have never ceased to thank God for the strong, stout anchor he has moored my nature by & will never cease to pray that it may never be torn loose from me. I see from the papers that the war in Mo. is becoming more & more bloody in its character & am sorry that it is so. The accounts I get from St. Louis alarm me for the safety of some of my friends, who are stated to be in the military prison. Clay Taylor is one among many others. Is it the son of old Mr. N.B. Taylor who was aid to Gen. Price? You must be under the weighty hand of a more than Turkish despotism. I am glad to see that your friend Mr. Brooks has been released. I feared they would send him to spend the _____ in Alton.

When you write to me, tell me all the news of interest. I love to hear news from St. Louis dearly and you know me so well that you know what will interest most. Tell me all about yourself & your health. And now in this connection let me remind you that you are a trustee for me of yourself & you must keep good faith to me in its management or when I see you I will hold you to a strict responsibility before the chancery of love.

But my darling to speak more seriously of a serious subject, you must not expose yourself. You told Florence that you had been sick from going to a party & dancing all night. Now do take care of yourself for my sake. It makes me very unhappy to hear that you are not well. So many lives are wrecked by just such little imprudence in going out to evening parties & taking cold when the system is relaxed. I will write a long letter to you before long & detail my plans to you in a short time.

I have to quit now. My health is fine & am comparatively safe, but my life is somewhat adventurous. Write to me very soon. Love to all.

Good Bye. Yours forever,   G.C.

Florence can put a letter through for me.

August 22. I had a chill yesterday but the large doses of quinine I have taken I hope will prevent a recurrence.

                    G.C.

Paducah, Ky. Aug. 26th, 61

My Dear Bettie,

    I have been very much of a wanderer since my last letter, going through the counties of the hundreds raising a military company for Camp Burnette, one of the camps of the Ky. Brigade, about 12 miles from Clarksville, and yesterday on my return received your letter. My company is intended for Col. Habins Regt., the 4th in the Brigade. He is anxious for me take the post of adjutant in his Regt. but I have made up my mind to take command of a company, as that position is in the line of promotion & more opportunities are afforded for gallant conduct. I desire very much to complete my company & be ordered off into active service soon, & I tell you that you need have no apprehensions for my safety, in case of a fight for I feel that I am not to be taken off in battles & that I will return from the war unharmed.

    If you know how much pleasure the receipt of your letter gave to me, I am sure you would write oftener. I read it over so often that I can almost repeat it. At the close of it you said don't forget the locket &c. I will not forget it, but you will never see it again except you see me with it, unless it is sent to you at my death, or when I go into battle if I am so fortunate as to be in one during the war. I will leave directions to send it to you in case I am killed, but this is the only event upon which it will be returned, unless you desire it after having ceased to love me & allied yourself to another. You must not let the fascinations of your beaux induce you to forget me who though absent loves you more than all the rest of them together. It is a popular fallacy that "absence conquers love." I know that it is not so, for the longer I am away from you the more anxious I am to see you, and the more clearly do I recognize your superiority to my other lady acquaintances. I have not been to see a single young lady since I saw you last, and do not expect to unless I go to Nashville where I will visit you & my friend—I saw Dr. Michel at Clarksville on last Saturday. He was from St. Louis & gave me all the news. He told me what I was very glad to hear that your father was rapidly recovering & that his physician thought he would very soon have full use of his leg. He gave me a very bad piece of advice, I mean that I should have wished to hear just the opposite, i.e. when I told him I wished to go to St. Louis soon to settle up some very important business he told me that he thought it would be impossible for me to go there & remain in disguises & that that if I was recognized I would surely be arrested & perhaps treated as a spy if they found out that I was in the Confederate service; no matter how foreign such a purpose might be to me. He said that the country also was under martial law; upon his representations & yours, I will delay my visit for a few weeks & wait & see if affairs improve in the city & if they do not I will try & see you in spite of the risk for you do not know how I do wish to see you once again before being ordered off.

I am glad to hear that you are getting to be such a good equestrian for I am sure it will be the best thing for you, but am sorry to hear that you go to the city to live as it will make it more difficult for me to see you without exposure. Affairs in Ky. are rapidly approaching a crisis & it would not surprise me to hear at any hour of war commenced in the center of the states. Down here in the western district we are happily united, all for the South & the people in this district are determined to go with the South let the course of Ky. be what it may. We had quite an excitement here a few days ago. The gunboat Conestoga came up from Cairo & captured a small stern wheelboat which runs in the Tenn. River called the Ferry on the ground that she carried a secession flag & carried contraband goods to the South. This caused great excitement but as the deed was over before breakfast very few people knew of it! At eleven o'clock in the day a large boat owned at Evansville, Indiana came down the Ohio & landed at the wharf where she was boarded by about 20 reckless men citizens of Paducah & the boat & cargo captured, the crew sent on shore & the boat & cargo were taken up Tenn. River into Tennessee & landed under the guns of Fort Henry. The prize was a very valuable one the boat a fine one & the cargo large, consisting principally of coffee. The H.K. did not make by the operation. This seizure of the Ferry was a very grave violation of Ky. neutrality. It remains to be seen what can be done by our Govt. whose hands are almost tied by a submissionist military council.

Around here we all have very much confidence in Mo. I believe that she will come out of this struggle for independence with honour & success. I was delighted to hear of the death of Genl. Lyons for he was the man most dangerous to our cause in Mo. I expect the Ky. Brigade will be ordered to Mo. If so the prayer of my heart is that I may be spared & allowed to march into St. Louis in triumph. I must close now & ask you to excuse this badly written letter and to keep your promise about punctuality.

> With much love
> Yours, Given

Paducah Ky. Sept. 2d, 1861

My Dear Bettie,

You see that I am making the promises, I made in my last, good i.e. to write once a week. I am very much afraid that the answer to it will not reach me, as the department at Washington has decided to close up all the offices west of the Tennessee River except the post office at Matfield in Graves Co: Ky: considering this part of Ky. as in a state of rebellion. Mr. Lincolns Govt. does not allow one pound of provisions or goods of any kind to come to this place; and the Military authorities at Cairo have threatened to shell & burn the town of Paducah to the ground, if the citizens offer any more indignities to the vessels of U.S. This is a large threat, but the people here are not the least frightened, and on account of these warm Southern sentiments the town is known in the South as "little Charlestown." Matters here are rapidly assuming a grave aspect, and we are all satisfied that this state will soon commence her ordeal of fire & blood. Many families have left Louisville, Lexington & other places in the state from a vivid apprehension of coming dangers. I am satisfied that Ky. will never be a reliable member of the Confederate States until she has gone through a bloody purgation. She might once have united with the South with honor & comparative unity but the people let the opportunity slip & they must drain the bitter consequences to the dregs.

But I will not dwell on this for I know you do not care much for politics. I long to see you—to hear your voice, if only for a short time, but there are obstacles which render it at present almost impossible. I have been informed that the Govt. has commenced a secret system of espionage, which is only one further step towards despotism. The Confederate States are not recognized by Lincoln as belligerent & he will not exchange prisoners with them. If he would do this I would not mind the risk, but to be taken & sent to his "Bastile" in New York & immersed in its dungeon til the end of the war is a danger worth a thought. I leave here to-day for camp with some recruits for my company which will shortly be full. They are all willing here for me to go, and I am anxious to be at work, not that I am afraid that I will not have planty to do, for I think that the North is just gathering for the struggle of which Manassas was but the introduction. I have great confidence in our cause & in its eventual success; but of all else I am most interested in my state Mo: & the Mecca of my hopes is to be able to march with a victorious army into St. Louis. I suppose that it will not be too prudent for me to write so plainly to you as St. Louis is under Martial Law & correspondence may be examined if so I promise not again to offend and in writing to me, it would be best for you not to say anything about St. Louis & its military condition. For you see by the papers that even Ladies are not exempt from the cowardly despotism of the Govt.

I have been to an entertainment lately, where there was wit & beauty the first & only one I have attended since I left St. Louis. I had a pleasant "hum-drum" time and was supremely indifferent. I really enjoy this feeling of perfect invulnerability. I am almost in hopes that you do not realize how secure your dominion in my heart is. I have no eye nor ear for another. But sometimes I have a fleeting fear that perhaps some one of your acquaintances aided by time & absence may obliterate the traces I left behind in your memory; but I banish these unwelcome thoughts & as the song goes "trust to luck."

I must close this hurried note with a request that you write often—

Yours with much love
Given

P.S. Direct the answer of this to me at Mayfield

Graves County
Ky
G

Sunday Afternoon
Feb. 1862

Sept. 26. 1861

My Dearest Bettie,

I have had no letter from you since the first you wrote to me, and do not know that my last three have reached you at all, but I intend to continue to write to you, in the hope that you may hear from me. I am satisfied that you alone can make me happy & without you I should be disparate. These desperate times have strange influences on men's souls, and I look to you & your love as the steel anchor of my soul. I have been a sad man about of late, and on yesterday saw your Aunt Mrs. Hamilton & Miss Ida who were very kind to me indeed. I love them not only for your sake but for their own intrinsic worth. Your Aunt had had the Rheumatism & was a little lame, but had nearly recovered. Miss Ida seemed to me to have grown taller, at times she reminded me of you & I could have faced all dangers to have obliged her on that account. She gave me the little gold lame' broach, and said I must give it to you as I would see you long before she would. I promised to do so & if you get it from my hands before very long, you must not be at all surprised. Mrs. H. told me that you still remained at Glencoe & would remain there all the winter, all of which I was glad to hear for obvious reasons. I called to see your Aunt Mrs. K. & Miss Sue & the young ladies but they were not at home. I did not see any of the male members of the family, but understood that all were well. Your Uncle James Hamilton was very well indeed & all seemed in excellent spirits. Mr. K. & your Aunt Lizzie & Miss Sue were on a visit to Mrs. K's father & had been absent for some time. There was no further news in the place of interest; generally all things were going on well when you see me I suppose you will hardly know me. I have tanned so much that I might well be called very swarthy, but the change is only in complexion. I am the same in feeling as ever & if I thought any change to my disadvantage had taken place in you I would not care to live longer. Kentucky is in a worse condition than poor Missouri. Many of her best citizens have been incarcerated & her fair fields will soon run red with her children's blood. Each side is rapidly concentrating for a battle which will decide the wasting of the "dark & bloody ground." Communication between the northern & southern parts of the state is almost impossible as the utmost vigilance is observed to prevent it. The Confederate troops have occupied Bowling Green & as far up as Green River. North of that the Federal troops have possession & their forces are gradually drawing nearer to the Confederate forces. So you may ask for important results in a short time. I have only time to write this little note to you as the bearer of it goes away in a few minutes. I am well with the exception of a very pertinacious cold and in very low spirits. If I could only hear from you now an than I should be better satisfied, and although I am of a sanguine hopeful disposition the hope deferred has almost made me heart sick. When you write to me again write to me at Paducah, Ky. care of Charles T. Bronson the postmaster there, that is if the place is not taken by the Confederates, for if it is, the mails will be stopped. I would give two years of my life to see you if only for a short time.

Write to me soon my dearest & believe me,
Yours forever
Given

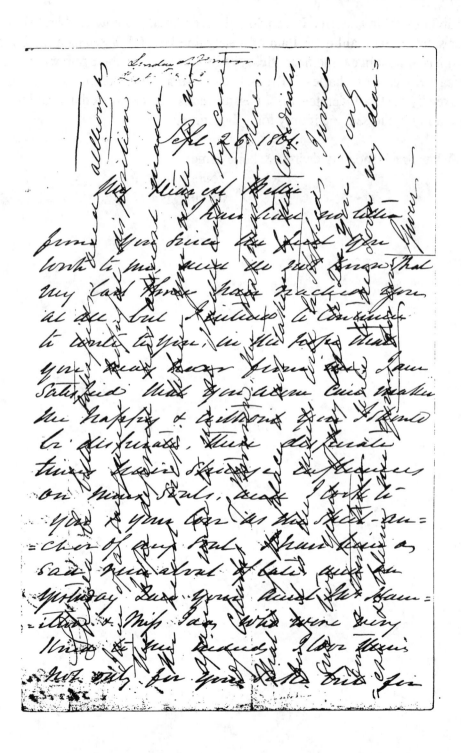

but for their own intrinsic worth.
Your Aunt had had the Rheumatism
& was a little lame, but had near=
=ly recovered, Miss Ida seemed to me
to have grown taller, at times she
reminded me of you & I could
have passed all day as to have
obliged her on that account.
She saw the little gold Curved
Comb, and said I must send it to
you as I would see you long before
she would, I promised to do so &
if you get it from my hands
before very long, you must not be
at all surprised. Mr H. told me
that you were rendered at Geneva
& would remain there all the win
=ter, all of which I was glad to hear
for obvious reasons. I called to see
your aunt Mr K & Miss Lee & the Young
ladies but they were not at home.
I did not see any of the male
members of the family, but under
= stood

that all were well. Your Uncle James Hamilton was very well indeed & all seemed in excellent spirits. Mr K. & your aunt Lizzie & Miss Sue were on a visit to Mr McFullen & had been absent for some time. There was no further news in the place of interest; generally, all things were going on well. When you see me I suppose you will hardly know me, I have tanned so much that I might even be called very swarthy, but the change is only in complexion, I am the same in feeling as ever, & if I thought any change to my disadvantage had taken place in you I would not care to live longer, Kentucky is in a worse condition than poor Missouri. Many of her best citizens have been incarcerated & her fair fields will soon run red with her childrens blood. Each side is rapidly concentrating for a battle which will decide the mastery of the dark & bloody ground." Communication between the Northern & Southern parts of the State is almost impossible as the utmost vigilance is observed to prevent it. the Confederate troops have occupied Bowling Green & as far up as Green River: North of that the Federal troops have possession & their forces are gradually drawing near to the Confederate forces. So you may look for important results in a short time. I have only time to write this little note to you as the bearer of it goes away in a few minutes. I am well with the exception of a very particular severe cold, and in very low spirits. If I could only hear from you, now an then I

Benton, Ky. Oct. 3rd, 1861
Sunday afternoon, Feb. 23rd, 1862.
Mr. Newbold looking out opposite.

My Dearest Bettie,

You will perhaps be surprised to get a letter from this out of the way place, but I am here to have communication with my family before leaving there perhaps forever. I was very near to Paducah on yesterday & sent for Mother to come here & meet me. She is here now and gives a sad account of the condition of affairs in Paducah. There are not more than half a dozen families of her acquaintance left there, all the rest have moved away fearing an attack from the Confederate forces. I am very *very* anxious to hear from you, and the time does seem so long. In my last I requested you to write to me at Paducah, care of Charles T. Bronson, but the mails are so uncertain that I am afraid it never reached you. I send, by private hand, a letter from your Aunt Mrs. Hamilton to your mother which will be mailed at Paducah, directed to the care of Mr. James E. Yeatman which with this I hope will reach you. For the first time for more than a month I saw a St. Louis paper to-day, and from it I see many familiar names in strange connections. But all these changes may be ephemeral, and when the sun shines again, the same things may wear a new aspect. I see that Maj. McKuntry has been promoted but it does not state who is provost marshall in his stead. I read the whole of the four pages advertisements & all and devoured its dull columns, with as much avidity as if I hungered for such literary food. I did not know how much I liked St. Louis & the people there until now for it seems that distance lends enchantment to the view indeed. In my last letter I told you all the news from your friends in N. & of your cousin Ida. I see in the St. Louis papers mention made of Lieut. Col. Thatcher & also Lieut. Tennent. Are they citizens of St. Louis & has Albert joined the army? He would make a capitol officer, his stature is so short that the balls would all range too high. Does he visit you at Glencoe as often as he did? Write to me & tell me what has become of Mr. Bouvier. I was rather favourably impressed with him. Tell me also what has become of Col. Churchill. I heard they had him in prison, along with many others of the prominent citizens of the city and when you write, write a very long letter, for you do not know how much I enjoy your letters, & how dear every line is to me. I have been very miserable for several days past and the reason is that I cannot hear from you. I am making my arrangements to come to Missouri soon, where perhaps we may soon meet. I would incur almost any risk to see you, if but for an hour. I did not think that I could ever desire to see any one half so much, as I do you, and I love you more now than ever. I must close this letter now as the messenger is ready to start with it. I am enjoying good health but am very much bronzed by exposure to the sun & air & now my dearest Good Bye, write very soon & a long letter & believe me

                        Yours affectionately forever,
                        Given

To Miss Sue Bettie Woods
St. Louis, Mo.

P.S. Excuse this paper & envelope. They are the best the village affords. G.

Benton, Ky. Oct. 19, 61

My Dearest Bettie,

I have just returned from a long trip on business connected with the new calling I have adopted. On my trip I saw many familiar faces & old friends, Clarke Kennedy & Mr. Decker & Dr. Bryan & Michael &c. I had to come back here to get some personal property of mine & on my arrival a package of papers & letters were handed to me. I looked over these hastily & among these recognized your letter of Oct. 10th. Oh I was so glad to get one more letter from you. I could not express to you my joy at hearing from you again & that you were well & was unchanged, though of a change I was not much afraid, for our acquaintance & my love was often confirmed & well tried to give way to any ephemeral circumstances. When I came here I did not expect to remain half an hour but I will stay here, almost in the lines of the Northern troops & write a letter to you, for I don't know when again I shall have an opportunity to write so that a letter will, with any certainty reach you. I leave here this evening to make my way to Missouri to cast my fortunes with the gallant army. Have resigned in Ky. & have better offers in Mo. I am in fine health and will stand the rough & long land trip well. If you were in the country I might see you & as it is if I can get news will let you know it so we may meet again & that before the winter is over. I feel that I have never loved before & believe I should never love another in the event I should be doomed to wear the crowning heart for my idol gone to heaven—you may think that I am foolish to let such an idea as death enter my head, but I love you so much that apprehensions vague & quick, sometimes attack my happiness. Your letters are always most interesting to me, and I have never since any thought or idea expressed in them which could be called stupid. I think you are as perfect as the Lord will allow to live under the grade of his angels & love you more than anything or being in the universe & do not like even to hear your own lips speak a charge which anothers folly would quickly repent having uttered. You speak of sewing a good deal—Now my own dear Bettie do not work at the stitch too much, for it will injure your health. You know how much I always hated to see anyone dear to me continually stitching away. My aversion to it runs in our family, for Father has the same feeling. I am glad to hear you ride so well & often it is such healthful exercise but you must not sit up to late at night, nor read too much by the gas light & above all keep up a cheerful heart for though the day may be dark & dreary, "Behind the clouds is the sun still shining." I feel that I am not destined to be hurt in this war & that for us is laid up abundant happiness. If the war does not look like there will be an end of it by the next spring, I wish to see you in the meantime & make preparations for our marriage in the summer or fall, for I should be most miserable to be away from you during the whole of a long war, where if you were my wife you could come to some neutral or safe ground where we could meet each other sometimes. If I do not have you for my wife, I shall never marry another, for I could never love another, and my days would be passed in other more peaceful pursuits for I should seek the deep excitements of danger & adoration & quiet would be a stranger to my soul. But I believe in the efficacy of my destiny, & that I believe is to be bright & happy. The sun is going down in the west now & I have a lonely ride through the woods of twenty miles & must bring this rambling letter to a close. You must excuse all its omissions & ingratuities—Write to me occassionally at Paducah as long as the mails go there & the letters will be saved for me or sent to me. I will not forget you, dearer to me than all the Earth & Heaven besides, and will write to you at every opportunity. Do not forget me & think often of the happy days we have passed together & remember me in your prayers. I shall never no never forget you and if it is possible will see you before I am many months older for I wish to see you more perhaps than you do me. Take good care of yourself & do nothing to impair life's greatest blessing—health, for I leave you as my trustee of yourself for I claim a valuable interest in you—Now Good Bye My Dear Bettie. When you hear of me again it will be in Mo.

Yours forever, Given

Miss Sue Bettie Woods
Saint Louis, Mo.

P.S. I send this care of James E. Yeatman who is a Union man & may be through him it will go safely.

GC

Paris, Tenn. Oct. 23rd, 61

My Dear Bettie,

Please wear this ring for my sake. I hope to see you soon.

GC

P.S. Florence will send it & explain. Write to me.

G.

Miss Sue Bettie Woods
St. Louis, Mo.

November 4th, 1861

My Dearest Bettie,

I wrote to you just before I left Ky. for Mo: but do not know if the letter ever reached you. I recd. your letter of the 10th & was more than delighted, just before I left I wrote a note to my sister Florence to send to you the diamond ring. You once had, by express, & to write a note to you explanatory. I suppose she has done so, as she would do anything for me in the world & in a matter of this kind would not fail. I left Ky. on the 23rd of the month of October & reached New Madrid on the 26th & remained there during the Sabbath. The next day I reached Bloomfield & was in Jeff Thompsons camp. That night his camp & its occupants reminded me very much of Simm's descriptions of Marion, his camp & men—You have had no doubt accounts in the city papers of his route &c. At Fredincktown, well the facts on his side were these. He had about 1100 men & about 700 of them took part in the fight. His loss in the fight was 19 killed & 25 wounded, and one of his surgeons who had remained with the wounded said he counted 40 wagon loads of dead hauled from the field by the Federals. Drake McDowell, as son of the old Dr. at St. Louis, is one of the aids to Genl. Thompson. He has also an Indian on his staff named Ajax & this one Indian has been magnified into 500 warriors by the fertile imaginations of newspaper correspondents. We left Bloomfield on Tuesday morning & about dinner time, we were overtaken by J.D. Clarkson, a brother to "Dave" & son of the old major. He & a young friend of mine & myself came through the country to this place (Yellville, Arkansas). We crossed a great many swamps & forded a great many rivers & one of these we crossed elev times. I never saw so poor a country as this South Mo: the people have as a general thing have nothing but a bare sustenance from the stingy soil, but nearly all of them have a lofty independence & a hatred to oppression which has drained the country of nearly all the men able to bear arms. This portion of the country is destitute of the luxuries & also of most of the comforts of life. They have many queer substitutes for coffee, one is corn meal coffee, another is rye, or wheat or sweet potatoes. I have partaken of all these different kinds, and also of a most villanous mixture which the old women here call "Store Tea," made of dried apple leaves, and "Sassafras Tea" is a great stand bye. It is an old saying that variety is the spice of life. If it is I am very well spiced by this time & as to bed's, we had all kinds. One night I slept in a room with a family of 13 men, women & children in a room no larger than 12 by 14 feet. I slept well & did not wake till the day was breaking. When I arose from my downy couch, for you know I am very industrious & such early hours do not at all incommode me, and to sleep all three on a pallet on the floor is our common fare. I am getting used to this kind of life, and my health is better than usual. I have a fine appetite & can eat almost any kind of provender, and one reason for all this I believe is that I feel as if I am in the path of duty, and as soon as I touched the soil made sacred by so many delightful recollections, I felt as if I was in a new atmosphere, an exhilarating delightful atmosphere, which came to me fresh from the home of my dearest idol. I feel more like I am near to you now than when I was in Ky. though here I am more than 10 days steady travel from you & there I was in about 24 hours ride. But now I believe I am on the road to St. Louis & I saw a wager offered of a basket of champagne that the Confederates would be in St. Louis in less than 25 days. But there were no takers. We are all Confederates now for the Missouri Legislature sitting at Neosho on Monday the 28th Oct. 1861 passed an ordinance of secession making Mo. one of the Confederate States. McCulloch & Price have formed a junction of their forces & a fight is expected to take place in the course of a week or ten days. I will without an accident be there in time for it but not in time to get a command. I am afraid, all people here are confident of the success of Price's army, who are supposed to be well armed & disciplined and equal in numbers to the other side, but I am afraid that our forces are over estimated both in numbers & efficiency, but if we have 2/3 of their number well armed, we are confident of success. If we go into St. Louis victorious I will see you soon. If not I hope to be able (& will do so) to come to St. Louis to see you this winter. I do want to see you so much, that I cannot express it to you—I have your watch charm (the currie comb) & all of the tokens you ever gave to me with me & if I am killed I will leave directions with some friend to look into my pocket book & there he will find directions what to do; and I shall leave directions to send all of these if I am killed to you and in the meantime if you do not get any letters from me do not fear for me, but I will seek every opportunity of writing to you, which may or may not be often, but during every vicissitude and danger I will ever remain the same in heart towards you, and my fear is that I love you so much more than any other, being that some jealous power may deprive me of you. I need no teacher to instruct me that I should not idolize any one but I do not desire to forego my love for you though it came under the ban as idolatry. I wish you would write to me sometimes at Paducah, Ky. for I have made an arrangement to have my my letters forwarded to me, and if you have time, or the inclination write to Florence occassionally she will answer your letters with pleasure. Well I must now close this badly written note. This place, the village of Yellville did not have a single sheet of paper & I borrowed this from Clarkson, who bye the bye wishes very much to write to his family to let them know he is safe & well & in hailing distance of the army which he expects to join in a few days. And now good bye my dearest one. May God bless you & protect you and not allow any evil to befall you.

And you must remember me often out here in this lovely country, for I feel that in this war I am fighting my way to see you once more. I shall never love you less though life should last a century. Your most affectionately forever,

Given

Miss Sue Bettie Woods
Saint Louis. Mo.

Camp near Pineville, McDonald Co. Mo:
Nov. 13, 1861

My Dearest Bettie,

I have just learned that young Von. Phul leaves here for Memphis in a few minutes & he has volunteered to take a letter for me. I have only time to write a hurried note; to tell you that I am well & in fine sprits and think of your own sweet self more frequently than ever. We have had no fight yet, but are anxiously anticipating an attack upon our outposts by the advance of the enemy. If I am slain in the fight I have left a little slip in my pocket-book, directing the gold locket & my seal ring & a few other things to be sent to you. I hope the contingency may not happen and if there is anything in presentiment, I am safe; for I feel that I shall go through unscathed. Our affairs are not as encouraging as reports have led me to believe, but whatever may happen I am fully of the intention to carry out my proferred visit to you, before the winter is over. I do wish to see you so much, and I believe that I would be happier than any other man if I could see you & speak with you for only a few hours. But my time has expired & I must close. Good Bye. Remember me & think of me very often is the request of

Yours most affectionately
Given

Miss Sue Bettie Woods
Care of Robt. K. Woods, Esq.
St. Louis, Mo.

Camp near Pinville . McDonald Co. Mo:
Nov. 13. 1861.
My dearest Willie

I have just learn=
=ed that young Van. Phul leaves.
here for Memphis, in a few minutes &
he has volunteered to take a letter for
me. I have only time to write a
hurried note; to tell you that I
am well & in fine spirits and
think of your own sweet self more
frequently than ever. We have
had no fight yet. but are anxious
=ly anticipating an attack upon
our outposts by the advance of
the enemy. If I am slain in the
fight I have left a little slip in
my pocket-Book, directing the Gold
Watch & my seal ring & a few other
things to be sent to you. I hope
the Contingency may not happen

and if there is anything in presentment, I am safe; for I feel that I shall go through unscathed.

Our affairs are not as encouraging as report had led me to believe, but whatever may happen I am fully of the intention to carry out my proposed visit to you, before the winter is over — I do wish to see you so much, and I believe that I would be happier than any other man if I could see you & speak with you for only a few hours, but my time has expired & I must close — Good Bye Remember me & think of me very often is the request of

Yours most affectionately
Gus

Miss. Sue. Hattie. Wood.
Care of Robt K. Wood, Esqr
St Louis Mo.

Dec. 7th, 1861

My Dear Bettie,

I have written to you twice, lately, from this place & hope that the letters have come to hand. I write a note to you now to find out where you will be about the first or middle of January, as I shall endeavor to see you about that time. Write to me & tell me where it would be best for me to meet you in the city, at your house, or in the country, for I must see you this winter. Direct your letter to "George H. Canter, Clinton, Missouri" who will have it forwarded to me here. I shall look for a letter from you in a very few days for it is important for me to hear at once, put nothing contraband in the letter for it may be examined and stopped. My health for the last week has not been so good, having contracted a bad cold from exposure. I hope this will go straight & your reply will also come safely to hand for you do not know how much I wish to see you & speak to you & hear your voice. You will understand why I wish the letter so directed, in order to ensure its safe arrival. Write me a long letter & tell me all about yourself & every body else of my acquaintance. I have no more time, for I have hurriedly scratched off this note while the gentleman is eating his breakfast & he is now ready to leave.

Good Bye my dearest & take good care of yourself. Be sure to write soon.

Yours most affectionately
GC

Jan'y 15, 1862

My Dearest Bettie,

I wrote to you a few days ago and today have another opportunity of writing. I never hear from you by letter or directly by information. Yet I have the utmost confidence in you & know that you would write to me very often if you had the facility of mails. I have occasionally opportunities to overcome these difficulties & shall in every instance avail myself of these. I would give almost anything in this world to get a long & sweet letter from you & if any chance presents itself you must not let it pass. I am yet at the same place & am very well & in good spirits. Tho' the winter here is severe, and the earth is now robed in its mantle of white I have for the last week or two days been an anxious watcher day & night by the bedside of my dearest friend out here, but thank God by diet of careful nursing & skillful attention he is now convalescing from the most severe attack of typhoid-pneumonia, loss of rest & anxiety have wore me down some, but I feel as usual and during the quiet hours of the night when setting by his couch I had most frequent opportunities of reviewing the incidents of the past years, and you have no idea how delightful the remembrances of our sweet intercourse were, and after each reverie I was compelled to admit that amid civil & political commotions & the upheavings of the wrath of a people & suffering & distress & death, I was yet the most fortunate of men in possessing a nature which the greedy grasp of war could not deprive one of, and that nature is the pure untainted love of a stainless heart. I live now in the future and many are the bright day dreams which flit across the disc of my mind, and strange to say the image of your own sweet self rests in the foreground of each of these pictures of the mind. I am truer to you today than I am to anything else in this world & all that I ask is that you will be true to yourself & to me. It shall not be much longer before I will see you & in your reply you must tell me how I can best accomplish that much desired end. This letter will be sent by private hand, and as soon (immediately) after you get it, if you will send a letter directed to me under the name of Given H. Caldwallader & place it in the post office at once directed to the above person at Pronkomme Post Office, St. Louis County, Mo. I will get the letter. Now my darling be sure & write to me by this opportunity for I long to hear from you. Now do not forget me & remember me well as your own true & faithful,

Given

P.S. I enclose my direction for the answer to this letter.

Springfield, Mo. Jan'y 26, 1862

Received March 17th/62
Miss Sue Betty Woods, St. Louis, Mo.

My Dearest Bettie,

Your sweet letter of Dec. 10th, 61 came safely to hand about a week ago and it made me happy very happy to know that you was well & that your family was well & had not been molested by the Fedl. Govt. authorities. I had not received a letter from you since one written Oct. 10th, and I received it with almost childish glee, for I read it & reread it until I could repeat to myself its contents. I wrote a little note to you on yesterday by private hand going to St. Louis. I could write no longer letter as the gentleman was about to start just as I came in town from a long scout, having been sent out by the Maj. General a few days before, so I had but a moment to write in. I am rejoiced that you & Florence have opened a correspondence & hope that you will not let it flag between you, for it is a strong link of sympathy between us two. I love my sister almost as much as I do you & if you knew her you would love her not only for my sake but for her own intense qualities. She is a great girl and loves me as well as a sister can love a brother. I am very glad to know that the ring came safely to hand though if I could have seen you I should have liked to have placed a gage d' armour more worthy of your acceptance, but I am proud to know that it now encircles the small finger of her I love most of all & the only one I ever loved, now you may not believe me when I tell you that I have never loved another than you. The first time I ever saw you coming out of the church door, a few days after I came to St. Louis to live I felt a singular attraction for you & my eyes followed that fair form as far as the distance would allow and when I was introduced to you at your house I talked long and attentively with you for I wished to see if the beautiful cachet contained a gem of a character to correspond with the cachet in which it was contained & went away satisfied that a fine intellect, a pure heart & beautiful person was all included in one sweet creature, & ever since that day I have felt towards you as I never felt for another & never expect to feel for another. Now you must not consider this as flattery for it is not & if you will reflect you will know it is not. You must wear it always & do not let the perpetual attentions & supplications of Bredell wear away the impress of the absent one. I know your opinion of him & do not deem it necessary to remind you that the perpetual dripping of water wears away the solid rock. We are of the opinion here that war cannot last very much longer & at its end will begin our happiness, but I am almost sorry that I made this playful caution to you for your acquaintance with me has been too long & your character is too high for me to doubt you for one moment, and as to reports of my death, believe none of these for fate has decreed a bright & honourable career for me & all that I ask is to have a portion for it of my hearts selection & that selection has been forever made. I cannot imagine how these foolish reports could have got such currency then, for a day or two ago a young Mr. Waples brought us news that they had us dead & buried & that a great many of my friends were lamenting my untimely death. He sd. that he had seen a photograph of me at Mr. Hardings & that he would not know me as the same person for I look like a border ruffian now—with a black hat & a black plume in it—a red shirt, military pants & horsemans boots—with large Spanish spurs, wouldn't you like to see how I look in such a costume with beard all over my face, for I haven't trimmed it for several months. I am getting on finely here & if I do say so myself, am becoming very popularly known here & have acquired a great many friends. I will not tell you what I am doing here, but you will probably hear before very long.

I am very sad when I think of the sickness in St. Louis & am haunted by occassional fears that you may be stricken by the pestilential agents, but I shall drive away all these unhappy misgivings & believe that God will protect you as in the hollow of his hand and in this connection I thank you for your good advice about reading my Bible. I love you for your piety, and you may recollect that remark I made to you in Sam Kirkmans parlor on that rainy Tuesday night which I so well remember, when I told you that I believed if I was saved itbe by the hand of a lady & that lady you may guess.

I am glad to hear that you like Wm. Saltlance for he is worthy of it, and I am gratified to learn that he remembers me. He is not like the small fry who skip around in society in St. Louis, but is a man of sterling qualities. I am not surprised that it did not occur before. I see that Miss Cornelia who you know I warned you against before I left was the first swift harbinger of my death to you. I cannot conceive why she should wish to be the first to break such news to you. You must keep watch on her & by no means allow any intimacy to spring up between you for though she is as fair as a May morning in her manners and talk, yet the deadly typhus is not more fatal in its effects. She is dangerous. Now Cates is a fine fellow & I thank him for his consideration in letting you know the report was false. You must love my friends too; you know I love my friends & do not love my enemies unscriptural though it is to say so—but I never concealed from you my imperfections & this revelation does not take you by surprise I know. Now let me doubly thank you for the language of affection in your letter, nor do I consider it unmaidenly, but I do think that it shows the true hearted & sensible woman & I love you all the more for it. Mr. Chiles told me he saw you & your mother only a few days before he left St. Louis about Dec. 22nd & has the little present you sent me in his baggage which will be here in a day or two.

He told me that your Mother (who I love) wished him to bring me a pair of blankets for which I thank her much. I have one pair of blankets & in camp sometimes sleep a little cool. But thus far I have had excellent health except for the last week I took cold in my head & settled in my lower jaw & gave me great pain for several days, and made my jaw so stiff that for several days I could not open my mouth wide enough to chew any food. I weigh more than I ever did in St. Louis. I send this letter to Paducah to be mailed to you & hope it will go safely to hand. I am now about to close this long letter my best respects to your Father & Mother & a kiss for the children and an inestimable quantity for yourself. Good bye now my darling. Take good care of yourself for my sake & remember me in your prayers. Yours forever most affectionately,

Given

Sunday Afternoon
Feb. 16, 1862
21 minutes past four

Springfield, Jan'y 26, '62
Miss Sue Bettie Woods,
St. Louis, Mo.

My Darling Bettie,

    I have just got in from a long tramp through the woods & find that a gentleman leaves for St. Louis in a very short time, only allowing me time to write a line to you. My hands are very cold for I have not had time to warm them so you must excuse the chirography. I was most delighted to get your letter of Dec. 10th, and oh you do not know how happy its contents made me. I will not die nor be killed, nor must you believe any such report, for "there is a destiny that shapes our lives," & that destiny has decreed that you & I shall pass this life hand in hand through its sunshine & shadows. I feel so much more love for you than I have time or could express if I had time, that I must bring this scrawl to a close.

    I heard from you & your mother by Mr. Chiles of St. Louis & now thank you for the beautiful present you sent to me which evinces so much thoughtfullness for your absent, but not forgotten Given.

    I will obey your injunction & read my Bible. Now good bye my darling—I have no more time as he is starting. Remember me in your prayers & I know I shall be blest.

                    Yours forever most affectionately,
                    Given

Received: 13 days on the way

Sunday Afternoon
Feb. 23rd, 1862

Camp Muriette, Sept. 9th, 1861
10 miles North of Clarksville
4th Regt. Ky. Brigade

My Own Dear Bettie,

I am writing this letter to you under manifold difficulties. In the first place my marquee is full of visitors, officers of other companies, who, though I leave them to entertain themselves, frequently interrupt me with questions & etc., and this letter is written upon the top of a cigar box, placed upon a valise on end, for a table. I have been here but a few days and am not as well fixed up as to tables, stands &c. as I intend. And in addition to all these petty inconveniences, I am very much troubled on account of a perfect ignorance of the condition & whereabouts of my mother, father, & sisters. I know that father has made himself very obnoxious to the administration on account of his Southern inclinations & the influence he has unwaveringly cast for that side. I have heard that he is safe & the papers have informed me that Gen. Grant said in his proclamation that he had come to "defend & protect the citizens" of Paducah. I have no apprehension of any present danger & in case the place is attacked by the Confederates, the women & children wd. be moved out, but the constant unsatisfied & disturbed condition of mind make me unhappy. Now while I am writing a thunderstorm with vivid lightning has broken upon us & I feel as if this discharge of the elements has in some degree cleared ups my feelings also for I delight to look at the sublimities of nature & the terrible magnificences of a real storm has a fascination for her which usually makes my spirits rise. However, if the style or chirography of this letter should fall short of a critical standard you must overlook its faults for my sake.

I wrote to you from Mayfield a few days ago and requested the answer to be mailed to me at Russelville, Ky. where I wish you wd. direct the answers to this also. I will go there in a few days & see if you have written & the letter is there. How long this avenue of communication may be open I know not, for I am afraid that the South part of Ky. is avowed to taste of the bitter civil war first. But I will continue to write to you whether your letters made me or not, for if you continue to love me you will be glad to hear of me & if you acknowledge these letters I will most probably get them & do not fail to write because you think that your letter might miscarry for you do not know how much I prize any little line from you. The daguerrotype and locket are great comforts for me & I carry them with me at all times & looking pleases me so much as to go out of the guard into the woods and take them & think over the pleasant hours we have spent together & in our walks & rides. These are the sparks of light which guide me on my way & without these happy reflections & the bright hopes ahead I would be more desolate than a shipwrecked mariner without his compass on an unknown ocean. I get to thinking of the hard fate which closed the door to any communication with you except by letter & of the idea that the homes of those that I hold dear & of you whom I hold dearest of all others, closed against me by the fate of war, almost makes me curse the authors of this horrid civil war; but then I feel that if I am beloved by you I am fortunate in spite of my misfortunes. I have just been informed that news has come that the confederate troops under Pillow are marching on Paducah & if the news is true I will leave here for Paducah & take a hand in setting fires the city—and if possible to get my Father's family out of the place beforehand. But I hardly believe it to be true, if it is confirmed by tomorrow, I shall leave a Lieut. in charge of the company & start. The drum has beat for Dixie & I must close this discussion note.

You must write to me at Russelville, Logan County, Ky. for I do wait to hear from you so much. Good Bye my dearest and believe me as ever,

Yours   Given.

Camp near Baldwin Tishomingo Co. Miss.

Miss Sue Bettie Woods
My Darling (Saint Louis, Mo.)

Genl. Price has just finished writing a letter to be sent to parts unknown & I have this pen & paper to write a note to you, though I cannot promise it will be either long or interesting, as it is late at night and very warm. I cannot impart as much intelligence to you as I would like, though the rumors which have just reached us make our prospects look bright indeed, for we have heard that "Picayune Butler" has been killed by some patriot of the City of New Orleans a fit fate for the traducer of our Southern women, and we have also heard, though I do not believe it, that Andy Johnson has been killed by ex Govr. Neil S. Brown of Tennessee again that Johnson has defeated McClellan & also the progress of Old "Stonewall." All these things go to make me feel more hopeful. We have fallen back from Corinth, but in doing so we gained a victory in generalship over Halleck. They must have been very much astonished at some of the ruses de guerre which were practiced on those at Corinth upon the evacuation. I came out here to headquarters to-day, in hopes of getting a letter from you as I heard that a number of letters were sent to Memphis by some of our officers who were held as prisoners in St. Louis & were exchanged and I was told that some articles of clothing were sent to me which are at Okolona as yet and I thought it but natural that any one who thought of me & my personal necessities, wd. also remember to drop a line to satisfy the longings of a soul thirsty for the communications of friends & one dearer than all friends—Although my dear Bettie I have not heard one word from you since Feb'y 8th yet I know and feel that all is well with me and am as confident of my being beloved by you as I know that you are ever the same in my heart—its idol—I hope & believe it will not be long—no not many weeks—before we will be in Missouri again, under one gallant old general, and when we return to Missouri we will go as conquerors to claim the spolis, and of all that in that dear old state, I claim only the hand & heart of one sweet little angel who once whispered to a breaking heart I love you & will never marry any other man. Oh how often do I think over that well remembered night in July, when I had almost given up all hope & dark despair had begun to hang its pall of gloom over my young life to darken all the patter of my future life, and when you told me those words of life & encouragement & I heard the sweet assurance dropped from your sweet lips that I was beloved I felt like the redeemed sinner or the long imprisoned bird set free. But I know you know how much I love you & prize your love and only hope & pray that you may remain as constant to me as I do to you. My candle is now nearly gone & I must close, write to me as often as you can for I have written to you very often & believe me whatever may happen yours forever

Given

Memphis, Tenn. April 17, 1862

My Darling Bettie,

I have only time to drop a line to you to you to let you know how I am. I left Des Arc, Arks. a day or two since & arrived here this morning and have just found the present opportunity. Oh my darling. I wish to see you so much, and would give almost anything in this world to see you, but honor calls me to take a hand in the next great battle & I must not disobey her calls. But my pride & the darling of my soul I promise you that I will take the first opportunity of seeing you. I passed through the dangers of the past unscathed & I want you to feel that amid death & danger I will escape unharmed. Rest easy I will not be hurt. Remember me my own sweet Bettie & recollect that amid all vicissitudes & troubles I shall never forget my pledge. I have no more time. I wrote to you nearly one month ago. Give my love to all and retain for yourself enough to satisfy your own heart for you have the key to it all.

        Good Bye
        Yours most devotedly
        GC

Corinth, Miss. May 11, 1862

Miss Sue Bettie Woods
St. Louis, Mo.

My Own Dear Bettie,

I saw Ge. Beall, bye the bye, the same one who used to flourish in Saint Louis as Capt. Beall and was devoted to Miss Mary Mitchell & Julia Barrett, and he asked me if I wished to send a letter to Saint Louis, and you may know that I sprang at the opportunity. I have not heard directly from you since the little note of Feb. 8th & have written to you several times since this period, but the letters, many of them, were sent by uncertain channels & perhaps have not reached you at all: but my darling I want you to know & believe that whenever an opportunity can be found I always write to you. I do not know, nor can my mind arrive at any probable period for the termination of this war and until then we can not be happy with each other but one thing I do know and that is if it lasts the year the time will not abate my deep & steady love for you. And if I have judged your character aright it will not change you.

Our gallant army was forced to retire from Missouri and oh how sad it made me when I crossed the borders of Mo. and took up the march through Arkansas but I remembered the consolatory verse of Longfellow i.e. "Be still sad heart! Cease thy repining behind the clouds is the sun still shining." I wrote you a full account of the difficulties and dangers of our retreat of the Battle at Elkhorn and the dangers & risks of it, through all of which I came out safely & unharmed, damaging my clothes and a shell cut my hat through & through. But in it all I have no apprehension of danger & felt as if I was not born to die by the hand of the country's enemies, and my darling I wish you to feel the same way & do not credit any foolish rumors to the effect that I am slain or wounded for I will not be. In the midst of all the fights I have been in your image rose before me & you may be sure that the apparition did not remove my angst. I have a source of consolation & pleasure which to my mind is more exhaustible & that is that though dangers & misfortunes may cluster round about me as a wall & though fate should frown on my fairest hopes, yet here is one heart far distant which responds in loving sympathy, & whose dear pulsations keep time to my own. I am tired of cavalry, and will resign my command to go into infantry or into the partisan service which has peculiar charms for me. I have been elected by the officers of the 7th Ky. Regt. as Lieutenant Colonel of the regiment but there are objections to the position. I will not accept it. The men under the organization have a right to elect, and though they have waived that right there are other objections I have little ambition for military promotion, and can get the position of Colonel of a regiment if I desire it; but I should prefer the dashing & reckless life of a partisan to any position in the regular line. All that keeps me here now is the prospect of a battle, a battle which will be the most bloody & the most decisive in the pages of modern history. I heard yesterday from Mr. Sam Kirkmans father & his family all were well and none of them had been molested.

Florence, the City of Florence, was captured by a scouting party of Federals composed of nine (9) men and surrendered "with all the honor of war."

The gentleman who told me of the Kirkmans, said he had not seen Sam for a long time & did not know when he had gone. Columbia, that you have heard Sally Polk speak of so often, was captured by our cavalry & the enemy's stores were captured with some hundreds of prisoners. I learned yesterday that our cavalry had also destroyed the US property at Paducah but this has not been confirmed. Oh I had almost forgotten to tell you that I saw Bredell at Memphis & he told me all the news. I asked him particularly about you but his replies were of a very general nature. He says he has come here to fight the battles of the South & intends joining a battery. I saw Dr. Michel yesterday. He holds the 3rd rank in the Confederate service as surgeon. He is surgical inspector for what the French wd. call Corps L' Armie, a corps of the army. He told me to send his kindest regards to you and to the family. We have a fine army here & ought to whip the Yankees if we fight them here. Now Bettie my dear I want you to write to me via Paducah, Ky. under cover to Florence, my sister. This will be the surest way to communicate with me. Oh how I long to see you, hear you speak. You first and family next are the only bonds which tie me to life and if they should unhappily be broken my life I would carry on my sword point, for I am becoming reckless & I had almost said desperate. I have been deeply stung by thorns through my family for they have insulted my mother & sisters & murdered my friends. But now Good Bye—take great care of your health & remember that you are held by yourself as trustee for me until I return & then I shall assert my title in my own name. Pray for me. I need your prayers. Yours forever, most lovingly.

Given

June 17th, 1862

Miss Sue Bettie Woods
St. Louis, Mo.

My Darling Bettie,

I have an opportunity of writing to you now with a certainty of the letters safe arrival, a certainty which I have not had for a long time. I have availed myself of every opportunity to write to you for several months past but do not know that any of my letters have ever reached you, and if you have written I have received not one of your letters, but when you get this if you will answer it immediately and mail it to me at Paducah under cover to my sister F. I will be almost certain to get it. I am in excellent health but rather depressed for my heart is the faithful barometer of my soul and it is sad indeed. One sweet affectionate letter from her I love would revive me, and I shall anxiously await it. You know I am nothing of a sentimentalist and that I have always been strongly practical and knowing this you would hardly believe it when I tell you that scarcely a night passes during which your image is not reflected in some beautiful dream. I have passed over many different lands & seen many changes & bold men with almost bursting hearts lamenting over all our troubles. I have been among men grown careless & reckless taking up the wild spirit of the times, and yet I cannot say that I have changed much in anything but one & that is that my affection, as days pass by, grows more & more—sometimes I chafe & a wild spirit of adventure seizes me, and if it were not for the silken chord which fair woman has wound around my life I would be as reckless & indifferent as the worst. Oh if I should be loosed from the sweet enthralment by a hard fortune, then indeed would all the wild passions of the times, run not through my veins. I remember well to have told you on a memorable night, that if I was ever saved it would be through the influence & intervention of an angel woman, and you know well who that woman is. But it has been so long since I have heard from you that I almost sicken at the ideas of such long silence & such protracted absence. I had hoped long before this to have seen you & pressed you to my heart, but the requirements of duty to my country demanded my presence, and I could not honorably get away. But my own darling it seems to me that when we do meet we can appreciate each other better, for these long absences try the human heart as the one is tried in the crucible, and if the matal is base it discloses the cheating. Many of the gentlemen got letters a few days ago from St. Louis & I hoped for one too, but it came not or if it did I could not find it. Though I was informed a package of clothes were sent to me by the adjutant of the 3rd. La.

Regt. I could not find out who from, but guessed very shrewdly; as yet I have not seen them as they are in the possession of Maj. Wms. about 50 miles from here. Your acquaintances here are all well. Mr. Bredell is a member of an artillery Co. and young Anderson I have not heard of for many weeks. Tonight Schaumburg, through the influence of Tom Snead, was appointed adjutant of Genl. Littles Brigade with the rank of Capt., and Frank Carter is aid de camp to Genl. Bowen with the rank of Lieut. and Ramey Hutchinson is his adjutant. I have been offered a staff appointment often but uniformly decline them professing the dangers & activity of the line, in all my conduct thus far I have never had an ambitious thought for myself and by a little management could have secured high places but I sought them not. I wd. prefer to serve my country first as a private soldier & then if merit demanded higher posts let them seek me. If you wish to know how I have acted ask some who have been with me. I will have to cut this short as the messenger is preparing to start. Do answer this letter immediately & write a long one, for the sake of your fiancee'. Good Bye my sweetest Bettie. May God bless & keep you as in the hollow of his hand, & make you a powerful instrument for the good of many, especially mine. Be sure and write when you can.

                    Yours most affectionately,
                    Given

Near Marietta, Ga. June 22nd

I am very much in hopes that you will get a letter from me as I have written this & another & both of them are sent by private hand though not by the same one, and also another by Flag of Truce. I would have written much sooner but literally have not had time to write for a long time, as our Brig. has been constantly engaged in active service in front of the enemy for nearly two months. I was so much delighted to get your letter of Feb. 22nd. It was like the well remembered voice of a friend long absent, age of more than a friend. I had almost given out the hope of hearing from you again when Col. Woodward handed me a letter which he said came from Miss. I looked at the super script and it was strange. Carelessly put it in my pocket & did not look at it for that day. On the next morning I tore it open and found that it enclosed another letter in another envelope and that envelope was blank. I tore it open and when I saw the handwriting was so delightfully startled. I could not cease reading it until I had read & reread it & had its contents written on my heart. Oh if you did know how delighted I was I know you would write again & often & try every expedient. Although I was rejoiced yet the tone of the letter and an illusion to delicate health made me feel very sad indeed and this impression was heightened by a letter from Miss Sussie who said that your mother had written that your health was not good & that you had been confined to your bed for a long time three weeks. It does hurt me very much indeed to know that you are sick and I unable to see you or even to communicate with you in any way or to hear of your health. But Bettie dear *you* must get well. I cannot bare to think that Death shd. have the power to strike so fair a form & to send so pure a soul away from its earthly casket but, I will not write on such a bad & distressing a theme. You asked me if I never felt like loving some of the Southern girls. I answered No! I have never seen one that could compare with the peerless one I left behind and it seems that absence has magnified every attraction and enhanced every virtue at this distance & time. I cannot think that there is any defect in your character and I know that I sould never be able to think so of another. I must see you soon though how it will come to pass I can not now see. I would surely see you if I could get leave of absence, but I have tried & failed & can get no leave till this campaign is over. But my precious one if you come South I will see you & Miss Susie says that you would come out with her & she promised to bring you out. Oh if you can come out do so. I saw some of the St. Louisians a few days ago & heard of one of your old beaux, Bridell, he is flying around in Richmond & report says that he has renewed his attention to Miss Lizzie Giles & she has discarded Genl. Quarles who it is said she came South to marry. Johnny Kay, your cousin, is adjutant of the 49th Tenn. Quarles Brigade & well. I have made diligent inquiries for McCane

& have been unable to hear of him at all. Isaac Haynes of St. Louis he is a Capt. in the 1st Mo. but I do not think that you know the officers in this rgt. & shall say no more of them. We have been having a lively time here and the skirmishes between Johnston & Shermans Army would one year ago have been termed battles, but all is yet indecision. We have a large, well disciplined & high spirited army and when the struggle does take place we hope & earnestly believe that the God of Battles will smile upon the efforts of a brave & struggling people.

I have written this letter under a perfect din of voices & hardly know what I am doing. But I know this that I shall always love you best of all. Goodbye—Love to all

Yours, G.C.

Glencoe, June 24, 1862

Two most welcome letters have just arrived from you, one yesterday written from Baldwin & another this evening dated the 17th of this month which I presume was of later date than the other. Although the other was not dated at all in your last I was glad to learn that by writing immediately there was an opportunity of sending you a letter, of which you see I am determined to avail my-self. I had just come in from riding on horse back with Mr. Dave Clark. So when your letter was handed to me, & as the house was full of company I concluded to wait until everyone had retired, & I could have a quiet time for writing. It is now after mid night & as I am going in town in the morning, & consequently will have to rise rather early (as you probably remember) I will not be able to write so long a letter as I undoubtedly would had I more time, however I don't doubt that I would sit up all night if it was necessary to write to you. I can scarcely give you an idea of my joy at receiving your letters. I had not heard before from you since this 17th of April, & that was but a note written from Memphis, & I had waited so anxiously & so long for a letter, that I had begun to look up on the reception of one, almost as a dream too bright to be realized, & when I actually held the letter in my hand & beheld your familiar handwriting once more, I could scarcely believe it. You said in your letter that you fear for these "long silences" & this "protracted absence." Why should you? I hope you do not doubt for one instant my constancy to you. You must not doubt me when I tell you that I have always loved you, though at one time, I did not think so, & as long as God gives me life & reason, I shall never cease to give you the affection of my whole heart, freely & entirely for the simple but excellent reason that I cannot help it, & I certainly would not if I could for it is a welcome bondage. I would not *for worlds* have written to you in this strain under ordinary circumstances, as I do not think such confessions ought generally to come from a lady's lips, but as you seemed a little low-spirited & rather doubtful of me, I feel that I ought to do any thing in my power to reassure you & make you happier. You see how shockingly vain I am growing in imagining that words of mine have any influence over you. As you are absent you cannot judge of my affection by my actions & conduct & can only know it by an actual expression of it. I would not have believed that any earthly power could have induced me to confess as much I have to you but these war times know no law & compel us to do many strange things, that at any other time we would have believed impossible. As you see by the date of my letter we are at Glencoe again. We have been out about six weeks & I can scarcely realize that a whole year has passed, since we were last out here; the time has passed delightfully thus far. We ride on horse back every day. Grand Pa sent me a present the other day of a check for eighty dollars with which I bought me a very pretty riding horse. He is perfectly trained to the saddle, delightfully gaited & very pretty, tho' I think too spirited for a coward as I am. I suffer perfect torture from fear every time I ride but am determined to persevere, as you seemed so anxious for me to learn to ride when you were here. Mr. Bryan (Nedwig) has also given me his horse for the summer, which is a splendid riding animal. I went in town a few days ago to attend a party given by Seddie Clarke out at Mr. Glasgow's. Mr. Lackland was my escort & we had a gay time. All of the gentlemen who are left in town were there though, as is always the case "nowadays" at parties the ladies were very largely in the majority. Picnics are very much in vogue this season. I have been to a great many. I believe there is no news at all that would interest you. Of course you have heard that Jellie & Mr. Carrare married. They are living for the summer out here at Jimmy's & seem to be very happy. When I was in town I attended the wedding of Mr. Wilcox & Mrs. Danjan, who were married on the same day with Mr. Jn" Clannahan & Miss Green. Mary Tarkin is the belle "par excellence" now, at least as much of a belle as any one can be during the present scarcity of gentlemen. Poor Mag & Mr. Thomson after enduring all the trials that all true lovers nave to bear, & perhaps even more than the usual share are at length to be married on the 16th of next month which by the way is my birthday in contemplation of which fact I am beginning to feel very aged. I received a letter this evening at the same time with yours, from your sister Florence containing her photograph which however was so indistinct that I could not judge any thing of her appearance from it. I am surprised that you have gotten so few letters from me as I have written quite often, tho not lately as I have had no opportunity, the last letter I wrote was sent by Col. Shernds. Did you ever receive it? Do you know Harry McCune? If not do try and make his acquaintance as through him you will have more frequent opportunities of writing. He is the adjutant of Burbridge's regiment. I will have a very excellent & certain opportunity of writing to you in ten days by a gentleman who is going South. But I have not the most remote idea of how to direct your letter. However, I will do the best I can but I fear not knowing your regiment & company that it will not reach you. I was sorry to learn that you are a private, as I think you deserve to be something higher & then too there are many advantages attached to an officer's position that a private soldier can not enjoy. I hope you may soon fill an office that is worthy of you. I had a few days ago a very flattering offer, of the hand & heart of a fascinating young Dr. from Virginia. I only made his acquaintance this winter. I of course declined the honour. I regretted very much to learn that your friend Dr. Harrison is a prisoner. I am glad to hear that your mother succeeded in sending you some clothes as I suppose of course they must sent by her. Susie Woods, who came from Nashville soon after the fall of that city sends you her kindest regards & says to tell you she is educating me to know what a "soap stick" is. Mr. James Clarkson has returned from the army & taken the oath of allegiance & by so doing has lost—as he deserved—the respect of all his friends, but I must bring this long letter to a close. Good night. If I write much longer I might be telling you my dreams. Take good care of yourself & think often of one who is truly & devotedly yours,

S.B.W.

July 1st, 1862

My Darling Bettie,

   Your letter was handed to me last night, & may God bless you for this sweet letter containing such gentle consolation. Oh how I was delighted to receive it. My heart is so full that I cannot find language to tell you all that I feel & if it is attempted I know you will think me crazy or very extravagant, but my darling if you have any idea of the suffering of a heart famished, and the joy it feels when supplies so pure are sent, then you may know how I feel. For months, long months, I have been a wanderer over a barren land & my heart has been encased in itself, extending its longing tendrils in but one direction, & that but to feel that between it & its mate a wide waste spread out to baffle its desires & disappoint its hopes. Now your letter as far as your woman's heart prompted by your womans natural instinct could, has supplied many of its wants. They say in books & it is the sneering remark of the rude world, that no human heart can resist the slow but steady encroachments of time, which with its ebbs & flows will surely erase any & all footprints on the plastic sands of memory, but thus far & I believe ever will I be able to fix the lie in their throats. Absence is the infallible test which enables us to distinguish between the pure & base metals of which poor mortals are composed. You ask the question of me, Why should I fear for this protracted absence? I answer because I had in the general estimate forgotten a very little. that there are angels sent by God to strew our earthly pathway with celestial flowers & you are one of these bright guardian angels sent to keep the heart true to its pole star. I am happy now & a deep & calm delight has sweetened my life since I have been away from you wild passions have attempted to master me but the evil spirits were exorcised by one little word "Bettie," & your sweet assurances have given to your fairy wand a sweeter power over me.

   Do you remember the night we first met after your return from Nashville, when an evil chilling blast swift over us & you told me you did not love me. I would not & did not believe you & begged your pardon for my unbelief. Who has proved to be the truer prophet? This was the first chapter in that prediction—the next was that one day you would bear my name & wear my honors. I believe that though it is dark now, yet the sun shines for me. I have great encouragement on all sides. All my friends say you will not be hurt. You are not yet to die but will pass through safely, and only a day or two ago I met an old man, a very old man, nearby. A century had left its traces on his face & form. He was standing by the grave of his son a gallant man who died at the head of his victorious troops. His eyes were dim, his frame feeble & tottering, & his voice weak & low & sad—I knew his son & stopped at his new made grave. I told him where I was going & my business on perilous & particular business & might never see my friends again. He looked at me long & attentively & said "go on you will not be hurt. No no you will pass through all that is sent." I thought that I stood before one of the old proophets, for when he spoke his whole person seemed inspired with a new life & vigor. Now simple as this was, it has made me believe certainly that no harm "lies wait" for me. I asked him for his blessing and he put his hands on my head & prayed for God to bless me. You may think me superstitious & easily moved by imaginations but it all, the place, time & man, made an impression on me not to be forgotten. My darling I have learned a good deal & been where men fell thick & have never in many fights been touched. You say in your letter you are sorry that I am a private. I have never yet been a private, though I do think that is the most honourable position & as easy as any—I have served for nearly a year as an officer & I know its duties & labors. I have had a command all the time except a short time when the army was at Sac River. I now hold the rank of Capt. in the Confedt. service and am here in Ky. on peculiar business of a very dangerous nature—so help me God I have not been ambitious in this war, nor have I sought office at all. But I have had many positions on the staff offered to me, but I prefer the dangers & hardships of the line to the soft sinecures of the staff. I was selected by the commissioned officers of the 7th Ky. Regt. as their choice as Lieut. Col. & at the time it was done I did not know any one of the officers in the Regt. But reasons of a private nature, connected with the weak state of the command, induced me to waive the offer. So you see my darling that if I chose I might have held a much higher rank & that without seeking it. When I do go in as a private then I should fight for promotion, and if bearing on the battle field could win it I would have it & that soon. I have a great notion to give up my present business and go in as a private & then you will see if I remain in the ranks. Col. Jno. W. Boone who may be in Saint Louis since day or other perhaps now, might tell you how I have behaved on the field & whether I have done my duty & you might ask any of my old regt. who led the charge at Elkhorn? You speak of James Clarkson— I am sorry for him, he acted badly & went home after his Capt. (Capt. Barry) told him if he went he would report him as a deserter, & Barry told me that he had so reported him on the muster roll, but in Clarkson's case there were mitigating circumstances. I do not tell this to injure him though I have good reason to believe that he is not much of a friend to me & you need not tell it on him. I would like so much to come & see you. Write what you think of it, & if you write at once I may get it in time. Direct to me at Paducah, Ky. under cover to Florence. I am willing to run almost any risk if you think it can be done. How I love you, you already know & you also know that you are not guilty of vanity in supposing that words of yours have an influence over me for as God is my judge I am speaking the truth when I say that words & wishes of yours have more influence over me than any one else in the world, and my dear Bettie I am very glad to know that you care for me & my wishes & that you are taking your rides regularly. If I could only be there to escort you I am certain you wd. not be such a little coward, but wd. soon acquire confidence & skill, but if he is too spirited you must be watchful & have the saddle particularly attended to and do not ride fast down those rocky hills. It is dangerous indeed. I have been in the saddle every day for a year & am a first rate horseman, and do not ride with all of your beaux for some of them cd. be of no more service to you in case of need than a 5 year old boy.

Give my love to Dave Clarkson and ask him for me if he still loves the same one. Give my love to Miss Susie, and tell her that I had hoped the disagreeable association of the "soapstick" has passed out of her mind as it had out of mine. I always liked her very much & had a great respect for her. I am indeed obliged for these clothes, though I am justly well satisfied that they did not come from the lady I now claim as my mother, though perhaps the day may come where the donor may bear that much honored name from me, if I divine aright who she is, it will be the happiest day of my life when I shall have the right to call her such a name—mother. Give to her my kindest regards & best love & many thanks. I am glad that you like my friend Lackland. He is a pure minded man & a gentleman, though you did not like Michel much. He is medical inspector for Hardee's Corps, a fine position & he has a fine name in the army. I am sorry to hear many people here despair of the Confederacy, for the motto should be "NIL DESPERANDUM EST." I have no such doubts nor has the army which is in fine spirits. I am very sorry to learn that Dr. Harrison is a prisoner. This is the first I have heard of it. He was another pure man, guileless as a child. Now my darling I must close this letter though I have not said half I desire, but I will inform you that this is written less than a mile of the enemy's camp & I have been here almost as long as is prudent to stay. Now Good Bye my own scout and may Heaven bless you and God make you happy. Give my love to your Father & all the family & retain a great deal for yourself.

Yours forever, affectionately   G.

P.S. I had forgotten to ask the name of the young Virginian, the Dr. who has exhibited such good taste, though I am sorry for him, yet I respect him—What was his name?

G.

August 30, 1862

My Dearest Friend,

I cannot tell you what a welcome surprise your letter was to me; after I had been looking most lovingly & eagerly for it & had almost given up the idea of ever hearing again when last evening to my great delight your letter of the 19th was handed to me. The last letter I had received before this one was written on the 1st of July. I could scarcely realize that it had only been two months since I had heard. That is the usual length of time that elapses between your letters, though this last interval seemed much longer than it ever has before, probably because I have been more anxious about you of late, as you have attached yourself to those terrible guerrillas who are so much more apt to be taken prisoners than the regular soldiers & so severely dealt with when captured. I have always been under the impression that those guerrilla bands were far from being any advantage to the Southern cause, in fact that they sought their own interest before anything else & went about for the purpose of stealing from, & murdering innocent citizens. You may consequently imagine my surprise when I heard that you were one of such a band, but to hear it was sufficient to change my opinion at once not of you, but of the guerrillas for all the newspapers in this world could not convince me that you would engage in anything that was not perfectly honourable & right but still I wish you had not left the regular army & your present kind of life exposes you to so much more danger. I do not think you have any right at all to run any unnecessary risks, for you must remember that you do not belong to yourself and that somebody else's happiness for life depends upon your safety & well being, every thing that is necessary to life done by a soldier fighting for his honour & independence of his native land. I am willing for you to do, but I entreat you to desist from any daring ruthlessness that once perhaps in a hundred cases costs undying glory upon the victor but in every other results in painful imprisonment or a terrible death & even if you should die gloriously & covered with honour what would that be to me if you were gone. But I must not continue in this doleful strain, & I know you will take care of yourself after such a lecture & I will now reward you for reading it patiently by telling you some news as you desired me to do in your letter, tho' being in the country I fear I am somewhat behind the times. To begin with, your friend Mr. Cates is certainly to be married very soon to Miss Kate Clemens. They both acknowledge it & he seems as he ought to be very happy. Miss Anna Polk & Miss Annita Alexander are both to be married next month to gentlemen that you do not know, both strangers in the city. Maggie Larkin is at length Maggie Thompson & for a month past has been the happiest little housekeeper in all the world. She has no communication with her Father's family. Lizzie Thornton is also to be married in November to a gentleman from Kentucky. There are various other reports but too groundless to mention. I suppose of course you have heard of Puss Flint's marriage to Ramsey Powell. I regret very much that I cannot tell you something about your lady love Miss Annie Patterson. She has been all summer in Canada with her family. I cannot tell you whether you have any rivals in that quarter or not, but for your sake I hope not. I am truly sorry to inform you of the death of Mrs. Chiles, the relative of the gentleman by whom I sent you a message. She died very suddenly. Mat. Scott died a few weeks ago at the Alton Prison. I think Mr. Brooke's arrest—the greatest outrage that has yet been committed—almost all the respectable people are in prison now. I cannot enumerate them however as I have not the time—I cannot refrain from mentioning some of the last names as they were arrested out here & are all friends of yours. They are Messrs. Jim Teatmann Jr., Dave Clarkson, Allen Pendleton & Tennent, & it happened in this way; the two last gentlemen had been ordered about ten days ago to report themselves to the Lieut. Col. for duty as clerks in the pass. office. They did not wish to comply & came out to Mr. Teatmann's to avoid compulsion. The day after they came out Seddie Clarke & Mary Larkin came out to pay me a visit & Annie Green was already here so with Sue & I we had five young ladies in the house & Mr. Clarkson & Mr. Andrew Stevens came over from their farms to stay with Mr. T. during the girls visit to me, & they with one or two other country beaux were in the habit of coming over here every day immediately after breakfast & stay till 12 & 1 o'clock at night. They all had gay times boating, riding & card playing &c. & on Thursday night they left us quite late promising to return early the next morning (yesterday) & take us riding on horseback. The hour came but not the gentlemen & we wondered at their non appearance until 2 o'clock when a note came signed by them all saying officers had come from town & arrested Messrs. Tennent & Pendleton for disobedience to orders & all of the others were taken for being in their company—we drove down to the depot to meet them & they were all marched in on the evening train & locked up in the Gratiot Street Prison. I do not know what the girls will do now, as these were literally the only gentlemen who remain in town that go into society or visit at all. There are no parties or gaieties of any kind, tho' one I wrote of to your sister is the last—we have had or are likely to have for sometime—fortunately for me. I am independent of such things, a letter from you is worth all the beaux & parties in the world to me. The Mr. Clay Taylor that you inquired about in your letter is a son of Mrs. Nat. Taylor & a son-in-law of Bernard Pratte. Col. Boone is held in very bad repute by the Southerners in this state, a great many of his recruits who have been taken prisoners as it is said through his instrumentality & thro' his own intentions to that effect are only waiting an opportunity to shoot him down. I dare not tell you what he has done as it might be considered treasonable to give you such information. Col. Johnson & his wife have both been in prison but are now released. The Southern people here are suffering for their opinions, as my Father has always been & is still perfectly loyal to the Government. I suppose we have nothing to fear. We have not heard from Nashville for a long time several weeks, as communication is cut off, as soon as it is open again Sue will return home & is very anxious for me to go with her. I think it quite likely that I shall do so, as I have been intending to for some time—Is there any more probability of my seeing you there than here? If I would be likely to miss seeing you by going of course I would stay at home—for O! how I long to see you, no one can imagine. I never know what it is to feel happy & I am sure I think of you every hour in the day. It seems to me a hard fate that I am separated from you. If I could only look forward to some definite termination to such a trial, but it seems instead of growing shorter it grows longer & is likely to last forever. I never dreamed until you left me of how much I loved you. Absence may break slender ties but it binds strong ones. I have written two letters to you lately—since the reception of your last letter, that is, but I directed them to Price's Army & I suppose you did not receive them. Shall I continue to send your letters there? How in the world did you manage to see your sister—it must have been delightful to both of you. How I envy her but I cannot help it. I was very sorry you have had a chill. You must take good care not to have another. Mother desires to be remembered to you. Please write soon & this volume deserves a long answer.

Good Bye. Believe me ever your own,

BW

Camp Coleman Near Trenton Ky.
Oct. 6th, 1862

My Darling Bettie,

Your letter of Aug. 30th was received and a few days ago I wrote an answer to it from Hopkinsville, Ky. but in that letter I did not tell you all the matters I discuss because I had not time. I now have time to write again & avail myself of the opportunity. I was mighty glad to hear from you, but I must confess when I saw the title you gave me I was troubled a little for you styled me *"Friend,"* and I told you once I was not your friend. If I were asked if my fathers wife were my friend I should say no she is my *Mother*. I do not mean to chide you my sweetest, you are too dear to me for that. I am writing this letter to you on a goods box & my seat is a camp kettle. I have a tent made of poles covered with wheat straw which tames the rains very well & keeps out the cold winds. We have a very active life which is munificent of health, but is hard on horses. We are on the scout but thirds of our time & the same covering that I wrote you from Hopkinsville. We had a fight in which we routed some cavalry killing a few. I have more than half of the time no shelter & the wind & rains blow & fall upon me unbridled. You would hardly know me now: Imagine a man 5 feet 10½ or 11 inches high, broad & more muscular about the chest with bronzed complexion & beard all over the face, and my hands that you used to flatter occasionally & as not at all judicious & very muscular from constant use of the _____ are as hard in the arms as steel. And again my darling I am a little changed by the life I have led in camps. I am not as good as I used to be, less iron hard & self willed about some things, but to you I am & always will be the same—for as Sheridan said in Pizzarro, all natures are soft beings & he illustrated it by these lines. "On iron pinions born, the bloodstained vulture cleans the stork, yet is the plumage closest to her heart soft as the cygnet's down & o'er her unfledged blood the murmuring ringdove sets not there gently." These are no doubt so familiar to you that it is idle to write them. I am in the midst of so much noise that I can hardly write for there is a parade & the articles of war are to be read to the soldiers, for discipline is rigidly enforced & yesterday a soldier had his head shorn & was disgracefully dismissed out of the service for drunkenness & disobedience to his officers—& again the rights of property are *rigidly respected*. And we are very far from being the *terrible* fellows you thought we were. I would like very much to hear from the way affairs are working in dear old Missouri. I saw some men from there several days ago & they said that it was a war of extermination on the side of the federals & that in consequence the South's policy was adopted. (On the other side).

I hope that the ravages of this war may never reach you or any of yours and that these series of horrors may now cease. I have longed to see you of late more than ever & I have almost concluded to run the hazard of imprisonment during the war to see you & if I can see you in any way do not fail to let me know. I am very anxious to hear from home for I have not heard since I saw my sister F. and as you desire to know how I came to see her I will tell you. I came to the point opposite Smithland & she came across the Cumberland & saw me. The town opposite was full of soldiers and several of them were on the same side with me but did not know me. She was delighted to see me & said she would have been frightened for me but she believed in my destiny which was not to be taken or harmed. I wrote to you to tell you if you could come to Nashville I could get to see you if I know when you are there—But if you can pay a visit to my sister F. I shall certainly see you if I can hear of it. I wrote to her this evening. When you write again please let me know all the local news in polite circles, and as much other as you can safely tell me. What Col. B. did, if compatible. I am sorry to hear that your father is such a good Union man & hope the last emancipation Proclamation of Pr. Lincoln may convert him to the faith. I suppose the people in St. Louis do mind the general declaration of martial law as they have by this time become used to the yoke. I have heard that the Inquisition has exhausted all of the male victims & now declare a grand *Auto da Fu* of the women of which they say St. Louis is full, nearly all of whom are heretical. I have a beautiful horse for you as soon as I can find a way to send him. He is very pretty & very kind, but all game, and riding him will be safe, but will appear dangerous. I am very anxious for you to continue that beautiful exercise & take as good care of your health as possible. Now in relation to myself, I acknowledge your proprietary right in me & shall take all the care of myself which may be consistent with the requirements of duty & honour. But rest at ease, I will return after the war to "the girl I left behind me." Pray for me my darling & I shall be blessed. Goodbye now. Love to your family & respects to friends,

Yours forever affectionately
GC

Charlotte Dixon Co. Tenn. Nov. 14th, 1862

Miss Sue Bettie Woods
St. Louis, Mo.

My Dearest Bettie,

I met your Uncle Andy this afternoon & came into town with him & take this opportunity to write a hurried letter to you. I have written several letters to you since I received your last dated Aug. 31st but have had no assurance that they have reached their destination. I would like very much to hear from you regularly and since I have I have met with Andy have hit upon a plan which may succeed, that is, for you to write to me and address the letter to "Mr. Campbell" and enclose it in another envelope to Andy. I have asked him whether I could pay you a visit & he tells me that it would be impossible to go & return again in safety. I cannot tell you how much I would give to see you only for an hour. I never dream but you are in the foreground and a hundred times during each day I find that my mind is busy with thoughts of those happy hours of you when we could meet & love each other. "Every danger I have known that a reckless life can lead." Yet your dear image haunts me still. I love you better now than at any previous time & if the theory of writers on mental physiology are at all correct I am afraid that the sudden interruption of a long continued reflection on the same subjects would be as dangerous to my mind as to the happiness of my heart & hence I love to continue to think of the one sweet subject—my love for the little dark eyed, fair haired girl I left behind me. You need never fear that I shall ever change and allow me to disagree with you that men are not as constant as women. If you are true to me, & I doubt you not, at the end of this war you & I will marry & be happy yet. I do not fear that I will be killed & I do not believe that God would be so severe & cruel as to take you away from me. I do not pray now very often, for the life I lead hardly allows me time or opportunity even if my wicked heart did not avoid them; but whenever I do you are always remembered and that too with earnest & fervent supplication. I live now in the hope of a future & brighter day when peace & honor shall crown our arms when I can consumate the promised gift of your heart & hand. I am very anxious whenever I can learn of any one who has seen you to know if you are well, for I have such perfect confidence in you that I know if you are only well, that all is well with me. I hear less frequently from home than I have ever done, it does seem as if communication is cut off from me entirely. But in any event never fear for me, I will always love you while you live & pray I meet you when you go to the home of the blessed—& my health has never been better, and the explosion which you would think would kill almost any one only toughens me. I am more agile & muscular but not quite as heavy. I have the most beautiful horse which I am saving to send to you by the first favorable opportunity. He is a young horse built like an Arab with head & ears like a deer and very fleet proud looking but as gentle as a lamb. I hope by this time that you are a fearless horse woman. I have become a very fine horseman, and when I get back we will have some fine rides.

Your Uncle Andy is on his way to Nashville but I do not know if he will be allowed to pass the rebel lines, as they are very strict in closing communications. He says all are well & his health appears to be better than it was when I saw him last. I saw the wife of your Uncle James a short time since & she was almost afraid to come & speak to me. I would like to tell you a great many things which would interest you, but I do not like to put these in this letter, for reasons you may understand. I carry your daguerrotype with me all the time & I have become to believe that it has a protecting & talismanic influence. You remember the little black ring made of gutta percha which you told me I might wear till you called for it. Well I lost that ring in creek whilst washing my hands & I looked for it every day for a week until I despaired of ever finding it. I never lost anything which I missed so much in my life & now when I am riding along I find myself involuntarily feeling for it on my little finger. I have the little locket and every one who sees it inquires whether I have my sweethearts picture in it, and think strange that I should so prize only a little lock of hair. When you gave that to me, did you think it would be so much cherished? No you did not think so for you did not appreciate me then. I will now bring this wandering letter to a close with the request that you give my love to your Pa & Ma & Miss Susie & kiss the children for me and take good care of yourself my little dear one & remember me all the time as,

Yours forever
GC

Dresden, Tenn. Dec. 26th, 1862

My Dearest Bettie,

I have only time to write a line to you—but will write again as soon as an opportunity presents & a long letter. I am enjoying fine health and am now under Gen. Forrest in his Cav. Division. Of our movements in this part of the state the papers no doubt have apprized you. I hope you are well for I never hear from you now—I love you more than you can conceive. I shall never cease to love you my darling, but oh it does seem that fate has erected a high barrier between us two, but cheer up—a bright day is coming for us, and I await it with an impatient mind. I would be willing to risk all dangers to see you, if you can write to me, do so often and some of them may reach me—I have been in five fights in the last two days, but I will never be hurt have no apprehensions for my safety. Give no heed to any anxiety on my account. God will protect me & I know he is too good to allow any harm to you my own Dear Bettie.

I hear from St. Louis now & then and weep on her hard fate. I never knew how dear the place was to me before I had to leave it & in it my treasured love. I wish I had some way to correspond with you regularly. I would feel much better, but my dear Bettie if I never hear from you at all I will never love you less, though ages of absence should intervene. I never loved but you & I am afraid I transgress God's commandment, Thou shall have no other Gods before me. You are my divinity & I worship at your shrine alone. Though I do not see you or hear from you, you are yet always present to my mind. Now in conclusion you must always remember me and love me. The war may last years now but its vicissitudes never will change me. Give my love to all the family, your father & mother & Miss Sue & the children. Take good care of yourself for my sake my dearest.

> Good Bye
> Yours Forever
> GC

Paris, Tenn. Dec. 28, 1862

Miss Sue Bettie Woods
St. Louis, Mo.

I wrote a few lines to you from Dresden yesterday, and will write again to-day. I have come to this place on business. Our command is yet at Dresden, but Gen. Forest will doubtless leave there to-day. It is Sunday and the first one for many long weeks that I have passed out of camp. There the days of the week are nearly always the same to us for we have no chaplain or religious services to mark the day a fact which is not very much to be admired for in the affairs of our young Confederacy God has taken a large part & we should acknowledge his intervention. It has been a long time since I heard from home, but the last time I had a letter it informed me that you had written to me and that the letter had been sent to me, as yet it has not reached me for my habits have been very migratory not remaining long at any one place. This wandering life has improved my geography very much for I have seen nearly all parts of the valley of the Mississippi but that part which my heart yearns to see; The City of St. Louis. Oh how long will it be before we will meet again. But my darling you must not despair of our happiness for we will be happy as soon as faith & constancy meet their just reward on earth. Our love my dearest Bettie has been tried and purified, and when we meet again we will then know how dear the one is to the other. I believe now & ever shall believe that men love only once, and that truth has been demonstrated by our experience. I love you better than any other being on earth, and it does seem so hard to be separated for such a long time from home & friends & from her I love best. But I am consoled in all this by the firm belief that let the arrows of fortune wound as they will, there is always one sweet ministering angel who will apply the value of affection. I never doubted that you loved me even when clouds overcast my happiness, for I did believe that the profound love of mine must demand & desire & compel a return. I never loved you as much as now & to lose your heart now would loosen the wild springs in a nature which requires the balancing influences of love such as yours. I must bring this letter to a close for I am in some danger in this place as it is twenty three miles to our lines and the Yankees scout in this country very often & I am afraid to stay too long behind.

Now my darling one, you must do all you can for our wounded and prisoners who come to St. Louis and remember that in each case you are pouring happiness into the heart of one of my comrades. Stand up for the truth of your principles when they are assailed and think that it is your duty to defend with sweet argument the same cause I have drawn the sword to defend. Now farewell my dearest, Bettie. Remember me in your prayers and be careful of your health: go to bed regularly and do not impair your health by going to parties too often. Continue your horseback rides for the exercise is the best. Give my love to your Mother & Father & the children and all the rest for yourself.

> Yours forever,
> GC

Camp at Antioch, Montgomery Co. Tenn.
Jan'y 29, 1863

Miss Sue Bettie Woods

My Dearest Bettie,

I had an opportunity of sending a letter to you today which was written at Williamsport. But for fear it may not reach you, I take an opportunity offered to send another line to you my dear. I have been in a very hard and disagreeable service for the last week or more on the Cumberland, blockading the river & firing into gun boats & transports. The weather has been very hard upon us rain & snow & cold & no camp equipage, i.e. without tools or cooking utensils, living upon the country. I have not yet despaired of hearing from you though it has been a very long time since I have had a letter. Oh so long! I wonder if you are as much changed as I am? I look much hardier & more weather beaten & graver & older than when we parted. I have endured much since I saw you last and the hope of an honorable peace within a definite period has turned to despair. In the cavalry we are always actively engaged in some kind of an enterprise burning trains containing army supplies, capturing boats tearing up rail roads, fighting Yankees on land & gunboats on water. The sound of the Yankee shells have become almost as familiar to my ears as the shrill cry of the katydid was when a boy at home. I will never cease to cherish the hope that we will meet before long though the how I have not yet figured up. I am glad to hear that the ball is rolling in Mo. again and hope that she may be enfranchised soon. My dearest Bettie I look forward to the day when I can come forward and claim you as my bride as the Mecca of my pilgrimage on earth. If we do not marry I know that I shall never get my own consent to marry anyone else. Do you remember what you told me on the step of your house not long after I was released from the arsenal when you told me I would never love you as another mans wife that if you did not marry me you would never marry any one else. You do not know the happy gleam it threw into my then desponding heart. This expression is only one of many others that are written on the tablet of memory. You must continue to write to me under cover to Paducah and they stand the best chance of reaching me. I have to bring this to a close for a friend is waiting for me to finish so that he can write home too. I must apologize for my paper for in Dixie's land paper is very hard to get. Good Bye my dearest one you are indeed the light of my eyes & the pride of my heart. Give my love to all.

Yours most devotedly,
GC

Road near Franklin, Tenn. Feb. 18, 1863

Miss Sue Bettie Woods, Nashville, Tenn.

My Darling Bettie—Care of Mr. James Woods

I have only time to write a line. I am well & dying to see you. If you can write to me & tell me where to meet you & when. I wish to see you more than anything else in this world. You must excuse my chirography as it is written on horse back—Try and find some way to write to me and direct the letter to Mr. Dr. Polk, Columbia, Tenn. on the outside & within direct to me. And if you can send me any message do so by any person. I will never cease to love you no not as long as reason is left in my mind or a heart in my body. Be perfectly easy my love. I love only you & you alone & you above all others on earth & would risk much to see you.

Good Bye my dearest one. Think of me & pray for me & take care of your ownself my own one.

Yours forever,
GC

Road near Franklin. Tenn., Feb 18, 1863

Miss Sue Bettie Woods Nashville Tenn
My Darling Bettie — Care of Mr James Woods
        I have only time to write a line —
I am well & dying to see you — If you can write
to me tell me where to meet you & when — I wish
to see you more than anything else in this world
You must excuse this chirography as it is written on
horse back — My and find some way to write to
me. and direct the letter to Mr Dr Polk Columbia Tenn
on the outside & within direct to me. and if you
can send me any message do so by any person
I will never cease to love you no not as long as reason
is left in my mind or a heart in my body — Be perfectly
easy my love. I love only you & you alone & you above
all others on earth & would risk much to see you
        Goodbye my dearest one think of me.
& pray for me & take care of your ownself my own one
        Yours forever
        GE

April 2nd, 1863

My Darling Bettie,

    I have time to write only a line by a man who is waiting impatiently for me to get through. I have written to you several times lately at Nashville & believe that some of the letters must have reached you but I have not had a line from you since the 24th Nov last. If you could have received my letters & replied to them when at N. I could have seen you. I know for many times I was not very far off from you & I would have risked all dangers to have spent one hour in your presence. Alas we do not value our treasures when we are secure in the possession of them, as we do when dangers & vicissitudes separate us from them. I think of you constantly & my mind has almost displaced the worship of my heart. I love you now more than I do heaven on earth, & with these feelings you must know how anxiously I awaited a letter to name the time & place where & when I could see you once again. I had been quite sick, but thanks to the kind attention of a dear old lady & my elastic constitution I am feeling recovered and at work again. I suppose you have heard of us of late, but I can't tell you now at some future time I will give you an autobiography of this part of my life. I once thought that a man cd. become resigned to separation when it lasted the very long time ours has, but the anxiety is like thirst which becomes more & more fierce till it is quenched in death. I never loved any one but you though at times before I saw you I had my fancies. They were ebullitions of youth but this is the fruit of manhood in its freshness & vigor and like the century plant blooms only once in a hundred years—But I must cease now for I could go on pouring out my hearts libations forever, but I am inconveniencing the gentleman—If you can write to me & provide some way we may meet I long to see you again & call you my own. Write to me if this reaches you at St. Louis & direct to me at Paducah under cover as before. If you are at Andy's write as I have directed him.

                                       Now Good Bye my Darling, Yours Forever
                                       G.C.

April 5th, 1863

I have one more opportunity of writing you before I leave & fearing my other two letters may not have reached you, I embrace it, if you received them all however you will have more than your share. I have been staying in "Dixie" for the last five days with a friend eight miles from Nashville on the Harding Road, & six miles beyond the Federal pickets, & had I only found any method of letting you know it, we might have seen each other once again, if only for one short hour. We have taken several long rides beyond here, & I felt that every step we took was bringing me nearer to you, & to be obliged to turn back without seeing you, caused me a feeling of intense pain, & will it flatter you too highly? Almost a tear I thought as I sat on my horse & my gaze wandered over the surrounding hills & valleys, that perhaps the very day or hour before, you might have stood up on the same spot & your eyes wandered over the same scene. I felt for an instant that I could not say with Pope "in erring reason's & spite, one thing we know, whatever is, is right." Sometimes I cannot keep feeling thus & then again my better nature leads me to feel that I can submit cheerfully to a destiny laid out for me, by a kind Father who does all things for the ultimate happiness of those who love, & try to serve Him. There were some of Ge. Van Dorn's men here this morning so intoxicated that they could scarcely hold their pistols & they did what I would not have believed a Southern soldier could do, cursed & threatened to shoot a lady—I only wish that the Federal accounts of the scarcity of whiskey were true. Our cause can never prosper if the men who are fighting for it so degrade them-selves—If it is possible to have such a thing done in the "Land of Cotton" do have your carte de visite taken, & send it to me. I long to see you once more even if it can only be done through the medium of paper. I will return to town tomorrow or the day after & expect to leave for home the first of next week though I am by no means certain that I will be able so to do. We are leaving today a beautiful bright Sabbath, & as I told you in the last letter I wrote you on Sunday, my thoughts turn to you oftener on this day than any other. Is it because I would naturally think on such a day of all things pure & good? I trust & believe that it is. I have many more things to say to you but have not time at present. Let come what may I shall always love you above all others.

> Good Bye
> I am your own as ever
> S.B.W.

If you will direct my letters enclosed to my Cousin Ida to Mrs. John Morgan wherever she is they will be sure to reach me.

April 9, 1863

Van Leans Furnace

My Dearest Bettie,

I have a good opportunity of writing a letter to you which will go straight at least it will have as good a chance as any will from this place. It has been a very long time since I have had a letter from you though I have heard of you incidentally from persons coming from Nashville and I thought it strange that my little darling did not manage some way to send a line to me. I have written to you often of late by different routes & by various persons and I am sure that some of my letters must have reached you. Oh how I long to hear from you and I was filled for a long time with the hope that you would communicate from Nashville with me & let me know where & when I could see you. I would give ten years of my life however brief its space to be restored to your presence if for only one short day. I love the images which memory shapes of all the little incidents of our acquaintance and many times when the cold moon & bright stars are my only companions I recall all the whole history of our love & feel that in it all is the house of God and that our loving must prosper well. I have had very youthful fancies but the ideal of my youth & the poetry of my heart was filled when I felt & knew how near & dear you were to me. I have never stood on a red battlefield but since here you were given to rise to my mind as an angel sent by heaven to move or impel me to honorable deeds in this cause I love next to you. I am in the Capt. Co(B) Woodwards Regt. Ky. Cav. the same one I belonged to last fall, but at that time I was acting Lieut. Col. of the Regt. Shortly after Dec. 1, the Regt. was refused to be accepted by Gen. Bragg because they were enlisted for 12 months & it was therefore disbanded and strange to say out of the whole we could gather only one company. This was commanded by Woodward. I joined it after its organization as a private & very soon we had enough men in this co. to make another over which I was unanimously elected Captain which position I now hold. We have gone on increasing till now we have nearly a regiment for the war and when it is organized if I desire I can be represented in any one of the new field offices. We have been down here on the Cumberland for a few days & have been blockading the river having sunk a gun boat & damaged two or three transports and yesterday we captured & burnt two transports loaded with Govt. stores & Sutlers goods. But I do not like this duty. I am not averse to making our battery play on the armed gun boats of the enemy but I do not like the idea of firing into the defenseless transports which carry women & children. I have never myself fired a single shot at any transport for I did not know but that I might cause the death of a relative or friend. The Yankees however are very much amazed at our presence on the river, and I would be very much surprised if they did not come out to see us before our painful duty to thrash them back again. I wrote a letter to Andy a few days ago enclosing one for you in which I wished to know if you were at Bellwood furnace. Oh you do not know how I do want to see you. I wish you would send me your daguerrotype. I wish to see how you look now after we have been absent from each other nearly two years—This separation cannot, must not, last much longer for if I stay away much longer I would go mad. Write to me my darling by every opportunity and if you are afraid they will miscarry do not sign your name to them. Good Bye my dearest & fairest one. May the angel of love bear watch over you and keep you from all harm. Give my love to all your family & kiss little Maggie for me

>   Yours most affectionately forever
>   GC

June 2d, 1863

Your beautiful letter of 10th & 12th May was received last night & Oh how delighted I was. I read it after night by firelight and thought that it was the most beautiful letter I had ever read from any one; it melted right into my heart & made that sad source of life bright & happy. I have read it a dozen times & think every time I peruse it that it is yet more beautiful. I received one letter from you dated April 5th written on the Harding Road, but alas not till it was too late to see you & not before I had learned you had gone. Oh you do not know how bitter was the grief of my heart when I read that letter. I had been trying to get a letter from you so long & had written so often & then when it was too late to ascertain that you were where I could have seen you so readily if I had known it in time, was a draught of bitterness indeed. I tried every available means to write to you but I now know I failed completely. I do not have much certainty of the attitude end of that letter but you requested me to write every opportunity and I shall do so. Could you not pay a visit to Florence next month? If you could and I can get notice of it I will see you or die. If you cannot do this then write how the matter can be best accomplished. If you can suggest any plan be sure I will carry it out if I can only know of it. Do try and assist me in this matter in the way you deem best, for I am so sad & long to see you so much. I believe that to live without you one year longer would be insufferable, and come what may I am determined to see you before the leaves fall unless accident unavoidable or disease prevents it. When you write to me again write the same kind of a letter as this last one, each line seems to be a balm to the wounds of the mind & heart. Women—true women—are much better & purer & more religious than men, but their affections are not so deep or painful as the love—the first & only love of a proud manly heart— you remember once I told you of the first time I ever saw you and how I followed you & your mother from the church to ascertain who you were, and then that the first time I knew who you were, was when I first saw you at your Father's house when Mrs. Kay was in St. Louis. Well now you have never known it but from that hour I felt that fate hath woven you & my destinies in the same woof, and how faithfully has the past fulfilled that presentment. I can never love any other though my life were as long as the patroarchs before the flood. Your dream was correct. I have no Bible for my Bible was left in my trunk & it is impossible to get it now, but for your sake & my own too I will get one & read it. I have read the verses in Matthew 5th Chapter 34 to 38 and my guardian angel I will abide by their precepts and swear "not at all." I am not as good as I ought to be yet I am better than a great many and you should have all the credit of it.

I am sorely to bear such bad accounts from St. Louis, and pity the poor women who are imprisoned. I could tell you how I feel with words on a living tongue to a listening ear, but not now. I know nothing of McCune & can learn nothing of him at present, but if I can hear I will be sure to send word.

I am truly glad to hear that you made the acquaintance of my Father & Mother & sister, for I know you could not help being pleased. You may smile at this and say this is just like him, for you used to say that everything I possessed I thought was better than any one else's, and you were to a great extent right. I concede to more in the respects above & you know that I think that I have the nicest, handsomest, most beautiful & intelligent & and loveliest little fair haired, dark eyed angel for a fiancee' in this Christian world & haven't I a right to think so too? Florence says "My admiration of her rivals yours." Speaking of you, she did not speak accurately then for she could not rival me in that respect. Now if this letter reaches you you must come over in July and see Florence & me, unless an accident should end my life, which I do not think probable. I saw a young Mr. Southall who knew you well & told me that he had seen you & all about it & promised to try and get the picture which you said J.H. was to send to me. He is a nice fellow on first acquaintance at least. He seemed so to me for he loaned me a carde de visite photograph of you which he says your Ma gave to him when he was sick in St. Louis, a very good likeness and one I prize above all my possessions except the one you gave me. I am to keep it until he gets the one you spoke of for me which he says he can do. If I can possibly have it done I will send you one though at present it wd. look rather badly for I have had a long siege of the chills & they have left me very thin indeed. I have completely broken them now and am improving rapidly. Give my love to all the family & take an inexhaustible supply for your heart. I will write you a long letter soon—when I am certain it will reach you and tell you all the news, but I have not much heart to write now for I am uncertain if you ever get it.

Good Bye my own & remember me always as yours forever.

P.S. This letter was very much hurried & you must excuse errors &c.

Afternoon, June 22nd

My brigade did not leave as we expected & I will add one more line. If you get this letter you must answer immediately & send it to my sister F. & she will be able to send it through to me. If I had time & cd. induce the messenger to wait I would go to Atlanta & have my picture taken & send it to you to let you see that although I am no miscegnator & hold all such in abhorence yet I am almost as dark as a "likely Mulatto" or intelligent contraband. Bye the bye does not the word "intelligent" in that sense mean "Mulatto."

I have been muddy & wet & dedraggled for nearly a month and have almost forgotten how a bed made with a dry blanket feels. You are aware I suppose that on moves of this kind we have no towels & scarcely any of the conveniences of life. But God has blessed me with fine health & I will not complain for he has been very good to me. I have been in the storm of battle many times & seen the brave & good fall smitten by swift death, & have not been seriously hurt, though I have scaped death narrowly & I earnestly believe that it is due to the prayers of a pious mother & to yours also. Oh how much I wish to see you. I can give you no idea. The South is a free land though alas not happy, but still if you come here I am satisfied that you will be restored to health. If you come I have the nicest horse to send to you to ride, & may be will be among the first to take a ride with you on him. Nothing short of my honor has kept me away from you as long as I have. When I was in Ky. I was sent on duty & could not consistently stay away any longer than I did & then if the river had not been frozen I should have stretched a point & came to see you any how & now if I could I would resign & and come any how. But officers in the service have to have surgeons certificate of disability to resign & go away from the army and I am healthy & as well as I ever was in my life.

I am getting prosy now & will not weary you with the perusal of a longer letter so once again good bye & believe me always yours.

Most affectionately. Give my love to your mother & father & the children.

GC

Athens, McMinn Co. Tennessee, July 26th

My Dearest Bettie,

I have written several letters to you of late & hope that you have received them. If you have not & they have fallen into the hands of the Philistenes I have the satisfaction to know that they did not find out to whom they were addressed or by whom they were written. I received your letter of May 12th which was the last I have had. Bye the bye I received a letter from Ms. Lucy Welsh from Mobile, Ala. in which she asked me for my address and said she had a photograph and several messages for me. I immediately answered and gave my address for I was certain the messages & photograph were from you. They have not been received yet. When they come to hand I write and let you what they were and from whom. I did not know Mrs. Welch. Who was she? We are at Athens, McMinn Co., East Tennessee to remit our stock which has been very hardly used of late and needed rest very much. We are encamped at a beautiful place, the site of an-old camp meeting place called Cedar Springs in a valley between the mountains and there are four large springs within one hundred yards of each other, the climate is delightfully pleasant & cool and at night it is frequently inconveniently so. Two blankets are required to cover with and not warm enough at times. The scenery here partakes of the sublime & now and then will spread out a beautiful landscape running up to the craggy hills in the distance. Athens is not the seat of learning in East Tennessee but has been misnamed, everything to eat has been exhausted and consequently I am living on army rations alone which is not like the fare at the Planters or Rest. de Paris. This war will teach many of us a great many valuable lessons. I will never complain of whatever I _____ to eat at home or abriad, and when the war is ended I have an idea of writing a treatise on the capability of the human constitution to sustain all manner of hardships and privations of hunger, thirst, cold, heat &c. I am well satisfied that man can endure more than any other animal, & if any one had have told me I could have had my health & endured what I have I would have been incredulous. Oh how I love to see you. I will be sure to forget all but my love which I bear for you. Love is one of the miracles of human nature. No other sentiment or feeling of the heart is comparable to it. It is the last & best gift of God to man & man though fallen in his nature in all other respects is the same child of nature in this respect as when Adam & Eve wandered in the Garden of Eden.

You remember when I used to talk of the fickle heart of woman—well isn't it strange that I have such complete confidence in the constancy of yours? Though strange it is it is no less true for I would trust you to all extent and God knows you may rely on the loyalty of my heart to its sovereign. No power ever had a subject so loyal as I am to you. I would regard it as a sweet privilege to risk my life to benefit or shield you in any respect, and when the day does come when I can before the world claim a protectorate over you, then you can rely on me as life lasts. When I see you again I will have much to tell you, and what I do tell you will make you believe that I never loved but one and that one you know is yourself. I would write more fully to you than I have done but you must know that opportunities of sundry letters must be snatched *en passant* and the time to write is very hurried. You must excuse this as it was written on my knee with a pencil, I sitting on a camp stool. Good Bye my love to all & remember me as ever your own most lovingly

GC

Kingston, East Tennessee
August 1, 1863

Miss Sue Bettie Woods
St. Louis, Mo.

My Dearest,

I wrote a letter to you a few days since, and promised to write again soon and a longer one than that one. I have an opportunity now of writing again through the kindness of Mrs. Lucy Welch who says she knows a sure conveyance to St. Louis and I hasten to avail myself of this chance. In my last I told you of having had a letter from Mrs. Welsh & that she said she had some messages & a photograph for me & that when they were received by me I would tell you what they were. The photograph was a bust & shoulders of a most exquisitely beautiful young lady in a riding dress with a palmetoo riding hat on certainly a most beautiful picture, yet not sufficiently si to do justice to the incomparable original. My darling Bettie I would prefer to lose all of my other possessions to losing this beautiful & life like picture. It is certainly the greatest of my pleasures to gaze on the bright eyes & happy expression on that great mouth; it shall be my talisman & on it will hang my present & noblest aspirations. Your friend Mrs. W. & my friend too for she has now very high claims to mine, said that you sent many sweet messages but all in substance that you were the same unchanged in your feelings. I was very much gratified to learn from her of your consistent & noble conduct to my enemies & the enemies of our country. She says you are one of the best women in the world, but she must not have told me that, for such has been my settled belief for several years. To tell you the truth, I felt some how the first time I ever saw you that you were to be the woman who was destined by the will of Heaven to make me a better & a happier man. I have no Bible but I remembers its teachings faithfully & read often in it and as soon as an opportunity presents will buy a pocket edition & make it my companion by day & night. I have much to thank God for & I trust I am not ungrateful. I have walked amid the storms of many battles & have never been touched, but I am far very far from being as good as I might be, and my sweet one I ask your prayers for me, and I know the request is already granted.

Oh when shall we meet again? I had perfected all my plans to see you during last month, but the unfortunate retrograde movement of the Army of Tennessee compelled a postponment of my visit & since then we have been so unsettled that I could find no opportunity to make any future plan—but I intend to see you before long though I am taken prisoner in the attempt, for to tell the truth it would be a great pleasure to me to be a prisoner in the hands of the enemy for a while, if I could only see you even thro' the grates & bars of a prison. Actually it looks like weakness of the mind to pay such constant devotion to a picture, but I say it & truthfully that I take your photograph and look at it more than twenty times every day, and it seems to stay the swell of a longing heart at least temporarily. As for myself my health is excellent but I am not as large as I have been represented. I am rather more compact & sinewy than when at St. Louis, but not much altered in appearance, except that two years constant exposure has bronzed my features. We are encamped at this place— the confluence of the Clinch & Holston Rivers which form the Tennessee and the scenery's grand & picturesque, the country is very much tendered with Unionism & many have run away & gone to the Yankee Army. The necessities of life are rather hard to get at, but the romantic mountains & valleys and beautiful water courses joined in one far stretching landscape remind me of the glens of Scotland & the rough & sublime scenery of Switzerland, and the imagination is very fruitful of both ideas. I think that if I had been born & bred in such a country, practical as I now am I should have been found writing poetry against my will. I have no news at all to tell you which would be at all interesting, for in my last letter I told you all the news I could think of. I hope you received that letter. I have written to you regularly all the time & shall continue to do so, though I do not hear from you, for I know how it warms the heart to get a letter from those we love, and I do believe & know that you love me. Write to me when you can and always think of me as your

                    Own Most Affectionately
                    GC

Courtland, Ala. Oct. 18th, 1863

Miss Sue Bettie Woods
St. Louis, Mo.

I have written so often & as yet have had no indication that my letters reached their destination, that it seems almost useless to write again but I have written & intend to write as often as a chance presents itself. I have great hopes that this will reach you & that you may be enabled to answer it also. It seems an age since I saw you and that I have not seen you since is by no means my fault, for I have applied for leave of absence several times & from the exigencies of the service my application was refused. I have got another one up through all the generals up to Bragg & have that yet to hear from. It is the dictator of honor & duty which prevent me from going to see you anyhow.

I think more often with sad delight of you & past happiness than ever and it is the ultimate aim of my hopes to meet you again & that not far off in the scale of time. If ever a human heart was true in its allegiance, mine is, & ever has been to you, my own darling Bettie. I suppose you may have been uneasy about my safety not knowing if I was engaged in the fights preceding and subsequent to the Battle of Chickamauga which was fought on the 19, 20th & 21st of last month. I was in it all. For five days prior to the battle Forests Cav. to which I belong was fighting almost constantly, and during that bloody battle we shared our part of it. The enemy were disastrously defeated and their loss was very heavy, losing about 12,000 prisoners beside great numbers killed. Our loss was heavy in killed & wounded, especially in officers.

In these different fights I never had any apprehension, though death blew his breath in my face as he passed on. In the last fight we were in which was about 10 days ago, I lost one third of my men in killed & wounded. I do not know that any of your friends or acquaintances were hurt in the battle. I have no news to tell about except that our troops are in fine spirits & equal to all emergencies. We are & have been bivouacking for over a month, no huts or shelters of any kind & no wagons so you see we must be leading a hard sort of a life. The hardships of the war have come upon us so gradually that I have not felt their weight so sensibly. This war makes men grow old very fast & though I do not notice it on myself but when I see my friends after an absence of some time they look so much older, the wrinkles begin to gather around the eyes and a gray hair now & then shines among the black locks of youth. If I do not get a leave of absence I will either be taken captive or killed before many months more for life with such a protracted absence from you is unendurable and relief can only be had by daring all dangers.

I have no news at all to impart and will close this letter my darling with an assurance of my everlasting love & devotion. I know but one love & will never know another. Good Bye. If this letter reaches you it will tell you on an accompanying note with how to write to me.

Believe me. As ever your own most affectionately,
GC

Glencoe, Nov. 15th, 1863

I again commence a letter to you without any prospect whatever of sending it but I can at least have it ready in case one should suddenly occur. I feel so restless & unhappy that it will be a relief to tell my troubles to you at least to write them on paper & think of you at the same time. Do you know it has been three months since I have heard from you in any way whatever. The last letter I had was the one sent by Mrs. Welsh & dated the 1st of August; sometimes I am almost distracted, with fear for you; if it were not for my faith in God, I could not bear it. Often in the midst of gay company I sit thinking of you until the room & every one fades from my sight, & I see you amid the smoke of the battlefield wounded or perhaps killed, or lying sick & deserted in some desolate place. A young gentleman friend of yours told me the other day that you were certainly engaged to be married to a young lady of Florence & that you visited her constantly. I also heard the same thing in a letter from Nashville. I thought when I heard this, but only for an instant, that perhaps that was the cause of your long silence, & what I felt in that one instant I can never describe to you & then came back to me with the radiance of a sunbeam my trust in you & I knew in my heart that it could not be true. Glencoe looks desolate now. Everything is covered with snow. The hills look much larger & are more clearly defined in their white robes & the whole scene is altogether wild & impresses me. Sadly, I often walk in the garden & stop at the spot where we parted—or at least where you told me Good Bye the night before you left. O! how the old torture revives with the old scene. I can almost feel again the soft firm pressure of your hand & hear your voice & remember well your words so full of tenderness & yet so free from that revolting sentimentality that others had offered me & my heart cries out in its loneliness. O! summer night come back to me. Nov. 25th I was interrupted in my letter & have not had an opportunity of resuming it for several days & in the meantime last evening much to my joy I received a letter from you dated Oct. 18th at Courtland. You said there would be a note enclosed telling me how to answer it but it was not there & I am still without any means of sending this letter. I am so anxious to see you as you are or can possibly be to see me but even if you suceed in obtaining a leave of absence I do not see how that is to be the means of bringing us together for it would be entirely too dangerous for you to attempt to come here or go to Paducah but I think the exigencies of the service must be great indeed if after serving faithfully for nearly three years you can not have a few weeks rest. I would do anything sacrifice anything to see you & be with you once for it is all I care to live for; but I see no way in which it can be accomplished, unless you should be taken prisoner & brought within the lines which I must confess I hope most devoutely will be the case, as strange &

perhaps even wicked as you may think such a wish. I would be thankful to see you even in a prison; the plan of not exchanging prisoners is thought by the Union people here to be quite impracticable; the people of the North will not stand it, & some arrangements will soon have to be made so that I feel even if you were taken you would not been kept long in confinement & I would have the intense satisfaction of knowing that for a while at least you were safe from Yankee bullets; but dearest it is all in the hands of God & if we trust in Him, He will bring it to pass for He has promised to hear those that pray to Him with faith. At some times I have a presentiment that I will see you soon & then I am so happy & the whole world seems bright & beautiful. I expect by this time you have seen or heard from Susie Woods. She is in Florence waiting for an opportunity to go to Lizzie. I asked her to write to you as I was not allowed to do so my self. It was a great temptation to me to go with her, & strange to say Father & Mother were both willing that I should. But just then a new order was passed not allowing persons to go South & return here to live so of course under those circumstances I was afraid to go. We are going in town for a week to stay at the Planters House for two months. I can not bear the idea. St. Louis is so gay now. Club parties, weddings, receptions, matinees, concerts, lectures &C. I can not of course live amidst all this gayity, & not participate to some extent in it, but society is as painful to me now, as it was formerly pleasant, & I have lived so very retired for the last year that I feel entirely out of place at a party & then I have not the spirit for such things. I am never happy now. O! when when shall I see you again! I had a letter from your sister Florence a few days ago; she writes such bright pleasant letters. I keep up quite an extensive prison correspondence now. Hugh & Jack Kirkman, Mr. Doc Vander & Mr. Rutledge are all & Johnson's Island & several others of my friends are at the Alton Prison. Hugh writes in fine spirits. I sent him a box of all sorts of nice things a few days ago. It contained various kinds of dainties, cigars, silk handkerchiefs & a great many interesting books, but unfortunately he never received it. The ladies here are very much interested in the prisoners & do all they are allowed for them. I sew a great deal but I can not beg money as the rest do.

Dec. 3rd. I again resume this endless letter after another interval of several days. I must not close my letter without telling you that Dr. Pollak is to be married on the 29th of this month to Miss Sallie Perry. Mr. Henry Nisbet was married last week to Miss Selby of Ken. Dr. Alexander & Julia Barret are to be married this evening, & Mr. Munford & Miss Erskine very soon. Mrs. Gen. Bowen came up from the South & staid a few weeks. Mr. Frank Noell came with & was allowed to remain at liberty about two weeks when to his great surprise he was sent to prison. Mrs. Bowen has returned. Mrs. Schaumberg has gone South to see her son. The Radicals (Republicans) here have carried this state & their measures are becoming so severe that it is thought in six months from now no person with any Southern proclivities will be allowed to remain here. Did you ever receive a foolish little work box I sent you by Mr. Chiles? If so you must have thought a strange thing for me to send you but it was sent through mistake. I had made a very pretty little thing for you called a soldier's companion which the ladies make a great deal for prisoners & I asked Mrs. Chiles to send to me for it when Mr. C. started which she did but I was quite sick at the time & told the servant to get it but she took my own work box emptied it filled it with buttons & thread & sent it off & when I recovered I was searching everywhere for my box & finally upon questioning Kate I found to my great amusement that she had sent it to you. I hope if it ever reached you that you did not think I had taken leave of my senses. Your friends very often inquire for you particularly Mr. Kennedy & Mr. Berry & Miss Cornelia. I have a cousin from New York spending the winter with me. She is a very sweet companion but rather too fond of society for my present mood. I have been in miserable health this fall & have just now recovered from a "spell" of fever which they thought at first was typhoid fever but I hope now to be entirely well again. I ride occassionally on horseback but the weather does not admit of it very often; but I am still a great coward about riding and now I must close this long letter which I do not suppose you will ever receive. Write to me by every opportunity. Many will fail but some of the letters must reach me. I love you more deeply & devotedly the longer this painful separation lasts; "Mine is an unchanging love higher than the heights, a love deeper than the depths beneath free & faithful strong as death." God grant that we may meet soon. Good Bye. Mother always sends much love to you.

I am lovingly your own

Nannie Bell is to be married on the 19th of this month.

Dec. 24, 1863

Miss Sue Bettie Woods
St. Louis, Mo.

My Own Darling Bettie,

I am here on leave and would give anything to see you. I have time to write only a line to you. I am well and have a little more time at my disposal & if you will write to me and suggest any plan for us to meet I will do all that can be done to see you. I would dare all dangers to see you for you alone know how dear you are to me. I get leave of sbsence solely to see or hear from you & my darling you must make some way for us to meet within the next three weeks at the fastest. Could you not come to see Florence or go to see Andy at Bellwood Furnace or the Rolling Mill. Either would do. Good Bye I will write again in a day or two. Answer immediately and under cover to Florence. She will send to me.

Of do not let this chance slip for it may be long again to another.

Yours forever
GC

Dec. 29, 1863

My Dearest Bettie,

I wrote you a short note from Paris, since then I have learned that it was sent to you by mail. I have not had a line from you for many long months and did not know whether you were dead or alive or well or sick, until today when I heard that you were well and that several letters from you to me had been sent nut not come to hand as yet. Oh my darling you can't know how deadly the pain of such uncertainty is. My letter since of these must have come to hand and you must have heard from me since I have from you but in all this dark silence I have never once doubted your faith and affection. But my darling it must be very trying to you to remain so long absent & so long ignorant of whether your soldier boy is alive or his bones with his ancestors. I wrote to you in the note before mentioned that almost my sole object is getting a leave of absence was to see you or hear from you, to hear from you any how & to see you if possible. Write to me at once whether I can see you and when it shall be, at some accessible place to be named by you. But as the time is limited when you get this letter if you could come to the Rolling Mill or Paducah or Nashville soon. Would it not be a good idea to telegraph to my Father the place & time & he will send it to me? If it is impossible then write to me & send your carte-de-visite or daguerrotype. I can have one taken and will do so & send it to you in a few days. I haven't changed as much as you may have imagined, for I resemble my old self more now than for a long time. I have not had very good health for the last month and weigh above what I did when we parted. My God help me for I almost fear that I shall lose my faith in his goodness, if He keeps up this anxious & painful separation much longer. I do not know what it is to love anything else but you, for I can truly say your image haunts my every sleep; I dream of you nearly every night and think of you every hour of the day. If we could meet together and talk matters over, I believe I could find some way of shortening our days of absence. The war is hateful to me because it separates us & has done so so long. Just to think what might have been if these troubles had not have overtaken our land. Long ago you would have been the sweet & loving wife of as happy & proud a husband as ever called Adam father, but this only makes the bitters more unpalatable, and let us look for brighter skies and happier days. I have faced death in many forms and would seek its unknown phases to get to see you. But my time is limited and I must not dishonor a name unspotted by taking time not honourably at my disposal and I know you do not blame me. I have written to you regularly and sent the letters by what several good carriers. But accident or misfortune must have befallen them as those sent by you to me.

I have seen none of my family, but have had a short note from home & will hear more perhaps. But Bettie, we must see each other soon. It must be so! You alone know how dear you are to me and frequently when at night I awake & hear the silent watches of the small hours pass by, I try to remember all of our conversations & your looks & manners, the tones of your voice its accents and the music of your laugh and the soft loving look out of the eye, and my memory is a very poor servant & not just to its mistress for I can not do you half justice, though in all of our long acquaintance I can see no imperfection in her I love. You do not know how you tried drowning the depths of my pride when for so long a time you would not acknowledge you loved me, but though the rebel pride wd. resist and fight desperately for independence, yet love was the stronger of the two & conquered the proud heart and bade it be still & have faith & patience & you know how well my faith was recompensed by you, deep pure love, now worth more to me than all else on this earth. I am in no condition to write a sensible letter to you & you must excuse the folly of this letter if it seems foolish for I am almost mad.

My candle is nearly out & I must close. Write to me at once and direct to me under cover to my sister F., enclosed in a smaller envelope to me. If you can suggest any way for us to meet do so and I will do my part to fulfill the plan. Nothing prevented us from meeting when you were in Nashville but the entire ignorance of your whereabouts & having no letters from you to tell me when to meet you.

Goodbye now my own dear Bettie. May God keep you & bless you. My love to all & remember me always as the true faithful & affectionate

GC

Tuscaloosa
Jan. 9th, 1864

    We are having a day of incorrigible rain & gloom, no hope whatever of a moment's cessation to the incessant pattering of the rain, no hope of a single gleam of sunshine, nothing to do but submit gracefully to the most disagreeable of things a long raining day. I can not think of any better way of helping it to pass away than by writing you a long letter at least I have started with the intention of doing so but whether my patience will hold out I do not know. Pray that it will not for I am in a very bad mood today & I fear if I write long my ill humor may show itself. I wrote you a few days after we arrived here which is now nearly four weeks ago, but the mails from here are so irregular that I doubt whether the letter has ever reached you. I also wrote & sent the letter to Mrs. Welsh to send you as I thought it very probable she would know someone going to the command—as she is now in Columbus—since then I have not written, waiting to hear from you, but I felt almost as much cut-off from you here as I was at home. Persons here who have relations in the army in Georgia say that they never hear from them at all but still I have an abiding faith & believe that it will all come right at last, that you will be shielded from danger & that the day will come when I can enjoy the happiness of being with you again. God grant that it may be very soon. We have quite a pleasant family circle here now. Jennie Bell who came through the lines with us is still here & a few days ago Charlotte Erwin came from Montgomery to pay us a little visit & these with Sue, Lizzie & myself compose the ladies of the family. The gentlemen are Mr. George Jackson from North Alabama, Mr. Jim Andrews of Florence & Capt. Jim Polk of Tenn. These two have just been released from prison & were on their way home when the army fell back, & of course they could not proceed as they are not yet declared exchanged they can not join their command. Col. Harry Yeatman & Hunt Kirkman are also here. He is still on crutches but able to about. Mr. Kirkman left last week for Richmond, but our family is so large that we do not miss him as much as we otherwise would. Tuscaloosa has been quite gay. Quite a number of parties & several weddings have taken place. I did not attend any of them, but have enjoyed myself walking, riding, &c. I took one ride on horseback with Capt. Polk & was to have gone again this morning had it not rained. I enjoyed the ride exceedingly as I had a pleasant gentle horse, but I could not help thinking that it would have been even more delightful if I could have substituted another Captain for the one who was with me. I had a letter a few days ago from Augusta & heard something of a lovely girl there who occupies the most stately mansion in the city. Her name is Jennie. The story goes on to relate that a certain Captain from the far distant West—perhaps Kentucky or Missouri—happened along there a short time ago, probably last summer & sad though it may seem, fell, a captive knight to the charms of the said Miss Jennie. Can you finish the story? I can not as my informant stopped there in his history of the affair & left the rest to my imagination. I hope you will be more kind & not leave me in ignorance of the finale of this interesting little episode. We all felt disappointed at Gen. Wood's utter failure in Tennessee. I felt that he never could take Nashville, but did not think he would have to recross the Tenn. this winter—poor fellows—they must have given up the contest with bitterness of heart. They might well have sung to their dear ones in Nashville the old song "Thou art so near & yet so far." We have been expecting a raid here for several days but I do not believe there is any thing in the report. I have seen your friend Miss Mary Martin several times. She is very pleasant & report says is very soon to marry Dr. Hawse. Miss Stafford spoke of you several times & of your having been sadly flirted by a Miss White of Talladega. I have not heard a word from home & feel very anxious about them all. Sometimes I almost regret having them, nothing but the hope of seeing you soon, who I love better than all the world besides, reconciles me to being so far away from home. O! do come to me soon. I want to see you more than I can tell you. I must put an end to this long scrawl as dinner is almost ready.

Good Bye
Your own loving S.B.

Glencoe Heights
May 22nd, 1864

I wrote several weeks ago by flag of truce & directed to Oxford, Ala. as I had received a letter from you there the evening previous & knew no other address. Yesterday however I received a letter from your sister in which she told me how to direct a letter to you with a certainty of its reaching so fearing you did not receive the other I write again. I have been very uneasy about you fearing that you may be in the battle now raging in the South West. I trust in God for your safety. I am better than I have been but I improve so slowly that the Dr. says I must have sea air, & in spite of all my remonstrances I am to leave in a week with Mother for the North. I don't know to what part of the coast we will go, but I want a quiet place if it can be found. I have been an invalid now for six or eight months & am very impatient to be well. If I can stand the journey by Fall (probably September) I am going South, They speak of Cuba but I prefer Tuscaloosa & think I will certainly go there. Can you "guess" the cause of my preference? There is some one there I want to see very much. St. Louis is very gay now with the races & the Sanitary Fair which even surpass in magnitude our old agricultural fairs. I am sorry the rules do not allow me to write you but one page. If I find that you get this I will _____ all desire to be remembered _____ but no room to tell it. Do not forget to read your Bible.

Hoping & praying that we may meet soon. I am yours lovingly

S.B. Woods

Near Chattahoochie River
8 Miles from Atlanta
July 6th, 1864

My Darling Bettie,

I have time to drop you just a line, & not to write a letter. I have had no time for several days past to do anything but fight & prepare for it, hardly to wash my face & hands but to day is a rather quiet day & I venture to commence a letter. I wrote several letters & sent them thro' a week or two ago & hope that they may be received. I am enjoying very good health & indeed I believe that the warm weather of this climate agrees better with me than does the warm weather of the latitude of Saint Louis. I have become acclimated to all climates & I am afraid that when I see you again you will turn this tough bronzed faced soldier away on account of his ugliness. When I saw Miss Susie I had been sick & was bleached, but the ruddy glow of health has come back over me & although I am frequently attacked with unhappy yearnings & anxious attitudes on account of you. Yet such is the happy influence of our elastic constitution in the pride of health, that my heart will not stay sad and I have too much confidence in the mercy & goodness of God to believe that he will take you away from me or make you endure a long languishing illness. I have not heard from you, i.e. have had no letter since Feb'y 22 but I will not despair & hope to see you in the sunny South soon & I can promise you that if you come I can get a furlough to go & see you. I was talking to Genl. Wheeler about it a day or two ago & he said I could get it.

I am fortunate in having a great many kind & influential friends in the army. And if I chose could get promotion at any time & I am candid when I tell you that you are & have been the reason why I did not desire it, I know if I held an office higher than I do I would not be allowed to leave the army as readily as I can now & I have all along cherished the hope of seeing you & paying you a visit. As Capt. I can get a short leave almost at any time, but if I held a high position I could not be spared so well. I must make up my mind that I will either quit the service or make it a vocation, if this war promises to last much longer & in the latter case I will pursue it with as much ambition, zeal & energy as I would any other business of life. But I do hope the war will not last long.

I have no news to impart except that Loyd Haynes, adj't of 1st Mo. was wounded & the Col. killed a short time since. Sally Polks husband has been seriously wounded & is at hospital near Griffin, Geo. Johnny Kay is adjt. of 49th Tenn. & is very well & is a large handsome young man. But scarcely any of my old friends recognize me.

They say I have changed so much & I believe that if I was to drop into your presence dressed *a la "raid"* i.e. like a cavalry man on a hard raid you would not know me.

I forgot to mention that I saw Col. Clark, Mr. Churchills Bro. in Law and your friend Miss Saddie's uncle. He was quite well & in his artillery uniform looked very red. Willie Clark his son is, I believe, a Capt. & stationed at some factories in command of the guard at these places. I have no more news. I have not heard from Mr. Kirkman lately & intend writing soon to find out the news.

If this reaches you & finds you as I have prayed it may, well—write immediately to me & send the letter under cover to Paducah & I will most probably get it. You do not know how I long to see you. I am coming to see you after this campaign at all hazards.

I must cease this brief and hurried note & let it make up in affection what it lacks in epistolary elegance. Give my love to all of your Fathers family & write to me.

> Yours forever
> GC

Near Chattahoochie River
8 Miles from Atlanta.
July 6th 1864.

My Darling Bettie
I have time to drop
you just a line, but not to write a letter,
I have had no time for several days
past to do anything but fight & prepare
for it hardly to wash my face & hand
but to day is a rather quiet day &
I venture to commence a letter,
I wrote several letters & sent them this
a week or two ago & hope that they
may be received. I am enjoying very
good health, & indeed I believe that
the warm weather of this Climate
agrees better with me than does
the warm weather of the Colledes
of Saint Louis. I have become
acclimated to all Climates &
I am afraid that when I see
you again you will deem this
tough bronzed faced soldier away
on account of his ughiness.
When I saw Miss Susie I had been
sick & was bleached, but the
ruddy glow of health has come
back over me & although I am
frequently attacked with unhappy
yearnings & anxious soli-
tudes on account of you. yet such

is the happy influence of an elastic
Constitution in the pride of health,
that my heart will not stay sad
and I have too much confidence
in the mercy & goodness of God to
believe that he will take you
away from me or make you en-
=dure a long languishing illness.
I have not heard from you & I
have had no letter since Feb 22
but I will not despair & hope to
see you in the Quincy [?] soon
& I can promise you that if you
come I can get a furlough to go
& see you. I was talking to [?]
wheeler about it a day or two ago
& he said I could get it.
I am fortunate in having a
great many kind & influential
friends in the army. and if I
chose could get promotion at
any time & I am candid
when I tell you that you are
& have been the reason why
I did not desire it. I knew if
I held an office higher than I
do I would not be allowed
to leave the army as readily as
I can now. & I have all along
cherished the hope of seeing

you & paying you a visit. as long
as I can get a leave almost at any
time, but if I held a high posi
-tion I could not be spared so
well. I must make up my mind
that I will either quit the ser-
-vice or make it a vocation. if
this war promises to last much
longer + in the latter case I will
pursue it with as much am
=bition zeal & energy as I would
any other business of life. But
I do hope the war will not last
long.

I have no news to impart except that
Loyd Haynes adjt of 1st Ino. was wounded
& the Col killed a short time since.
Sally Polks husband has been se-
-verely wounded + is at hospital
near Griffin Geo. Johnny Kay is
adjt of 49th Tenn + is very well & is
a large handsome young man.
But scarcely any of my old friends
recognize me. they say I have chan
=ged so much & I believe that
if I was to drop into your pres
=ence dressed a la "raid"
i.e. like a cavalry man on a
hard raid, you would not
know me.

I forgot to mention that I saw Col
Clark Mr Churchills Bro in law

and your friend Miss Peddies
Uncle he was quite well in his
artillery uniform looked very
red. Willie Clark his son is,
I believe, a Capt. & stationed at
some factories in command
of the guard at these places.
I have no more news. I have
not heard from Mrs. Kirkman
lately & intend writing soon to find
out the news.

If this reaches you, & finds you
as I have prayed it may, well—
write immediately to me & send the
letter (under cover) to Paducah & I will most
portably get it. You do yet know
how I long to see you, I am coming to see you after this campaign at all hazards.
I must close this brief & hurried
note till I make up in affection what it lacks in
epistolary elegance. Give my
love to all of your fathers family
& write to me.

Yours forever

We —

Near Atlanta
July 26th. 1864

My Darling Bettie,

I am going to write you a brief letter this time for I did not know till now that I could send a letter thro'. I have had unequalled health till yesterday when I had a slight fever, occasioned by having taken cold from the sudden change in the weather. On the last night the thermometer was nearly low enough for frost & you have no idea of the disagreeable nature of such changes. I wrote to you a few days since by flag of truce & told you about all of the news. Bye the bye, have you ever written to me by Flag of Truce? I have sent several letters to you & had none in reply. I have letters from home now & then & if they will not allow your letters to go from St. Louis send them to Paducah & they will come thro' from there.

I was very much rejoiced to hear thro' Florence that you were well, for I was so uneasy about you. I am almost broken down, for I have been on duty & in active service nearly all the time for 75 days, constantly under fire, sometimes the steady pop pop of the skirmish lines & then the heavier & duller boom of artillery with the shrill hurtling of shells as an accompanying terror. But so far have not had "a hair turned." We have had a great many gallant young men sent to the "Elysian Field" since this fight commenced. I believe that the morale of our army was such that we could have beaten the enemy at Resaca or Dalton or at any place between there & here, but it was Genl. Johnston's place to cripple them by a Fabian retreat & if their papers speak correctly, their loss must have been very great indeed. Genl. Hood a Kentuckian born & bred is now commander in chief of this army & he is as dauntless & skillful as any one in our army excepting always Robert le grand Lee. The army was loth to part with Genl. Johnston as we are always to part with friends we love, but I believe that Genl. Hood will inspire more enthusiastic ardor among the troops than Genl. Johnston. At all ends, be whatever may come & you will see the South still as resolute & determined as now & in my opinion more so as this contest is prolonged. This war is working much sadder ravages than the same time would in peace times, in the appearance of the soldiers, for the hardship & exposure to winds, rain, cold & heat have turned many black hairs prematurely grey & made many smooth faces hard & indurated. I believe that I wear as well as any & I am very much weather beaten. It is also making even the female children, old women for it is no uncommon sight to see a girl of 12 in the hospitals of the mortally wounded sweetening with her attentions the fleeting last moments of some dying soldier's life and then closing his eyes as placidly as an experienced death bed nurse. The women here deserve the manly defence which is made for them, for they nurse the wounded soldiers like mothers & sisters. One brigade has made a great name for itself on this retreat both under Col. Grigsley & Genl. Williams ("Cerro Goods") who now commands us, but this fame has been dearly bought. Many very many of our dearest friends & bravest have bit the dust. I think that this campaign will prove a decisive one if we can weather the storm, but if Atlanta & Richmond are abandoned the administration of Mr. Lincoln will last four years longer, then, another term of war. I have no more paper to write upon as we are bivouaced all our baggage with the trains in the rear. I wish to see you more than anything else & if you can you must come out with Miss Susie. I have so many things to say to you which I cannot put in a letter & then I believe that the sight of my eyes would last an age longer if I could only get to see you. I love you and only you & have never had any temptation to love another. I have seen no one so handsome & none so entirely good & just to my taste & if I live a hundred years never expect to see another like you. But you know all this & hence I stop, my kindest regards to your Father & Mother & the children. If you write an answer to this immediately & send it to Florence I will get it.

> Good Bye Yours Forever
> Most Affectionately
> GC

New York August 6, 1864

My Dear Brother

We were so rejoiced to hear from you yesterday through Mr. Roche, even so far back as the fourth of last month. He reports you looking well and in fine spirits; but I believe your spirits are always good.

Florence has written several letters which she sent by the way of Fortress Monroe, and we have started some by private hands, so I hope some of them have reached you.

We have had no letter from you since the one sent by Flag of Truce last April. And as you may imagine were very glad to hear Mr. Roche's news.

You will probably be surprised to see this letter dated from New York; but we are here on our way to Canada. General Pain took possession of our house two weeks ago for his residence while he remains at Paducah. So as we had no home we left there immediately. General Pain is the Commander of the District, and I have no idea how long he will retain the house, but I hope not long.

Uncle Gus with his family have left Paducah and is now keeping house in Montreal, where he is anxious we should join them. He says there is a small house near theirs that Father can get and he wants us to rent it. I don't know what Father will do about it; but we expect to leave here next Wednesday for Montreal, where we will remain for the present either keeping house or boarding. We are looking for Jimmy over in a few weeks and Father and Uncle Gus want him to remain in Montreal and study law there, if we settle there it will be so much pleasanter having him with us.

Here was the last accounts we had from him, traveling through Scotland and intended after finishing his tour through that country returning to America, his heart seems set on going to the Army, but Mother & Father are opposed to that.

Aunt Kate is the only member of the family left in Paducah now except Marian McLeilland and Joe Fowler's family. Hizzy has taken to drinking regularly and Aunt Kate thinks if she can get him off from his associates there he may break himself of the habit, but I am afraid it has become too confirmed on him; I feel so sorry for her.

Uncle Henry and his wife are living in Louisville now at the Gatt House; they left home last spring. So you see we are a scattered family. Sister and George are still down the river, where I expect they will remain until the fall. Sister feels very hurt at not hearing from you. She says she has written repeatedly to you and never had a reply, and she says she is sure you received the letters. I wrote to her I didn't believe you had, or either you had answered them. If you have not written to here do write for she believes you think hard of her, and I am sure you do not.

Florence is with Aunt Clara in Canada. They left Paducah a few days before we did. But I will close now for Mother to add a short post script. Good bye my dear dear brother. Your loving sister Carrie.

My Darling Son,

I was so glad to hear by Mr. Roche that one month ago you were safe and well and thankful we have an opportunity of writing. Carrie has told you the news I expect. We will remain in Canada the remainder of the summer and fall. After that time Mr. Watts can tell where we are. You know what you told me last winter that it would be easier to see us then than where we were and I do so long to see you again without constraint or fear to hold your precious hands in mine and tell my noble boy how inexpressibly dear he is to me, to us all. All are praying for you and Omnipotence is pledged for your safety. Only don't forget to pray if you know that can be done at anytime on horseback on the eve of battle or in the quiet night. We can come to you at any time or in any place.

Mother says don't be uneasy about us that we will be well provided for.

Your sister Carrie

New York August 6 1864

My Dear Brother

We were so rejoiced to hear from you yesterday through Mr Koehn, even so far back as the fourth of last month.

He reports you looking well and in fine spirits; but I believe your spirits are always good.

Fannie has written several letters which she sent by the way of Fortress Monroe, and we have started some by private hands, so I hope some of them have reached you.

We have had no letter from you since the one sent by flag of truce last April, and as you may imagine were very glad to hear the Koehn news.

You will probably be surprised to see this letter dated from New York; but we are here on our way to Canada. General Ben took possession of our house some weeks ago, for his residence

While he remains at Paducah
For as we had no home we left there
immediately, General Payne is the
commander of the district, and I have
no idea how long he will retain the
house, but I hope not long.

Uncle Gus with his family have
left Paducah, and is now keeping
house in Montreal, where he is
anxious we should join them.

He says there is a small house
near theirs, that Father can get,
and he wants us to rent it.

I don't know what Father will
do about it, but we expect to
leave here next Wednesday, for
Montreal, where we will remain
for the present, either keeping house
or boarding. We are looking
for Jimmy over in a few weeks
and Father and Uncle Gus
want him to remain in Montreal
and study law there, if we settle
there it will be so much pleasanter
having him with us.

He was the last accounts we
had from him, traveling through
Scotland, and intended after

finishing his Tour through that Country, returning to America - his heart seems set on going to the Army, but Mother + Father are opposed to that.

Aunt Kate is the only member of the family left in Paducah now except Marian McLelland, and Joe Fowler's family. Lizzy has taken to drinking regularly. And Aunt Kate thinks if she can get him off from his accosiates there, he may break himself of the habit, but I am afraid it has become too confirmed on him; I feel so sorry for her.

Uncle Henry and his wife are living in Louisville now at the Galt house; they left home last Spring. So you see we are a scattered family. Sister and George are still down the river, where I expect they will remain until the Fall.

Sister feels very hurt at not hearing from you. She says she has written repeatedly to you, and never had a reply; and she says she is sure you received the letters, I

wrote to her I did not believe you
had, or either you had answered
hers. If you have not written
her, do write, for she believes
you think hard of her, and I am
sure you do not

Florence is with Aunt Clara
in Canada, they left Paducah a
few days before we did.

But I will close now for Brother to add
a short post script. Good by my dear
dear Brother, Your loving sister Carrie

My darling son   I was so glad to
hear by Mr Ralhe, that one month
ago you were safe and well, and
thankful we have an opportunity
of writing. Carrie has told you the
news. I expect we will remain in
Canada the remainder of the sum
mer and fall. After that time
Mrs Watts can tell where we are
You know what you told me last win
ter that it would be easier to see
us there than where we were. And I
do so long to see you again without
constraint or fear to hold your precious
hands in mine and tell my noble
boy how inexpressibly dear he is to us to
us all. All are praying for you and Omnipoten

Augusta, Georgia Aug. 9th, 1864

My Dearest Bettie,

I commence now to write and I intend to write you a long letter which I have every reason to believe will go thro' safely, as the young lady who is so kind as to carry it says she will be sure to take it to you. I suppose you will be surprised to see that I am at Augusta. Well the way I happened to be here was thus, our brigade has been in very hard service for a week or ten days, after a large body of raiders under Genl. Stoneman & others. About a week ago we overhauled Genl. Stoneman & his command, whipped them severely and forced Stoneman & about half of his command to surrender. The other half made their escape from us then but the next morning we were hot on their track and after riding after them three days & nights we overtook them, and about one hundred men constituting the advance of our brigade charged them in camp about daylight completely routing them & capturing about three hundred men & six hundred horses & equipment, killing about forty with very small loss to ourselves. After this our brigade moved to Athens Geo. to rest & shoe the horses, where I asked for eight days leave & came to Augusta, where I found a great many friends & acquaintances, and among the others Miss Cornelia Polk, who has very kindly offered to carry a letter thro' to you. My health is excellent though I am thinner than usual, but one cannot wonder at this seeing that the weather is so hot & the exercise extreme. I have had a photograph struck off which will give you a pretty good idea of what I look like when off of duty. I was slightly wounded a fortnight since by a shell, but my usual good fortune attended me & I suffer very little serious inconvenience from it. I am delighted with this part of Georgia, and am very glad that I came down here, for I had no idea of what nice people there were here. I am satisfied now that the Southern women of themselves are worthy of all the sacrifices which have been made. They are kind humans, hospitable & handsome too. As I told Miss Polk, I have never seen any Southern that can compare to the beautiful flower of the West. Bettie you do not know nor would you believe if I told you how entirely true to you I am. I go thro' all sorts of assemblages & have had some compliments made to me but I speak only the truth when I say that I never think of any of them. Miss Polk told me that she began to be afraid for me once when you had a wounded sick soldier at your house by the name of Southall from Nashville, but I know you too well to believe you care for any one by that name. When our brigade reached Athens with our prisoners the Ladies Aid Society felt very grateful to us for their safety & made us a very handsome bouquet, a dinner sufficient to feed the whole brigade. A presentation speech was made on behalf of the ladies to the brigade & I was selected to return the thanks of the brigade to the ladies, i.e. to make the reception speech & you would have been a little jealous to have seen me a few minutes after, the centre of a circle of the handsomest girls in the city who presented me with flowers &c. & requested me to drink a health in their wines, all of which I got through little to my satisfaction. I was repeatedly asked if I was married & of course told them I was not & this you know being leap year I expected a proposition but much to my sad disappointment none came.

Our prospects look brighter to me now than for a long time past & the campaign around Richmond seems to be a grand failure at least it is so regarded by us. The enemy may take Mobile but let it go we can do without it. But I do not believe that they will take Atlanta, for Hood is bold, audacious, prompt & steady & has inspred some of the same indomitable spirit into even the very cowards of the land. We needed a young man here at this time one whose age did not make him too cautious.

George Allen is here & is doing a fine business. He is I am afraid a cripple for life, but a finer fellow never lived. Mrs. Welch is still at LaGrange, and I am very sorry that I cannot tell you something of your Uncle Sam & Aunt Lizzie. I have not heard a word from them.

I have been enjoying myself a good deal for the last two weeks though the service has been very hard. We have lived on the fat of the land & this is as great a land for vegetables as it used to be for cotton and melons of all kinds are very abundant & ripe peaches & apples & grapes make up the Bill of Fare which nature presents to the wearied soldier for his refreshment. The crops in this country are spendid. We have never had a more farmable season, unless the mere weight of numbers can crush our armies. The North cannot succeed in subduing the South, for it is amusingly ridiculous to hear them talk of starving us out.

I am sorry to hear that persecution & tyranny have become the order of the day in Mo & Ky. I see that the Lincolnites have discovered a "treason nest" in Mo. of a Northwestern Confederacy & in Ky. the authorities are doing a great deal of mischief to innocent & inoffensive citizens. While I think of it, let me tell you if you want to write to me by Flag of Truce to endorse your letter to me to Florence & she will mail it from P. for I have been informed that they tamper with them in the office at St. Louis. I have written to you by Flag of Truce repeatedly & have never heard whether any of my letters came to your hand. It is dinner time here & I will close, though finish after dinner.

After Dinner

If you had have seen the talk of the Southern States Hotel today you would have smiled at the gaunt caricature of famine conjured up by the Yankee press. I am very much afraid the war will last four years longer and the election of Mr. Lincoln will alone determine the question. If he is elected he will of course carry out his plans through his term & that plan is ruin or subjection of the South. If he is defeated then we may looked for the white winged dove of peace some time in the spring or summer of 65. If Lincoln is elected I must make some arrangements & then I must see you as soon as I can & we ought to get married, don't you think so too? If I could have seen you when I tried so hard, I intended to try & persuade you to consummate our engagement at an early day. I do hope you will come out with Miss Susie. I want to see you oh so much more than I can tell. If you were to die (to prove false would be impossible) I would have no aim in life and I do not know what would become of me. I believe God would snatch you from me as an idol is taken away but that you are destined to be the lamp to my feet & the light to lead me to Him. Every letter I get from you makes me so much better & indeed I tell the truth when I say that your counsels & advice have more weight with me than all of the rest of man or womankind. I have written a long, dull letter because I had nothing but myself to write of & that is a dull subject. Write to me my precious one & come out if you can.

Yours affectionately forever,
GC

An original envelope used by Sue Bettie to write to Given. Note the extremely small size to accompany the traditional manner of folding the letter in six or more parts.

Bordintown, New Jersey Aug. 12th/64

I received your letter of June 21st a few days ago, & hasten to write you, as I now have your address which has been the only reason I have not written before—in fact I did send you a letter some time in April & knowing no other way directed it to a place in Georgia from which your last had been dated which I suppose was why you never received it. I have been a great invalid, spent the whole winter almost on the sofa & finally in the spring was too ill to be even there & had to submit to the horror of being in bed for nearly seven weeks about the first of June. However I rallied suffi- ciently to obey the Dr.'s orders, & came North where I have been ever since & I am happy to say am very much improved. I had a delightful trip on, stopping at Niagara, West Point &c, & then paid a very pleasant visit to a friend here, of four weeks at the end of which we all went together to the sea shore from which enchanting spot I only returned yesterday. We had a most charming party of friends there. There were fif- teen girls from Baltimore with a sufficient number of married ladies to matronize the party. I can not tell you how I enjoyed the sea. We did nothing but enjoy ourselves yachting, driving, rolling ten pins, bathing &c. The bathing was splendid. We went twice a day. The war has made gentlemen very scarce here, & we had about ten ladies to a gentleman which made the bathing a little dangerous, as ladies had to go in alone. I was very fortunate in having a devoted cavalier, who bathed me always delightfully. He was an expert swimmer & we went far out beyond the other bathers. Instead of stay- ing at the hotel after tea in the glaring gas light we generally made up a party for the beach of some five or six pleasant people. You can not imagine how delicious it was to sit there by moonlight listening to the ever varied music of the waves breaking on the shore at our feet. Of course my bathing friend was always of the party, & while he sat pouring soft nonsense into my ears I was thinking of you so far away. He was a student from Princeton, N.J. & very handsome & agreeable. I have not been so well since we left, & my aunt wants me to return again for a week or two before I go home but I am quite anxious to get back as Sue, Grand Pa & Grand Ma are there. I had a letter from Ida H. today. She said that she had lately seen one of your friends. I think I will probably return to St. Louis in a week, but I can not tell exactly. If it is possible to get a pass Sue & I will go South the last of October. I do not think Father will be willing for me to stay longer than I am, & O! how I hope in that time to see you. We must not be so near together without meeting, must we? I try to imagine how you have changed in these three years, & now we are entering on the fourth. I can not say what I want to writing in this way but I live on the hope of seeing & telling it to you before long. Why don't you send me your photograph. I hear constantly from pri- soners especially Hugh K. Good Bye. Write as soon as you receive this. Yours lovingly

Sue B. Woods

Glencoe Sep. 20th, 1864

I received your letter by Miss C.P. last week & the one of Sep. 6th by flag of truce last night. I suppose you had not received mine written Aug. 12th. I can not understand why you do not get my letters when I receive yours so regularly. However I will make one more attempt. I can not send them to Florence as you suggest as I do not know where she is. I reached home just a week ago today after an absence of three months. I am entirely well & had the most charming time. I spent a month at the seashore, & the rest of the time between New York & New Jersey. Mr. H. was mistaken about seeing me the middle of July as I left home the first of June. I was so glad to see Sue once more. She has told me a great deal about you, which of course was very interesting. Were you not broken hearted when Miss White was married. Sue & I will leave Nashville for Tuscaloosa about the middle or last of October. I believe the trip usually requires about a month but it depends entirely on circumstances. We will go by Florence & hope to be in Tuscaloosa by the last of November if not sooner. I hope Father will consent to my going but he has not done so yet. Your photograph I think is excellent. You have not changed at all judging from that. Good Bye

> Yours with love
> S.B. Woods

Sue sends her love. She is entertaining Mr. Clarkson in the hall. He is still devoted & she is inexorable—Write me again soon.

> Yours
> Bettie

LaGrange, Geo. Oct. 7th, 1864

My Dearest Bettie,

I wrote to you yesterday by flag of truce acknowledging your letter written at Bordenton, N.J. and of date of Aug. 12th. I need not tell you how joyfully it was welcomed—for I had no letter from you since July last, and my sister F. told me in a letter of the date of July that she had heard no news from you for a great while. I had very gloomy misapprehensions for your health, but thank God you write cheerfully once more & assure me that you are nearly restored. The long period of rest which I have had has done much for my general health, before I was wounded at a place called Sunshine Church. I was very sallow and very thin and I tell you that the rocky soil of Georgia was most unpleasant to my bones at night, but I had a very pleasant place to recruit in, and good diet and fine water with pleasant associations have reinvigorated me so that I am capable of enduring the hardships of another winter & spring. I have been having a nice time and several young ladies have been making inquiries as to who I am & what his lineage &c. but you must not be jealous for I have not even felt the slightest sensation, of interest even, for any of them, and to show the singular perversity of the sex I believe that is the reason any of them felt any interest in me. I am now reporting to Genl. Johnson who is commanding the residue of the cavalry of the Army of Tenn. which did not go off with Wheeler. My brigade is in the side of the enemy & I am cut off from it at present—I arrived at this place under orders to attend to some business today & have just returned from a visit to Mrs. Welsh who you remember was exiled from St. Louis & who is kind enough to lead this letter thro' for me. She gives me a very gloomy account of the affairs at St. Louis, and to my horror tells me that there are two large prisons in St. Louis filled with the sweet ladies in the state. She gives a peculiarly favorable character to James E. Yeatman and her description of his many kindnesses to the poor confed's make me love him. But seriously he must be the meanest man north of the "lower regions." She was very entertaining, knew all about all of my acquaintances, and is decidedly the best posted of any one I have seen. She appears to be an admirable character indeed. I know very little of any of your acquaintances except Johnny Kay is well & adjt. of the 42nd Tenn. He makes a fine soldier. Is very popular—George Allen who married Miss Greenfield is at Augusta on business and doing very well, though he has yet to use his crutch & stick & his left hand to be very bothersome when he uses it any more than the most absolute necessity compels.

Eddie Bredell & Thomas Courtenay are in the "secret service" of the C.S. What that means I do not know for from all I can learn Bredell does nothing else but loaf around Richmond, and I have heard imputations of a pack of men urged against him, and I believe that he has renewed his affair with Miss Lizzie G. I don't now remember of any others whom it would be interesting to write to you about. I suppose you know that my Father's family have left the N.S. and my Uncle. I have not heard that they were banished, but shrewdly suspect as much. I am glad they have gone away & got out of this trouble. I am so glad to see that you & Miss Susie intend payg. your Aunt Lizzie a visit & bye the bye I heard from Sam K. a few days ago. He was very well. You know that if you come no earthly person can keep me from seeing you— and when you were at N. if I could have communicated with you I should have seen you in spite of the fates I think of you oh so often and as you say try to imagine how time has changed you. Oh my own darling you must not be sick any more, you must get well, keep up a brave proud heart, and be cheerful under these seminary adversities for our happiness. I know its decreed & the Gods will not give us grudgingly. I am writing this in a store and they are waiting to close it for dinner & I think I had better slip away now for I did not sleep a wink on the horse & my letter must be very stupid indeed. Good bye my darling. My love to all the family &c.

Yours as ever,
Given

Augusta, Ga. Jan'y 4th 65

My Dear Bettie,

I leave Augusta day after tomorrow for Tuscaloosa, and will be there in six or eight days—Mr. Kirkman's letter of Dec. 13th was received on the first of Jan'y & I immediately got leave to see you—I have no time to write now but hope my darling to see you in a few days & tell you all I feel & know.

Yours affectionately
Given

I would have sent a whole sheet but George Allen is so stingy he made me tear half off.

G.C.

Greensborough. Feb'y 9th, 1865

My Darling Betties,

After a slow, but safe & not very disagreeable stage of 25 miles we arrived at Havanna where we were to meet the stage up from Greensboro, but it failed to come and we remained at Mr. Sheldon's the Post master. I introduced my Aunt Miss Woods & they treated us very well & made us very comfortable. So after a pleasant nights rest we started this morning after breakfast to this place where we arrived about dinner time.

Susie is fortifying for the nights ride (for we ride from here tonight to Marion) by taking a nap while I write to you. We have had quite an agreeable journey thus far taking all things into consideration. I thought of you oh so many times and dreamed of you last night. I do not know how I can endure to be separated from you. The dispatch from Richmond relative to the Peace Commission puts an end to all speculations concerning peace, by reconstruction, and peace by any other means is in the remote future. I have been thinking of all things that have happened and the more I think of our affairs, i.e. our marriage &c. the more reason I have to rejoice that we are married now. Bettie you must write to me very often, and tell me your whole thoughts & feelings. If I could see you now—this afternoon I would answer any questions you might ask of me for my love could not refuse you anything.

I told Susie about your trip out on the porch in your bare feet to listen to the serenades and she was completely horrified. She said that she saw you go out & asked you if you were warmly wrapped up & you did not reply.

But you must be very particular about your health and remember always that you do not belong solely to your self but that you have a partner who will be always a deeply interested party in whatever pertains to your health and happiness. But I must not go on to lecture on your health any more for fear you will mentally say— "Do hush old crabtree." It promises to be right cool tonight, and it is eighteen miles of the very worst part of the road so you must not be surprised to hear that we fail to reach Marion in time to make the connection, and then we enjoy the sumptuous luxuries of one of the most elegant hotels in Dixie.

It is getting so dark I can scarce see how to write so I will have to stop and say give my love to all & keep it always in your own memory that I love you best of all on this earth.

Good Bye. Take care of yourself & pray for me

Your devoted Husband
Given

Mrs. Given Campbell
Tuscaloosa, Ala.

On board Str. King 20 miles
below Montgomery, Feb. 11, 65

My Dear Bettie,

I didn't promise to write to you *in transitu,* but at every stopping place, but I wish to see you so much that I will see if it will not be a relief to write to you. We had a very pleasant trip from Greensboro to Selma and remained there four or five hours, during which time I went with Sue to see Mr. Cross, who was very polite & showed us thro' the arsenal and I was very much pleased to see that everyday the CS are progressing in manufactures & improving on all its past exploits. You would be surprised to see how much & how well we do in Dixie in our machine shops—but still it is mortifying to see that nearly all of the most skillful mechanics are Yankees. I hope to live to see the day when we will be independent of Yankee skill & industry as well as Yankee rule. We had quite a race to the boat which started sooner from the wharf than I expected, but you know your Aunt Sue is right quick & we made the connection. While on the boat I met one of our old Captains of 2nd Ky. & he came up & sd. you have "gone and done it" & congratulated me. I asked him how he had heard it & he said he heard it at Mobile, and was very much surprised to hear I was going back to my command so soon, for sd. he, if I were you I should have gone into winter quarters. I have learned from a soldier of the Army of Va. that in the new consolidation act of the army, officers who are supernumerary have 60 days to select a command to join. I would be willing to be consolidated out of my command for I know I can always get a position when I desire one & can't get a leave for 60 days when I want it.

I am very anxious to return & will make every effort to do so though the Yankees getting possession of the R. Road between Augusta & Branchville will make it difficult to get to Richmond, but if that is all that is in the way, I will not be deterred for love laughs at all such feeble barriers. I am not at all surprised at the result of the Peace Mission and from what I can see & hear I believe that it has been the means of strengthening the spirits & fixing the purposes of all classes. The soldiers are all determined to die before they will disgracefully submit, and so are the people, tho' I overheard a conversation yesterday between two old men in which one of them said that there was a grave question in his mind & that was whether this thing called "priceless liberty" might not be too dearly bought. I looked at him & if a look could have transfixed him he would have been a dead man, & he was too old to insult by word but it made me very indignant to hear such sad sentiments. I am whistling now to keep my courage up so you must excuse me—Good Bye my dear darling wife.

Love to all
Yours, Given

Macon, Ga. Feb. 13th, 1865

My Dear Bettie,

You will no doubt think that I am faithful to my promise to write at every stopping place for this is the third letter since I left Tuscaloosa. I arrived here this afternoon on a special train with Genl. Lorings staff & leave him in the morning at 8 for Milledgville. Thus far the trip has been quite agreeable but I have wished to see you a thousand times & never before knew what a deep place you have in my heart. I think of you every hour in the day & do not believe that I will be much account as a soldier until I see you again. I saw Miss Susie safely housed at Dr. Wilsons in Montgomery and called to see her when I met her, Mrs. Wilson, & Miss Charlotte Irwin who does not look like the same person I met in St. Louis. She looks much older & rather a hard expression lurks around the corners of her mouth & eyes. I made a conquest on the train coming down of a very handsome young lady from South western Ga. and she asked me when I became acquainted with her if that photograph the one I had been looking at was my sweetheart, I said that it was not but was one of my wife. Now don't you think that was good in me. Just to think a very handsome young lady requests an introduction to her & is very gracious and offers a splendid opening for fun & I decline having too much love for my wife & respect for myself. I saw Ony Barrett and told him a great deal of news from St. Louis. He is very well & was not on the campaign with Genl. Hood but was left with the reserve artillery at Macon. I will go to the theatre to night. Just behove it to say that I have been at a theatre in Dixie. I don't believe that I will have an opportunity of writing as often here after as I do now, for in moving around in the field in active service it will not be possible but I will always try to write at least once a week & you must do so also for you do not know how much I wish to hear from my darling wife. The weather is charming and I only regret that I am not with you to enjoy it.

It is very nearly dark now and I must close this hurried note. Give my love to Mrs. K & Sam & Miss Mary & all the others. Good Bye my darling,

Your affectionate husband
Given Campbell

I enclose three letters. Please send them thro' if you can.
GC

Augusta, Feb'y 17, 1865

Mrs. Given Campbell

My Darling Bettie,

I write from Macon and had no opportunity of writing till now. I had a terrible trip from Milledgville to Aparta in an open wagon & the weather wretchedly cold & rainy on the greater part of the trip in the night. I can not say that I didn't experience any inconvenience from this exposure for I had neuralgia horribly and on the next day started on my horse from Sparta to Augusta. I took some morphine & quinine and it made me sick at the stomach and gave me an awful headache. I couldn't eat any supper and was quite sick this morning but thank God and a good constitution I am now well—I forgot to tell you that I found my horse all right, but my halter and blankets were stolen by some public spirited soldiers. I had hardly got in town before I met an officer of our brigade. He came up and shook hands & said allow me to congratulate you. I accepted his congratulations very gracefully and he then told me that he had heard it from Miss Carrie Campbell. I came on and when I got to the hotel every Negro in the place came grinning up and offering me their humble congratulations, and every man I saw on the street of my acquaintance seemed to have been just made acquainted with the facts. I hadn't been here but a few minutes when I was invited to a "winding party." I had an explanation of the meaning of the word "winding" but have forgotten it. I declined to go for I much preferred writing to my darling wife to any such gayety. I paid a short visit to my old friend who wrote me the letter I showed to you in which she said she was on a "rampage." She was delighted to see me and asked me a great many questions about you. I find a great many of my old acquaintances have and they are as a general thing having a very gay time. I had no idea I was so widely known or that my character was so much observed. I must be on my "p's & q's" and be very particular not to transgress in any way, shape or form for if I do you will be certain to know of it, but you need not to be at all afraid of me my darling for I am more & more in love with you every day. George Allen is here. He is not very well tonight. I do not know if he is really in love with Miss D'Autignoc or not but he pays her very assiduous court and that you know is a sign now adays. I haven't been able to hear from Mr. Reeves at all. I would like to see him just to get that last letter you wrote to me. I see that Miss Jenny Bell has gone to see her father at Flatshoals on Flint River not far from Newman, Ga. Our brigade has had several fights lately and Wheeler's cavalry has covered itself with glory. I leave here in the morning for Columbia, South Carolina where the brigade is said to be and as soon as I can I will go to Richmond to fix up my papers for the Regt. and if I am successful you will see me in about one month. Oh I long to see you so much. You are much nearer & dearer than ever before—I am so glad that I obeyed your instructions & followed your wishes when I was with you. You know my heart better than I do myself. I should be watched if I knew you had to suffer on my acct. and I far away from you. You must take the greatest care of yourself and take your walks regularly & recollect that I shall be very much disappointed if you do not weigh 130 when I get back to you—With the warmest love to Mrs. & Mr. K. & Miss Mary and the children. I remain yours most affectionately,

Given

I read my testament & have
read a good deal in J.W. Brookes "How
to be Saved."

GC

Danville, Va.
March 25th, 1865

Mrs. Given Campbell
Care Saml. Kirkman

My Darling Bettie,

I have written to you repeatedly lately, and by pretty good hands but I think this letter will beat either of them for I got Mr. Matthew Sonlard from Miss. to mail it at Motgomery. Richmond is the most wretched place to have to remain unless you are always busy, the cutting of the canal by the raiders under Sheridan cut off a great part of the family supplies from the city & the necessaries of life are very high. I shuttled thro' the markets & priced different articles. Sweet potatoes $100 per bushel, eggs $25 per doz. and flour $1200 & 1000 per barrel &c. The people are all confident, but their confidence is based upon McCawber's proposition, "waiting for something to turn up" from Johnston, from whose condemnable means, most incurable, are constantly flowing, but our officers from what ?I can learn are in a more healthy situation than they were a short time ago. Genl. Johnston has ingrained confidence in the troops & has increased the morale in the army & among the people also. Genl. Hood has made a most unfortunate blunder in incorporating into his regiment a secure & stringent criticism on Johnston's campaign & won for himself many active enemies who sympathized with him before. I have not yet succeeded in accomplishing my purpose to go to Ky. & call by & see you. The Sec. of War was opposed to the policy motive & would have positively refused but I had an interview with him and he then ordered me to report to Johnston authorizing him if he will prefer to grant the commission &c. I have letters to Johnston from his staunchest friends in the Senate— Whigfall of Texas & Burnett of Ky. in which they give me the highest recommendations, but my darling I am by no means certain of success but failure will not by my fault. I will reach headqts. tomorrow & as soon as I hear definitely I will write to you & let you know the result. I saw Miss Lou Randolph a cousin of Ann Patterson and she was perfectly surprised to hear I was married, every one I saw was in fact. You remember old Mrs. Giles the mother of the beautiful Miss Lizzie. She was very much surprised when she heard it, for said she, "I didn't believe that she would have had him. He was so stuck up." Poor old lady how egregiously mistaken she was in her estimate of your humble servant.

I saw McCune & so did Kennett & McCrea & Bernard Pratte & wife & several others, but have no particular news of any. I wrote a letter to your mother while in

Richmond. Active operations are taking place among the Yankees and you may expect a fight at almost any moment.

I have not heard one word from you since I left and am so anxious to have a letter from my wife. I suppose when I reach head quarters that I shall find letters waiting there. Oh Bettie you can't imagine how irksome it is for me to stay away from you & how I long to see you. I thought I loved ma fiance' but I didn't know what the word meant for I love my wife a million times more than even I dreamed I could. I haven't flirted or had any inclination that way at all—I must close my letter now for my time is out—Remember me kindly to all friends & give my love to your Aunts Lizzie & Tessie & Mother. Good Bye my dear dear wife

Yours Given

The following poem was written by Sue Bettie Woods for her husband Given shortly after their marriage. It graphically portrays the horrors of the Civil War and its impact on those who fought it.

The Guerrilla

1

Awake! and to horse my Brother
For the dawn is glimmering grey
And hark! in the crackling brushwood
There are feet that tread this way.

2

Who cometh? A friend—what tidings?
O God! I sicken to tell
Earth seems earth no longer
And its sights are the sights of Hell.

3

There's rapine and fire and slaughter
From mountain down to the shore
There's blood on trampled harvest
And blood on the homestead floor.

4

From far off conquered cities
Comes the voice of a stifled wail
And the shrieks & moans of the houseless
Ring out like a dirge on the gale.

5

I've seen from the smoking village
Our mothers and daughters fly
I've seen where the little children
Sank down in the furrows to die.

6

On the bank of a battle-strained river
I stood as the moonlight shone
And it fell on the face of my Brother
As the dark waves swept him on.

7

Where my home was glad, are ashes
And horror and shame have been there
For I found on the fallen lintel
A tress of my wife's torn hair.

8

They are turning the sword upon us
And with more than friends worst art
Have uncovered the fires of the savage
That slept in his untaught heart.

9

The ties to our hearts that bound him
They have rent with curses away.
And madened us with their madness
To be almost as brutal as they.

10

With halter and torch and Bible
And hymns to the sound of the drum
They preach the gosepel of murders
And pray for lust's Kingdom to come.

11

To saddle! To saddle! My Brother
Look up to the rising sun
And ask the God that shines there
Whether deeds like these shall be done.

12

Whenever the vandal cometh
Press home to his heart with your steel
And when at his bosom ye can not
Like the serpent go strike at his heel.

13

Through thicket and wood go hunt him
Creep up to his camp-fire side
And let ten of his corpses blacken
Where one of our boys have died.

14

In his fainting foot-sore marches
In his flight from the stricken fray
In the depth of the lonely ambush
The debts that we owe we'll pay

15

In God's hand alone is vengeance
But he strikes with the hands of men
And his blight would wither our manhood
If we smite not the smiter again.

16

By the graves where our Fathers slumber
By the shrines where our Mothers prayed
By our homes & hopes of freedom
Let every man swear on his blade

17

That he will not sheath nor stay it
Till from point to hilt it glow
With the flush of tardy justice
In the blood of the felon foe

18

They swore and the answering sunlight
Leaped red from their lifted swords
And the wrath in their hearts made echo
To the wrath in their angry words.

1 9

There's weeping in all New England
Any by Schuykill's banks a knell
The widows there & the orphans
How that oath was kept can tell.

Author's Note: The following poem was written by Given Campbell to his wife Sue Bettie shortly after their marriage. It celebrates her influence on him and is a tribute to their love.

To My Wife

Who first stirred the blood in the heart of my youth
In my path strewed the roses of beauty and truth
Who caused the first grief that harrowed my soul
Then checked with a smile its dark dangerous roll

Mid the dangers of strife her image was there
Forever to cheer and rebuke black despair
Till at last cross the borders of wars dark dominions
She folded in peace on my breast her sweet pinions

And twice in his flight more mercy has shown
More oft in his custom for lovely has grown
Me fair plighted bride into mother's serene
Reserving her charms and her beauty so coy

To lavish them all on her bright handsome boy.

Tuscaloosa, May 21st, 1865

I have at last concluded after weighing the matter for several days that it is best for me to go home, & my constantly increasing longing to be there renders a longer delay here, painful & almost impossible—So soon as we heard Gen. Lee's surrender we knew that Gen. Johnson would be obliged to do the same. I knew that your brigade was on this side of the army & supposed that you would start immediately for Tuscaloosa. Two weeks ago the soldiers of Johnson's army commenced to arrive here & then I began looking hourly for you but as day after day passed & still you did not come, hope which at first was so high gradually diminished until at last it sank altogether leaving me in the most painful doubt & uncertainty with regard to you, which feelings were greatly increased by a visit from a Lt. Bradford who told me that he had left you in Georgia & that you intended sending Mr. Davis to where-ever his destination might be. I can not believe that you would go to the trans-Mississippi without sending me some definite word of it when you must have passed with in a few miles of here to reach the river, & yet I can in no other way account for your strange absence—perplexing doubts, hopes & fears wigh upon my mind with such intensity that at times it amounts almost to agony to think at all—& I try to shut out the subject entirely from my thoughts, but of course that is a vain attempt, for I can not sleep at night, nor have a moments peace in the day for thinking & wondering where can he be. O! my dear husband may you never experience the painful & wretched anxiety that I have suffered during the last week. What a long week it has been the longest & sad of my life—I think.

Everything concerning you now is a mystery to me. I know not where you are nor how you are, & the more I think of it the more perplexed & anxious I become but thank God it is all in His merciful hand, & I trust & believe that you are safe under the shadow of His wing—my only consolation now is in prayer & my bible.

Susie wants me to scold you for not coming directly to Tuscaloosa but I can not blame you until I hear your reasons—We leave on Tuesday or Wednesday & I write this note to leave with Lizzie in case you should possibly arrive after we leave—if such should be the case come on as quickly as you can, & if you can not come to Kentucky or Missouri, I will meet you in Tennessee or any place you choose— I sincerely hope you will be paroled. Sue leaves much love for you. And now dearest I have opened my heart to you; perhaps too freely—I may have exaggerated my troubles, but if so you must excuse it, for it is all through the fondness of your loving—Bettie

Sunday afternoon—Hope is not quite gone yet as my foolish fast beating heart testifies because some one happened to knock at the front door but it is only a stupid Col! another hope disappointed.

Glencoe
June 25th, 1865

My Darling Husband—

I suppose by this morning you are safely over your journey, & once more at home—I can imagine you about this time at church with your Mother & sisters. I wish I was sitting there by your side, to cast a reproving glance, when you look at your watch, which I know you will do at intervals of five minutes, if the sermon is any thing at all on the Dr. White order—I can not pretend to tell you how much I have missed you—you know we been so much together for the last four weeks, scarcely being separated for an hour, that it makes me feel your absence now the more keenly—it really seems more like two weeks than two days since I have seen you. This is my first Sunday at home & we highly prize Sunday because Father can be at home with us—he has just gotten his morning paper from the train & is reading it in the parlor—the children have all gone to walk, & Mother is playing on the melodeon, & so I slipped off to devote an hour to you dearest, for my thoughts are with you all the time.

This morning it was uncomfortably cool. We were all wrapped up in shawls & for a while thought we would be obliged to have fires—but it is warmer now & though there is a pretty stiff wind blowing it is very pleasant. I only hope it will remain this cool all the Summer though I suppose that is rather more than could be expected.

Mother is beginning to yield some what to the plan of going away this Summer, tho. not quite given up yet, but I think I can persuade her to go in about two weeks. Her cough is not so well in the last two days-& she has no appetite. I am better than I was when you left. The Dr. was here yesterday, & I have been taking the medicine he ordered all day yesterday & to day just as regularly as if you were here to threaten me with all sorts of things if I didn't take it. I take it because I am so anxious to be well when you get back. I already feel the benefit of it I think—O! I long so much to see you & hear you say *"it is, in the cool"*— I hope this will be the last separation we will have to bear—*please* do not stay long—I will look for you the last of the this week. & in future you must always take me with you. I see by the paper that your boat passed Cairo at 11, o'clock Saturday so I presume you reached home about dark. I will enclose a little note to your Mother if I can get up the courage to write it. But if it is not here you may know that I tried & failed—but I want to do it, because you asked me to & I intend to strive to do always what will please you. Mr. Clarkson has called & I will have to see him so I must close. I was so much obliged for the chocolate—Give my love to Florence & tell her I hope she will return with you & pay me a visit. Good Bye my own darling,

> Always your loving
> Bess

I look for a letter from you day after tomorrow. O! *please* dont stay long. I cant bear to think of not seeing you for a week & any longer than that is out of the question. I am never going to let you go off & leave me again. I have made up my mind. I hope Dr. White would not think me a "love sick young matron," but I can not be happy away from you—

After tea. Jellie, Mr. C., Mr. Tennent, Jim Teadman, the Misses Sonlards have just left & I opened my letter to add just a line to say Good Bye—

Paducah, Ky. June 26th, 1865

My Darling Wife,

I arrived here safe and well about twenty-four hours after I left St. Louis and found all well, but not looking for me on that day. You have no idea how rejoiced they were to see me "& looking so well." Many & affectionate were the inquiries made for you and all were disappointed that you were not with me, but I readily explained why you did not come, for you were just off a hard trip and not rested sufficiently for another—and besides you had not seen your mother for a long time &c. Mother & Father are very anxious to see you—and Florence particularly was very much disappointed. Carrie is engrossed with her bridegroom & they seem very happy together.

I find the place a good deal changed especially in population, but the home of my father is not so much changed as I feared, the garden & flowers were tramped & expired but the spring weather has made it look swell again & the trees are all here. When Payne took possession of the house he demanded that it should be left completely furnished & his demands at that time were despised only at the risk of your life, so that he destroyed nearly all the furniture and committed heavy acts of vandalism but the house is furnished again & all is shipshape again. I attend the Presbyterian church last night & heard an excellent sermon from Dr. Henricks who is still the Preacher here. He preached on one of the Psalms and in it he explained the meaning of "Selah" which he said was a musical note which meant (repeat this) used to give emphases to certain verses or clauses. I came here feeling very much edified & informed and sat down and read a chapter in the test. you gave me and then said my prayers. Within this are improvement for me. One of my old sweethearts here says she does not wish ever to see you because you are my wife. What do you think of that. I find the people here all very kind to the returned rebels and in fact I feel like I am in a truer Southern town here now than when I was in Tuscaloosa. The streets are full of returned rebels who are high spirited & not at all subdued in appearance. It is the first place I have been where I have breathed free since I left Columbus. The weather here is very cool & pleasant. We had a hard rain on yesterday which did the growing crops in the country great good.

Business is increasing very fast & since the military rule has been withdrawn everything seems to thrive more than before. I am so very anxious to see you that I cannot stay here as long as I originally believed, and I think I will compromise the visit by getting father & mother to come over with me to St. Louis. They have not yet determined to go but I shall try & persuade them. Oh darling I pray for you at night

& long to see you & hear your sweet voice. Give my love to your father & mother & Aunt Lou Maggie & Robert & reserve a thousand more for yourself.

> Good Bye—
> Darling—
> Yours affectionately
> GC

UNITED STATES OF AMERICA.

I *Given Campbell* of the

County of *McCracken* State of *Kentucky* do

solemnly swear that I will support, protect, and defend the Constitution and Government of the United States against all enemies, whether domestic or foreign; that I will bear true faith, allegiance, and loyalty to the same, any ordinance, resolution, or laws of any State, Convention, or Legislature, to the contrary notwithstanding; and further, that I will faithfully perform all the duties which may be required of me by the laws of the United States; and I take this oath freely and voluntarily, without any mental reservation or evasion whatever.

Subscribed and Sworn to before me at *Nashville Tenn*

this *19* day of *June* 1865. *Given Campbell*

Capt ..... *Provost Marshal General, Dept. Cumberland.*

The above-named has *fair* complexion, *Brown* hair, and *Hazel* eyes; and is *5*

feet *10* inches high. Was formerly a *Capt* in Co .. .. 20 *Kentucky*

Regiment *Cavalry* in Rebel army.

The original Oath of Allegiance signed by Given Campbell on June 19th, 1865 in which he swears allegiance to the United States. It lists his Confederate service as a Captain in the 20th Kentucky Regiment of Cavalry in the Rebel Army.

Paducah, Ky. July 4, 65

My Darling Bettie,

This is the "glorious Fourth day of July" and the streets are thronged with troops with drum & fifes and the flag of our country waving over them. And all the Sunday school children are having a picnic, and to make the day more interesting, the thermometer is °95 in the shade—I am rejoiced to hear by yr. note of 28th that your health is so much better, and am really very uneasy to hear that your weather is warm, but I knew that if she get much warmer you would have telegraphed me. All out here are so well except myself, and I look so much thinner than I did when I left that you will think that I had better not come over again as it does not agree with me. I have eaten too much fruit lately. It is so abundant. We have the greatest quantity of sugar pears. I wish you were here to enjoy them. I am sorry to disappoint your expectations, but I found it impossible to get away from here before the fifth or sixth of the month. I have to have my teeth fixed tomorrow morning & if I can get a boat will leave the afternoon for St. Louis. I am so anxious to see you—I dreamed of you twice last night and they were pleasant dreams too. I have just finished reading or rather rereading Warren's great novel of 10,000 a year—but I don't intend to read any such novels when I can get anything else, for I will have to study very hard if I go to New Orleans to get up the Civil Law & Code of Louisiana. I am very sorry to see that count fests up a majority for the new Constitution—

My father rather favors the idea of my going to N.O. But he says he is pleased with any place that pleases me—I suppose you will see me almost as soon as you do this letter. I can not endure to be away from you any longer & no one can persuade me to stay away any longer—than Wednesday or Thursday.

Good Bye my darling. God bless you & all the family,

Love to all,
Your faithful & most
Affectionate husband
Given Campbell

Mrs. Given Campbell
St. Louis, Mo.

Paducah July 22/65

My Dear Son,

   Your letter came to hand yesterday. Your horse arrived safe last Sunday. He is very poor in flesh & a good deal chafed by harness, but in good health. I am having him well cared for & in a few weeks will have flesh on his bones. Florence returned yesterday from Dickson Springs, very pleased with her visit. The family are all well. I will write to N. Orleans as requested. The foolish Restriction Laws in the States will no doubt be repealed by legislators the ensuing winter. They were enacted in the midst of war by violent radicals & I think a more conservative policy will be adopted hereafter. I was very much pleased to hear that you found your books etc. all safe. The weather here has been very warm & sultry, with heavy rain storms. Will the constitutionality of the 3d Section of your new Constitution be tested. I have heard some of your lawyers design doing so.

   George & David are doing well in their grocery and George seems very much incouraged and is very attentive and industrious. James has been since you left very studious. He has a very fine mind, and after the cloud that hangs over the study of law with all new beginners passes away, he will comprehend the symmetry of the science. We were gratified to learn that the health of Mrs. Woods was improving, and that you & your wife were well. Your mother myself & the girls will go over about first Oct. when the weather will be pleasant and bring Bettie back with, and you can spend that month on the land in clinch. I have notes there for about $15,000 & will give you all you can collect. I want that business closed up & you & James can after a while sell the land. If you remain in St. Louis or go to N. Orleans, it will be a pleasant & healthy retreat for you & your dear wife in the hot months, and you can then combine health & business and sell out to advantage. Tell Bettie we all want to see her very much. It is not you know curiosity as we know her, but tis love for her as your wife. All send to her & you their best wishes & love.

                              Your affectionate father
                              J. Campbell

Given Campbell
c. St. Louis. Mo.

St. Louis, Nov. 27, 1865

My Dear Daughter,

Among the letters enclosed to Mr. C. with this is one to Mrs. Railey from Mrs. Day, her sister I think. Mrs. Day says that she is thoroughly posted in New Orleans & will be of service to you in obtaining board & in otherwise informing you about the city & its people. I think however you will have friends enough there when you & Given have mixed among the people enough to become known. You must remember that you can contribute to yr. husbands success by making friends for him & yourself. Be cordial, meet people half way, in short recall your mother & do as she does.

We had a glorious day yesterday, Sunday, in the country. The weather continues fine. Your mother is in really fine health & seems now to enjoy life. R.K. fattened very much on his trip East & has grown more in the past two months than for the whole year before. He has a fine puppy given him by Mr. Whittaker which now engrosses his whole attention except his book which shares part of his mind. He came to me a few days since to show how much he had learned & was spelling the names of various things, birds, animals &c. which he pronounces very glibly aided by the picture which was on the right of each word & which I supposed he was doing from a knowledge of the sound of the letters until he came to J.A.Y. which he called Jay-bird. This rather staggered me, but I had to laugh outright when he came to WOLF which he pronounces with little hesitation after glancing at the picture "Fox." He certainly learns very rapidly & promises to become a fine scholar. He is looking handsomer than ever before—fat & with fine color. Maggie is also looking very well & making fine progress with her books. Annie Lou is quite the young lady. Geo. Moore was out yesterday. Your mother & the little ones come in to night & will not go out again until Thursday. They will stay with Mr. Whittaker. We are very well fixed with servants. I expect to go to Chariton in a short time & may be back in time to go with your mother to Nashville. Love to Given.

Affectionately your father,
Robt. K. Woods

Sue Bettie

Paducah Feby. 10/66

My Dear Son,

 Your letter to your mother was received to day, giving an account of the great misfortune to you and dear Betty in the loss of her child. Your Mother when she heard of the recent illness of Betty had apprehensions that the child would be still born, & they have been true. It was a great blessing to Betty that she had her Mother with her at such a time. We are all truly glad that she is so much improved and hope that the dangerous time with her has passed. The submission of Betty to this heavy affliction, and sad disappointment, shows a truly pious heart, and we have all since we know Betty well and opportunity to study her character congratulated ourselves that you had such a sweet of a wife. All her influence my dear son over you will be good, and altho. you have been disappointed in the hope of a little one to bless you both, you have every reason to thank God that your wife survives.

 Your sister Mary is with us, but is expecting George every day and is preparing to leave for the cotton farm. Carries little boy is getting along, about as well as any baby with half dozen nurses. Carrie has regained her health and strength. David leaves in a few days for N. York. Jimmie seems well absorbed in his profession, and has several cases. We have at last got clear of Emily & her husband & children. We had got heartily tired of such a servant & nuisance. She was a rogue and the imbodiment of laziness. Your Mother laments very much the loss of her little grand child. It grieved us all for we wanted to have it with us next summer. You must and your wife write us often. It is a source of great pleasure to the family to receive letters from you & Betty. There is nothing of news to relate. Our town is quiet, & business men seem satisfied. Nothing disturbs, but now & then the Bureau puts on the big law maker & judge and creates confusion. I do think the Bureau is a great nuisance to the White & the Negro, and the contrabands, or freed men would do much better without that with them.

 We all write in love to you and Betty and send to Henry's wife and her Mother our thanks and gratitude for their kind attentions to Betty.

       Your affectionate Father
       J. Campbell

Given Campbell Esq.
Atty. at Law
New Orleans. La.

St. Louis, March 16, 1866

My Dear Daughter,

I have not written to you for a long time as I have considered that my letters to your Mother would serve to let you know what we were doing here. I have felt your past suffering & sickness my dear daughter very keenly, although was spared some uneasiness by getting telegrams advising of your being better before I received the letters speaking of your worst attacks. I do sincerely hope that your trials in this way are now over & that you may soon gain health & strength. I think that as soon as the weather is entirely settled it would be well for you to come up & try Glencoe air for a tonic that will not make your head ache & has no nauseous taste. I am satisfied country air & country food will contribute more to your entire convalescence than anything else. Any time from the middle of April to the 1st of May I think you may feel entirely safe to come up. Given I suppose can leave by the 1st of June. I go about so little—in fact into society none at all—I pick up very little news that would interest you. Anna Ewing & her husband have gone to New York. He on business. When they return from there they will be here but a short time before setting out for Santa Fe. Rachel Miller & her mother returned home on Wednesday last. I chanced to be that afternoon at Anna Mullens to see R.K. & went in to see her. She was as bright & cheerful as usual & gave me a full account of all that she saw of you & your mother. She says that she never saw your mother looking so well, so much color & so much flesh. I was sorry that her account of you & dear Maggie was not so flattering. We must bring you both up to her standard this summer some how. I have no letter from your mother since hers of the 5th & 6th. Last Monday or Tuesday week. Annie Lou had one a day later. We might have duty here now as late as the 11th. I hope I may have a letter to-morrow. Her last letter spoke of you as not being very well, suffering from head ache &c. & I feel anxious to learn how you were some days later. I have had my business arranged to leave here by the 15th, yesterday for New Orleans & on Monday last—four days ago— I telegraphed to Given asking if your mother was still in New Orleans & to let her know that I was coming & desired to know if I should meet her there or at Mr. LaBourgeois. To this I have received no answer. Whether Given has left New Orleans with you for the coast of whether the fault lies with the telegraph office I cant well divine, & until I get letters to throw some light on your movements I am at a loss what to do. I have telegraphed again to day to inquire if Given is in New Orleans but am told I must not expect any answer before to-morrow afternoon as the line just now is not working. I wish very much to make the trip & would greatly prefer to be with your mother when she makes the trip up. I wished to make the trip particularly to see you since you have undergone so much danger &

suffering but do not like to risk meeting your mother on the way without knowing it. If I had been sure of keeping your mother in New Orleans until I could go down there I would have been now two days on my way there. Annie Lou is very well as is also R.K. He seems very bright & happy but frequently wishes to know when his mama will be home. He is now under some excitement by reason of a circus being established in the neighborhood. Since last Saturday until to day, Friday, we have not seen the sun. The weather of course disagreeable in the extreme but not cold until to day. This morning gave promise of clear weather but cold enough to make some ice. But it has again become cloudy & threatening snow. Give much love & kisses to your dear mother & to little Maggie for me. Much love to Given.

> Very affectionately
> Your Father
> Robt. K. Woods

New Orleans, La. May the First, 66

My Darling Bess,

    I wrote to you yesterday or sent a letter to you written on the boat, and told you of my trip & safe arrival.

    To day I will write you a short letter to tell you that I am well, and how much I have missed you. I went home yesterday to dinner and ate dinner and went to Uncle Henry's and talked a while to Mrs. Gregory & Dr. Pierce, but they did not satisfy me and I left there, and went towards home, & met Annie Given & she wanted me to go back with her, but I declined. I went home & saw Miss Sally Fee sitting on our gallery, and it made me feel so home sick to see any one there but you. I went up and talked to Miss Sally of you until the mosquitoes drove Miss Sally in, and then old Eliza came in to fix my bed, and I lit the gas, and talked with Eliza & made arrangements for her to leave me a pitcher of ice water every evening when I came home. Then I commenced a Journal, in the Journal you gave me, & wrote two pages and ½ of foolishness in it & then tea bell rang & I went down. Mrs. Fee did not come down as she had tired herself too much, & Annie had passed two very bad nights Saturday & Sunday & was a little out of her head, but was much better when I left, and running about the room. Charley has appropriated the gallery, & is a very disagreeable child. I sat out on the gallery & smoked a cigar to keep off the mosquitoes, and thought of you & it almost made me crazy. I thought I would give anything to hear from you & the world to see you, and then went in & went to bed, but before that I paid Fee yours & Maggies board & made arrangements to stay at the same rates, $100 per month. It was long before I could sleep, but at last I slept & waked in the morning to miss you so much. I was busy yesterday, and have some business today. I must close this hurried & foolish note—with the earnest hope that it may meet you at St. Louis well & strong.

    Good Bye Darling—love to all,

> Your devoted Husband,
> Given

Mrs. Given Campbell
Care Woods & Christy & Co.
St. Louis, Mo.

New Orleans, May 2, 1866

My Darling Bess,

I have not time to write you a long letter today, but will let you know how I am. Very well, but very anxious to see you. Yesterday during business hours was right busily employed. I bought me some linen drawers & they are large & fit well & Eliza says are well made. When I went home they were all at dinner. After dinner I found that Eliza had made me a pitcher of ice water. I stayed at home a while & then went down town for I get the blues when I am in my room alone. At the St. Charles I found one of the numerous family of the Flournoys, and he told me that two of the Paducah Flournoys were with him—cousins of David. I went to see them & had a pleasant talk for half an hour but they commenced to bore me & I left. I can't stay long with anybody but you without getting bored. Whilst I was there saw Lucius Terry & his widow bride & she looked well. Brother Terry invited me to come to see him after. Also saw Frank Armstrong & his wife. He is in commission business in Mobile. Came home had tea and stayed out on our gallery a while but Oh it was dreadfully lonely. You shall never leave me again summer or no summer. Then I went over to the church to a wedding, and it was very amusing, for when the ceremony was over the groom saluted the bride & it made as much noise as the popping of a cap, and to crown it all as soon as he had kissed-her, he took out a great white handkerchief & wiped his mouth well. I staid up till about 12 & then retired, after reading my chapter in Romans. I find that you have left something. Your little paper box containing something of yours—and a pair of stockings. I will send the paper box & contents to you by express to day, to St. Louis care Woods Christy and Co. I only took two claret punches yesterday. I enclose you a letter from Mary that I opened on yesterday. Sent you another batch.

Good Bye my darling wife. You must take great care of yourself for me,

Your own loving husband
Given

Mrs. Given Campbell
St. Louis, Mo.

ATLANTIC & MISSISSIPPI STEAMSHIP CO'S
STEAMER
"OLIVE BRANCH"

Wednesday just after dinner (May 2, 1866)

My Dear Husband,

I wrote you & sent off the letter last night at Memphis & now I am writing for Cairo which we will reach before day light tomorrow. We are making first rate time & Mr. Shaler says will reach St. Louis by 6 oclock Friday morning. O! darling I want to see you more than I did at first. I feel so lonely & lost without you tho. everybody on the boat is very kind to me (I mean our friends) & there is somebody almost always with me, but all the people in the world cannot make up to me for one minute with my own precious chere'. O! it seems so long since I have seen you tho. I can see your dear face in imagination distinct by now & nothing makes me so miserable or so happy as to shut my eyes & call it to mind. Chere' dont you think you will certainly be up by the first June. Your "little stick" cannot do any longer with out you. It is very cold to day. Fire in the cabin all day & ladies sitting by it wrapped in shawls & cloaks. I hope you have felt the change tho. not to the same extent in N.O. I wonder what you are doing now my own darling in your office I expect. Dont forget to take that hymn book back to Mr. Palmer's church & I hope you will go tonight yourself chere'. Did Elisa mend your drawers? I have not cried since you left me except just at the time awhile but I have swallowed down many a sob & oceans of tears. My room mate has taken Mrs. Furney's room to day.

Good bye my own darling. Write me every day & I will do the same until we meet again—soon God grant. I love you too much darling. There is no news. Mrs. W's baby is improving.

Your own loving stick-bake Bess & best of all your *loving* wife.

4 oclock.

The babies & children are all tired out with the trip & as it is so cold they are all obliged to stay in the cabin & I assure you it is a perfect bedlam for the boys fight & the girls quarrel & the babies yell &c. Maggie & Maimie are excellent friends & very good but chere' there is one baby just three months fat, pretty & as sweet as it can be. It is just the age our little baby boy would have been if God had seen fit to spare his life. We are stopping to wood now. We have stopped a great deal to day. I long for our baby more than I did when I was with you. I am lying down. That is the reason I write so badly. I imagine you at dinner now. Dont forget the 50 cts. to Mrs. Fee for

Kate. You must take rides either on horse back or in a buggy every evening after dinner. You may take old Mrs. Gregory but I dont think I could stand Carrie Campbell. You might take Miss Sallie she was so kind to me but I doubt if she would go. If you leave the Fees you must be sure & go to see them often. They are mighty clever people. Dont forget about going in & having your picture taken *just as you are* some day, just one, dont primp a bit. There are about seven babies now screaming. Who do you love precious? I can hear you answer. I love my little stick. Dont put on your white pants unless it is very warm & chere' do be prudent about your health in every way. 6 oclock. Good Bye darling, your

Own wife

New Orleans, May 3rd, 1866

My Dearest Wife,

    I have just come down to my office & it is only 8 o'clock. So you see that my habits are very industrious. We breakfasted at 7 ½. I was not very well yesterday. It was one of those close cloudy hot days that induce an irresistible languor, and I felt badly. I had not much to do during the day & time hung heavily on my hands. I will send you the paper box containing your aroma by the porter of the Atlantic and get him to deliver it at Woods Christy's and Co. I went home early & took a cold bath & lightened my clothing and felt better afterwards. I have had another pair of white pants made & they are prettier & much more genteelly cut & made to fit me to perfection. I did this to please you. After tea I paid a visit to Mr. and Mrs. Geo. Langstaff from Paducah. You remember Mrs. Langstaff, and she told me a great deal of home news. I passed a very pleasant hour, came home to tea & had the blues, for it is so hard for me to get used to being away from you. I looked anxiously for an acct. of the Olive Branch having passed Vicksburg & Mr. Fee saw it. I suppose you are this morning about Cairo, & Oh I do hope you have passed a safe & pleasant trip. I read a chapter in Romans every night & never forget to say my prayers.

    Last night Eliza had a tub full of hot water & I took a hotfoot bath & after it went to sleep & slept soundly till morning, but when I wake up & do not find you it makes me feel so disappointed. I long to have you put your head on my shoulder & go to sleep. I had a letter from Jim yesterday & all were well. Your acquaintances are all well. Mrs. Fee looks right pale & badly. Annie Given is improving very much, and the baby is very well. I shall be tolerably busy today. I have no more news of interest to impart. I hope & believe that this will find you in good health. I enclose a letter from your mother. It seems your father is not at home, so he will not get my dispatch telling of your being on the Olive Branch. Write every day darling, to your own,

Given

New Orleans. May 3d 186_ –

My dearest Wife
                    I have just come
_____ to my office – it is only 8. O'clk
_ you see that my habits are
__ industrious, we breakfasted
__ 7½. I was not very well yesterday, it was one of those close
_____ hot days that induce
__ irritable languor, and I
__ badly – I had not much to-
__ during the day & time hung
_____ on my hands. I will
____ you the paper box containing your Anemia by the Porter of
the Attacka & get him to deliver
it at Woods Christy's & Co –
I went home early & took a cold
____ & lightened my clothing –

and felt better afterwards. I have
had another pair of white Pants
made & they are within much
more gracefully cut & made & fits
me to perfection. I did this to
please you — after tea I paid
a visit to Mr & Mrs Geo Langstaff
from Paducah. you remember
Mr Langstaff. and she told
me a great deal of home news.
I passed a very pleasant hour,
was home then & had the
blues, for it is so hard for me
to get used to being away from
you — I looked anxiously for
an acct of the Ohio Branch her
ing passed Vicksburgh & no He
saw it. I suppose you are this
morning above Cairo — & oh
I do hope you have passed a
safe & pleasant trip. I read a
Chapter in Romans every night
never forget to say my prayers

Last night Eliza had a jug full
of hot water & I took a hotfoot
bath & after it went to sleep & slept
soundly till morning — but
When I wake up & do not find
You it makes me feel so dis-
=appointed — I long to have you
lean your head on my shoul-
=der & go to sleep. I had a letter
from Jim yesterday & all
were well — Your acquain-
tances are all well, Mrs Lee
looks right pale & badly —
Minnie Grove is improving very
much — and the baby is very
well — I shall be tolerably busy
today, I have no more news
of interest to impart —
I hope & believe that this
will find you in good —
health, I enclose a letter from
your mother — It seems your
father is not at home, So he

Will not let any despatch
telling of your being on
the Ohio Branch —
Write every day darling — to

Your own —
Gen —

May 3rd, 1866
Thursday after Dinner

My Own Darling Husband,

This is the last letter I will write you from the boat as we get to St. Louis tomorrow morning at day break. I will stay on board till 7 & then if Father is not there I will go with Mr. & Mrs. W. to the depot as the cars leave at 8 I believe. I write this in case I should be too hurried in the morning. I am writing on the guards right by my room door. Maggie is busily packing just inside under my directions. It is just three oclock & much more pleasant than it has been for two days past. Warmer I mean but not all too warm. O. Chere' I am so far away from you & the farther I get the more I want to see you. I never shall forget how I felt the day you got on to that boat, & I sailing off in the other direction. The distance widening between us every second, but never mind that pang is past & it is the 3rd of May, only 28 days before I will begin to look for you. Know you promised me you would leave the first week in June. Chere' I think it would be nice if you would keep a sort of journal to show me when you come. Write a page every night before you go to bed of what you have been doing all day. You will have plenty of time. I wrote you a long letter from Memphis & also from Cairo. I hope you will get them. Mr. Shaler said that he had put on the outside of them return to the Olive Branch if not called for in 30 days as he thought you might forget to ask for them but I told him his trouble was entirely unnecessary. He was in fun you know of course. Mr. Woods has just come up & taken a seat on the guards & he tells me the cars leave at 7 instead of 8 so we will have to make a very early start. We have passed & repassed the Magenta half a dozen times & at dinner to day we were stopping to wood & fire a wheel & she came up & passed us. The churring was deafening from both boats & the excitement ran quite high. Mr. Shaler says he thinks we will not catch her again. She may get in an hour ahead. We are just passing along by those magnificent bluffs between Cape Girardeau (I dont know how to spell that name) & Selma Devil's bake oven one of them is called & O! darling how I long for you to be here to sit by me & look at them & talk about them. Everything looks just as green here the grass & forests I mean as in Louisiana which is quite a pleasant surprise to me. It is 4 oclock now & I imagine you just on you way up to dinner probably standing up on a car. Chere' can you realize that it is only 4 days & a half since we parted. It really & truly seems to me like a month without the least exaggeration. O! Darling I do want to see you so much. Dont ever send me away from you again. There is a woman on the boat who asked me if I was not Sue Bettie Woods. Said she lived near Ft. Donaldson & knew me when I was a baby. I have been taken twice since I have been on the boat for Mrs.

Ben Thurman tho I cannot imagine how any one can see a resemblance. Darling be sure & go to church on Wednesday nights, Sundays & Sunday nights. We must not expect to enjoy the benefit of religion when we shirk or neglect its rightful demands upon us. We must not be Christians only in name. Read your Bible every day or night darling & dont forget to say your prayers. It is now 5 oclock & time I was closing this letter but I will leave it open & say good bye after supper. Chere' you are the most precious thing in this world & you are never entirely out of my thoughts night or day. Be sure & shave at least every other day because you look so shabby if you dont. I am very well indeed this evening. I know you miss your little Bess between dinner time & dark. How thankful I am that I have got God's care to trust you to. I pray for you through the day & every time I wake up at night. If it were not for this I could not live away from you a week.

Friday morning, 6 oclock. St. Louis.

Arrived at 4 this morning. Am up & dressed waiting for breakfast & Father. O! Chere I want to see you so much.

9 oclock.

I am just going to bed. Will mail this in the morning. Capt. Jones has just been up to tell me he will have coffee prepared for us in the morning at 6. I have just finished reading the 4 Capter of Romans. Isnt it beautiful chere'. Good night precious.

Your own loving wife.

New Orleans, May 4, 1866

My Darling Bess,

Your letter written on the boat & mailed at Memphis, I got early this morning, & it was such a joyous and welcome letter to me for it relieved a great portion of my anxiety. I was afraid that you might be sick or unwell. But now that I know that you were very well up to Memphis, I have little fears for you till you get home. Home sick is not the word for me. I am home crazy, and it is too bad for me to have to stay away from you so long. I wrote to you every day & you will get a cloud of letters when you reach home. I have forwarded every letter sent to you, but one from your Mother, which I send with this. I took the liberty of opening & reading it. I knew you would not care if your cheri did read it, and was very much shocked of the acct. of young Washingtons treatment of his wife. Oh Bess the time does hang on my hands so heavy & I go to places & they afford no amusement. I get restless & get to shaking my foot & then think of you & quit it & get up & go some where else. Yesterday after dinner went to see Dr. Scott & Pine & saw Mr. S. & Mr. Dean, and it looked so pleasant to see Scott with his wife happy that it made me feel half mad & envious, for I did not see that he had any better right to happiness than I had. I stayed till 8 ½ & went home. The family had had tea but Miss Sally came down & served my tea to me, and talked of you. I adore to talk about you to everybody. I went up on my gallery. It used to be ours and sat down & smoked a cigar to keep off the mosquitos & blues and thought it so strange how much more I loved you now than I did a year ago. You need never fear my love & truth to you, for I could as soon be false to the mother that bore me, as to have a shadow of an idea fall athwart my heart in which your image was not beautifully portrayed. You need never have any doubts of us any more for I have none at all of myself under any possible circumstances. I sat and listened to Mrs. Clark, the bride, sing till nearly eleven & then I went to bed. I read my chapt. every night & never fail to say my prayers, night & morning. I would have gone to Wednesday prayer meeting but I forgot it. Shame on me. Oh I could write you more but I must go to my business now. Give my love to all.

Your true & loving Husband,
Given

New Orleans, May 5, 1866

My Darling Wife,

   I will write to you though I am very busy & can't write as much as I would like. I have got some two new cases today & have had to go to court & other places & am right tired & hot, and my old complaint is annoying me, the back ache.

   I was at Annie Givens a little while yesterday and met Mollie Dreux and she called me cousin Given & was so friendly I believed she would have kissed me if I had made an offer but I wouldn't kiss any woman in the world now and never will until I see one sweet little one that is now far away. When I look at a woman now I don't take any more interest in them or their movements than I do in the movements of the leaves on the trees. Annie G. invited me to come up & stay for three or 4 weeks. She said she could not make me as comfortable as I am but would do her best as I was lonesome &c.

   I politely declined & told her that I was very comfortably fixed up &c. I went to bed very early at about 9 o'clock & slept well till day light. The 4th District looks like a great garden now. All those shrubs that we see in the yards are covd. with beautiful flowers and oh I long for you to be here so much. We had a delightfully cool night. Was cool enough for you & Maggie.

   The dispatch of your Father that you had arrived safely lifted a great weight from my heart. I was uneasy & anxious about you. Jones has not sent in his bill though I sent word to him to do so. Your friends all inquire very affectionately if you have arrived & are well &c.

   I read in Romans every night & will continue to do so, and you are much surer to know that I do this regularly than if you were here, for I regard my promises to you as peculiarly sacred.

   A letter from your Mother came today & I will wait until I get all of them together & send them to you. I know you are now happy & gay in the midst of your friends & family while I am here with a chronic fit of the blues. Oh Bess I would give almost anything to have you here again. I get on partly well by day but after dinner I am entirely lost without you.

   Good Bye Darling,

                                        Yours Forever,
                                        Given

New Orleans, May 6, 1866

My Darling Bess,

This is Sunday morning and I am in my office before church writing this letter to you. I have just come from the post office and have just finished reading a letter from you mailed at Cairo. Oh Bess you don't know how it delights me to get a letter from you, and such a dear sweet loving letter too. I shall leave here just as soon as I can possibly arrange my business and will continue all my cases that I can so as not to be delayed. I have paid Eliza the money for Kate, and have done everything you asked me to do but return the Hymn Book, which I will do on next Wednesday night. I have not taken any rides yet but will go soon and take Miss Sally once. I can't stand it but once. Carrie Campbell I have heard has gone away. I have not seen her or her mother. Annie G. has invited me to dinner today at 1 o'clock and I accepted for half past one. Uncle Henry came up yesterday afternoon & bought his little girl a beautiful cap that he pd. $25.00 dollars for. It was a little beauty. The baby looks very sweet and fat. You must write to me and tell me if you are regular in your habits & if you have been taken sick &c. All about yourself.

I am still at the Fees & will remain there until they wish the room I occupy of which I have as yet had no intimation. Mrs. Fees waist is growing visibly larger but she keeps very well. She is now talking of going over the lake to spend a short time in July or August. I didn't think she has any idea of going up the river. Eliza has mended my drawers & keeps my room very neat & has water for me to take a bath every day, and I tell you it is very refreshing too for we have not had the cool weather you complain of. Miss Sally Fee will go up the first good chance & from what I see I think that Mrs. Fee would not care how soon that chance presented itself. I have not been to see Mrs. Kennard yet tho her husband told me that she was very well. I was out last night till a very late hour for me, 9½ o'clock. I was so terribly blue & wanted to see you so much that I could not talk to any body at all & I concluded to go down town. There were two large political meetings one at the Clay Monument which was held by the Nationl. Democratic Party & one at Lafayette Park which was held by the working men and after watching these a while I went to a fair and stayed about 20 minutes & got bored & came home & sat on the gallery & talked to Miss Sally & Mr. F. till bed time then read in Romans & retired. I stopped here to go to the front of the office to look at the procession of the Turners and Sangers German infidels who celebrate their great Volks Fest today at the Oak Grove out by the half way house. You passed it with Maggie & I in a buggy. It is a great shame that bands of music and processions should be parading the streets any Sunday. In one of the cars was a group of girls & on a pedestal was one holding the US Flag dressed as the soldiers of

Liberty. It was a handsome time out. But it is getting church time & I must draw this rambling letter to a close. Oh Bess I love you more than ever & want to see you worse than ever. You must keep your self in health & write to me every day, & pray for me every night. I will now send love to all and to you my darling I will ever be your HUSBAND.

S.B.W.

[1866]   Monday   Glencoe, May 7th

My Dear Darling Husband—

I sent you quite a long letter yesterday & consequently have very little left to tell you to day. I am improving. Missed my chill to day & am dressed & sitting up but of course feel very weak & badly. Have no doubt I will feel better tomorrow. It is a lovely day—cool bright & spring like. I am so sorry you sent the paper box & contents by express as it is an old broken & useless one I left on purpose & brought the one I use with me. But I suppose it is too late now & probably it will be out this evening. I hope for a letter from my own precious black eyed sweetheart this evening. Mother is splendidly fixed with servants. Susie & the children & Mary Woods (black) will be here in ten days. I have nothing left to tell you, but that I love you better & better every day.

You are the most precious thing in this wide world & I can not do much longer with out you darling. Don't think of staying any longer than the first of June—*now remember Cheri.*

I am going to write in a few days for Florence. Please be sure & take care of & bring Maggie's fairy tale book I left—Everybody sends love to you

Good Bye My Own Dearest
Your loving wife

Evening after tea—Father came out & with him Annie E. & Mrs. Kennedy. Annie's husband is away & she is very sweet, but Cheri I had no letter from you & consequently I am not glad to see them & mad at every body, & O! darling I am so disappointed.

Your Bess

Author's Note: Glencoe, Missouri is located approximately twenty miles west, southwest of St. Louis on the Meramec River.

New Orleans May 7, 66

My Darling Wife,

   I have little to tell you today except that I have a great deal to do. Will have to take depositions all day and file some suits. The weather is sultry & warm & no breeze. My health is very good. I looked anxiously for a letter from you this morning —yesterday was our Communion & oh how I wished you to be with me. We have never taken Communion together. I am glad you are not here today. It is so hot. I did not go to church last night, but went to see your friend Mrs. Kennard. She did not know that you had been sick & said if she had she wd. have been to see you. I took tea there, and then went home & sat out on my gallery till about 10½ & then read my Chapter & went to bed. Eliza says to give you her respects & tell you she would like to see you so much. Dr. Palmers sermon was the most powerful I ever heard him preach. His text was "It is a faithful saying & worthy of all acceptation that Christ Jesus came into the world to save sinners, of whom I am the chief" (Timothy). I long to see you all the time, but if you gain strength and health at Gelncoe I will fear the separation.

   Maggies little friends inquire for her & all of yours do so. Mrs. Singleton says she does not blame you a particle for not coming to see her & knowing your condition did not expect it, and says that Mrs. Woods was mistaken in what she told you. I have at last had a letter from Harry Courtney & he refers me to their lawyer. I will close this hurried note my dear dear Bess with the love of my whole heart.

Your Husband   Given

I enclose a letter to Magqie from Mattie Tarlton.

Glencoe, Tuesday, May 8th, 1866

My Darling Husband,

 I had no letter from you Sunday evening nor last evening & it seems like an age & O! cheri I do want to see you so much. Never send me or let me come away from you again. If Father does not bring me a letter tonight I will____well I will have to try & be patient & wait till tomorrow. I am up & going about today, & much better but feel very weak of course. It is 5 o'clock now & I think you are just finished dinner. I know you miss your good for nothing little wife just at this time more than any other. Please be making your arrangements to be here by the first few days of June. I think about you so much. Annie Mitchell & Mrs. Kennedy came out last night & have been chatting & laughing all day. Mr. M. is in Washington. Annie looks very well. How do you get along without me now that you have tried it this long. Do you miss me more or less than at first. I miss you a thousand times more. I am sorry Charlie annoys you on the gallery. Why dont you go to Annie G's? The weather is so pleasant here. Dr. Johnson is coming out tomorrow evening just to pay a friendly visit & see if I need a tonic &c. I am not quite strong enough to write a long letter yet. I have written every day since I left you.

        Good Bye My Own Precious,
        Your Loving Bess

After Supper—

 O! darling I got two letters from you May 3 & 4-& I am so glad. I feel better already. They have been dancing, playing & having a gay time in the hall but I left to come to bed & write this to you. Annie sleeps with me, & we have great talks but at night I think of & long for you. O! but it is no use for me to try & tell you what I feel. I could only do it with my head on your shoulder & your arms around me.

        Good night—say your prayers,
        God bless you my darling,
        Your own wife Bess

New Orleans May 8, 66

My Dearest Wife,

    I went to the P.O. this morning fully expectg. to get a letter from you and when I took my letters out of the box saw one from your Father & one from your Mother but none from my own wife, & for a minute my heart sank for I thought perhaps you were sick & they had written in your place. But on examination I found that you had not reachd. St. Louis at the time the letters were written & I shall wait till tomorrow for a letter from my own. I wrote to so that you would get a letter every day after you arrived. My time is filled up now with business. I have three cases to try & in one of them the highest ability at the bar is against me alone (Rozelius Phillips & Hunt) are the opposing counsel, but I have a good case & am not at all afraid. The weather was very warm yesterday & I had to move about a good deal, but when I went home Eliza had a tub of cold water for me and I took a bath & put on a pair of white pants & no vest & went to dinner much refreshed. After dinner Uncle Henry came & asked me to go riding with them & show them some of the pretty drives. I drove them up Magazine to the St. Vincents Academy & across the River Road & as high up as the Seagewich Hospital, and the air was very fresh. Annie G. talked of furs &c. The ride brought back so vividely the delightful rides we used to take. I thought of you so much when I looked through the Grand Avenue of Live Oaks at the Hospital. I drove back home & it was the night of Miss Annie McCleans concert. You remember she was the principal singer at the Episcopal Church. Uncle Henry & Mrs. Gregory & Mary Francis went from there & Mr. Fee & Miss Sally & Mrs. Fee from our house. I did not feel like going but staid at home & sat on the gallery and looked at the passers by, read the stars & wondered where you were & if you were asleep & who slept with you if Maggie or Annie Lou, and my heart yearned for you & I thought that life would be a dull dreary drag without you. Oh Betsy I do want to see you so much. Bess I would write longer letters to you but I haven't the time. I feel very well. I will answer your Mother & Fathers letters soon.

                        Good Bye Darling
                        Your Own
                        Given

Glencoe
May 9th, 1866
Wednesday

My Own Dearest Husband,

I have just written a letter to Florence begging her to come round & pay me a visit. I am still a little better today than yesterday but am very thin & extremely weak. I never was so weak before. Mr. Kirkman took me a little ride this morning which tired me a good deal but I am benefited by it this evening. Dr. Johnson is to be out this evening & I will tell him every thing & get his orders for the future. I have had to take four toddies today. I can see that Mother & Mr. Kirkman & Father & all of them think I am in a very bad way but I have unlimited faith in God & what He has promised He will perform & He has promised if we have faith to grant us the desires of our hearts—of course if they involve no sin. I read all of your personal letters over every night. I miss you more every day darling & last night I was so cold & did long so inexpressibly to crawl up into your bosom & be wrapped up in your arms & get warm & go to sleep. But I wrapped my feet up, put on more cover & thought about you & that was the next best thing & then Annie talked me to sleep. She went in this morning but Mrs. Kennedy will remain through the week. She is a very sweet woman & I feel so sorry for her. I am sorry you did not feel well that warm day. I know you wanted your little Bess to comfort you & rub your head. I am looking for a letter this evening. I do hope the mails will not get out of order. There are a great many flowers here in bloom & it is beginning to look lovely—it is generally supposed that Ned Washington is crazy—his poor wife is still suffering from the bruises he inflicted. Tell Mrs. Fee I will write her as soon as I am able. St. Louis is more gossiping than ever. It is quarter past 4 & I think you are just on your way up to dinner. O! darling, my own darling, you have no idea how incessantly I think of you. I am glad you got another pair of white pants. You are just the very handsomest thing on Earth with them on, but Oh chere I am getting so ugly. Have you gotten your new straw hat? I read my chapter every night. I am so glad that you do too & darling never forget your prayers. Go around & see people & enjoy your self & make haste & get ready to come to me. Don't stay at home & get the blues. You say I need not have any fears about your constancy. I have none. I trust you with the most perfect confidence & would under any circumstances & forever. Good Bye dearest. All send a great deal of love to you. Your own "little stick." after tea. Good night darling. I didn't have any letter from you tonight. I enclose one that was advertised & Father got out of the office. Dr. Johnson came out, has examined my lungs, says they are sound now. I will write you more tomorrow about what he says. You are the dearest thing on earth.

Your own wife.

New Orleans, May 9, 66

My Precious Wife,

How I do earnestly wish that I was with you now at Glencoe. I have missed you so much, and last night when I was alone in my room I longed for your sweet cheerful conversation to enliven & arouse me. I did not feel very well last night & did not sleep well & had a nightmare, the first I remember ever to have had. I suppose I must have eaten something that did not agree with me but I feel better this morning & came to my office. I was disappointed again in not hearing from you. A St. Louis mail came but no letter from my dear dear wife. Uncle Henry told me that his wife was very sick after she came home from the ride on the day before yesterday & had a very bad night & the doctor was with her for almost all day. It was a violent diarrhea. She is convalescent this morning. I passed by Dr. Jones office this morning & he told me I had better look out for intermittent fever, that it is very prevalent. I asked him for his bill and it was Two Hundred & Fifty Dollars, less than I thought it would be. Dr. Scott was to see me last night and we sat out on the gallery for an hour. He told me that young Washington had to leave St. Louis, or had left it & was notified not to return.

I have had no letter from home since you left and am beginning to get home sick for news from you. The Dr. said he was very glad to hear that you were so well when you left & when you arrived. We are having doleful weather, cloudy & damp & warm. There was a report that there was a case of Cholera here, a Mr. Thosen who lived on the corner of Philip and St. Charles, but I believe that it was Cholera Morbus that he died of, so the Drs. say.

I have a good deal of business to attend to today, but as it is so damp will not go to court. I wish that you would write to me & tell me all about yourself, how you are & how you pass your time & if Florence is coming to see you. I suppose you have Susie with you by this time. Try & persuade your Father & Mr. Kirkman to come here to live. This would be a great place for them. Business is getting dull now in commercial circles & law business is almost at a stand still, I have however had some new business lately. I will close this short note with the love of my whole heart.

Your Husband.

Glencoe
May 10th, 1866 Friday

My Dearest Husband,

I sat down to my writing desk about two hours ago to write a letter, first to Dr. Johnson, then to Sister Mary & when I had finished with duty, to take pleasure in the way of writing to my own chere—& what do you think I did? Opened your journal forgot everything else & read an hour & a half when I suddenly remembered that I had some thing else to do, & found I had only time to write to the Dr. & to you before car time so I will have to postpone the other one until some other time. We are having the warmest day of the season. I find even my calico wrapper oppressive. We started out at 8 o'clock this morning & took a long ride, as far as the blacksmith's shop beyond Mr. Hutchingsons & we returned a little after ten. I laid down & rested an hour & then roamed around the house awhile & finally settled down with "Ten thousand a Year," (speaking in a figger as Sam Weller would say. I laughed till I cried over poor Tittle-tat's agonies with his green hair & white eye brows & by the time dinner was ready had gotten up a fine appetite. Since dinner I have been lounging, talking, reading your journal & finally arrived at my invariable afternoon occupation writing to you. I was interrupted here by Mary (the cook) bringing in a saucer of ice cream & some lemonade as a surprise & you may imagine it was a very pleasant one & both of the aforesaid disappeared in a trice. It is very warm this evening which made it all the more agreeable.

It is now 5 o'clock. You have just finished dinner & are thinking what you will do with the rest of the day. I do hope you will get a nice horse & buggy & take some friend (gentleman preferred) to ride on the shell road & home by the river. Oh! how I would love to be by your side in a buggy, but I believe I would rather be in our own room, sitting in your lap with my arms around your dear precious old neck, & I know I would not miss such a good chance to kiss you right in that place where it makes you feel so funny. I know you want me now to talk to you, & I wish every day that I had never left you. Cheri I feel like taking my hands & just pushing all the days away until the first of June when I certainly look for you. Everything is so intensely quiet out here. I can hear nothing but the twittering of the birds, the occassional sighing of the wind through the trees. I am all alone and as I look out on the beautiful earth & the blue sky I can not help thinking how happy I would be if I had my little baby to play with & to love. But God knows best. It is nearly 6 o'clock & car time & I am all impatient for my letter. It is time to dress & I will finish after tea—

After tea—

My darling Cheri. This evening my heart was gladdened by two letters from you—one 13th a delicious long one, with a P.S. of 14th & the last one amused me darling & grieved me too, I am sorry you have been made uneasy but nobody says I have consumption, & Dr. J. is a man of great judgement & caution. He knows the whole state of the case & the toddies & every thing else I do is by his order, & I am daily gaining strength & health. I have no cold & not a symptom of a cough. Mr. Jarret came out with Father this evening. He & Dr. Hendricks came over to the assembly which is causing great excitement in town. He says that just before he left P. Florence & Jim had started to Judge Flowler's to a party given to Laura & Gus. Fowler at Judge Fowler's—says they are all well—he looks badly I think, says his wife has been out of health all winter.

Good night my own most precious one. I wish my head could be as you say pillowed on your shoulder tonight. Oh dearest why don't you ever say a word about when you are coming. You never say a word about when I am to look for you. You must start by the First of June. I cant stand it any longer. I am now going to bed & to pray for you my darling.

Good Night
Your own little Bess

New Orleans, May 10, 1866

My Darling Wife,

Your letter mailed at St. Louis the day you arrived was received this morning, and I was more than rejoiced to get it, & one from your Father the same date, for it relieved my mind a great deal. The mails are irregular & the letters were delayed on the way. I am a great deal better & feel quite well today. This is the 10th day of May. The day I was captured at Camp Jackson & also the day that my connection with the Confederacy was ended by the capture of Presdt. Davis, and it is a beautiful warm moist day for we had rain yesterday and last night. Last night I spent at home & talked to the Fees, and then went up stairs & longed to see you. I have thought of you so much in the last two days that it interferes with my business, and this morning when I waked up I missed you. It seemed more than ever. I had commenced a Journal the day I returned here & have written in it every day. I say my prayers every night & morning & read the Bible every day, or rather night. Andrew Erwin Esq. was in to see me. He has just returned from a visit to his daughters and looks the worse for wear and speaking of the looks of one &c., I do shave every other day. I keep my accounts faithfully with the Deposit Bank of yours, and it is increasing right fast. I am getting tired of being away from you & will return to you just as soon as I can possibly do so. I have something to do every day, and am busy now preparing some cases for trial. I see Maggies little friends every day playing on the "banquette" and Louis has won Mr. Sears heart. It is amusing to see what an interest he takes in the child. The bride looks quite disconsolate, & her husband does not stay with her much. Mrs. Charles baby is thriving & daily growing more like its father. Mrs. Fee looks right pale & delicate & does not always come down to breakfast. Eliza says she can't come up, as Mr. Fee wants her to stay and go over the lake. But I doubt very much if she goes over to the lake. Jennie has taken a wonderful "fancy" to me and bores me dreadfully with her attentions. I get on about as usual in my home affairs. I now look for a letter from you every day, & you must be sure to write to your loving and true Husband.

Given

New Orleans, La. May 11, 1866

My Dear Wife,

I was bitterly disappointed in not getting a letter from you this morning. You arrived in St. Louis on the 4th & now it is the 11th and your letters have not reached me. I am afraid you are not well enough to write, for I see a letter here to you from Lizzie Hunt, post marked the 7th of May, only 4 days out. It is so hard to be so far away from all I love. I feel adrift & lonely & if I did not have a good deal of business to occupy my time during the day I don't know what I would do. If I do not get a letter tomorrow I shall telegraph your Father. The weather is clear again & appears to be settled. I was a great deal better yesterday than I was the day before, and my genl. health now is good. Last night I went to the theatre. I was so lonely, and I don't like Annie G. well enough to go there every day, and I didn't feel at all like visiting, & I don't think it is much harm to go to such places now & then. This is the first time since you have gone away. All things seem to conspire to give me the blues today, but I will drive them away and think of you at Glencoe well & happy in the midst of friends & family, but I know that there will be a dark corner in your dear little heart that will silently entertain the memory of your absent husband. I slept after dinner yesterday for an hour & felt rested & refreshed, but my sleep was not disturbed, for Jimmie and Charly were on the gallery in front of my window seeing which could shout the loudest. They have appropriated it since you & Maggie left, and asked me to let them come thro' my room as a passway to the gallery which I declined to grant. I wrote a good deal in my diary. It is the same book that you began your's in, and it is with a sad & mournful feeling that I read over the pages you wrote, during your "dark ages" but I see thro' all this sadness glimpses of sunny happiness & it makes me happier to know that I was the moving cause of some bright & happy hours for you. It is now nearly two weeks since I left you & it seems a long long time, but I am delighted that that length of time has dragged its weary length along. It only makes the day when I shall start to meet you nearer. Now Bess it is near court time and I have to close this. Write every day to your dearest Husband,

Given

Glencoe Friday May 11 (1866)

My Own Dear Husband,

　　Here commences the regular bulletin of the day. I am sometimes almost afraid you will get wearied with so many letters but then I know that I receive every letter from you with more pleasure than the last so I judge you to be the same but then you have so much more material for your letter than I have. I am much better to day than I was yesterday. I take six grs. of quinine in the morning & an iron pill morning & evening three toddies a day containing each a teaspoon full of pepsin. My appetite is quite good. Mr. Kirkman says he can see me improve every hour & Lizzie Hunt says I look much better to day than yesterday. She & I have just come in from the nursery to my room to lie down. We left Mrs. K. Mother, Bede & A.L. busily engaged sewing & Mr. Kirkman amusing the crowd he is such good company. That was just like Annie Given to say. She could not make you very comfortable when she invited you to stay with her. It was equivalent to say it would inconvenience her but she would stand it. I cant see why she could'nt make you comfortable with a large house plenty of money & plenty of servants. I am glad you didn't go. You say you have a consti-tutional attack of the blues. Now darling you know that is not right. When you feel that way go to see some body & laugh & talk & you will soon get over it. I would have the blues all the time if I didn't struggle against it for I can not be happy away from you. Poor Ned Bryan is in town & drunk all the time. Chere' why dont you ever say any thing about coming. Do you think you will certainly be here by the first week in June? If you are not Oh chere' I cant bear to think of it. You must be sure & write to me *every day*. I get some of your letters in 3 some in 4 & some in five days. Maggie is writing to you & you must be sure & send a scrap of an answer. She writes on her gilt edged peper out of her portfolio. Mrs. A. McDowell has great expectations. Good Bye for the present dearest. I will finish after Father comes.

　　It is just 4 & I suppose you are on your way or maybe not quite started. Have you been to see the Kennards & Terrys? It is just after tea but not quite dark. They are all going or gone walking in the garden. Father came out bringing me two letters from you 6th & 7th. Oh! darling they made me so happy. The box also came. Jimmie Yeatman came over to see me this morning & took tea. He & Lizzie have made an engagement for a fish in the morning. I have taken two drives to day one with Lizzie & one with Mr. K. Everybody waits on me in the house from Father to R.K. They all seem to study my health pleasure & comfort above everything else. I am in a fair way to be spoiled. Good Bye now darling. Oh how I long & long to see you. No body knows. Good Bye my own darling.

Your Bess

Glencoe May 12th, 1866 Monday

My Dear Husband,

I have literally nothing in the world to put into this letter to day except that I love you better than I did yesterday & every day & every hour that I live I love you more. To day I long especially to see you. I don't know why but I am thinking of you every moment & wondering what you are doing, how you look, trying to recall the sound of your precious voice &c. I look for you now in less than three weeks or about three weeks. This morning Mother & I took our drive over to Mr. Graham's. The old couple look well & are getting along nicely. The made great mirations over my appearance, could not believe it was the same "lass" so thin so pale, &c &c. I felt like an exhumed mummy when I left. When we got home found little Doxie right sick. I think she has taken cold. She is in bed now with considerable fever but hope she will be well by morning. No one comes out this evening but Mr. K. A.L. R.K. & Father stay in to the theatre. Father leaves on Wednesday for Oceola, & Mr. K. for Memphis from thence to Florence, & returns by Nashville with Sue & the children. He will be gone about two weeks & Father only 4 or 5 days. I feel deeply interested to hear the result of your case where Rozelius Phillips & Hunt were the opposing counsel against you alone. You must write me about it. Chere' please look in my trunk in that bundle of the baby's little sacks, & woolen things & bring me that little pink & white shawl Maggie Collier sent me. I wrote in my letter yesterday of blanket shawl, but forgot to mention this. I wrote to Mrs. Fee on Saturday. I am so sorry you have to bring suit against the Courtneys. I was in hopes matters could be arranged without it. Don't forget to have your photograph taken for me & colored, & now remember chere' that is all I want you to bring me. Mother's thinks something of letting Nance go on a visit to Spring Hill & Mrs. Handy's this Summer. Who do you love darling & who does your own little Bess love?

Oh! Chere' Chere' I want to see you so much. Do you ever see any pretty women now? You must be prepared dearest to see me very ugly, worse than when I left you, *so* thin, & so dark under the eyes. I think I am improving in health every day, but not gaining flesh. I have a pretty good appetite. I expect a letter from you tonight. The last was the 8th (last Tuesday). So I may have two. Oh it is delightful to get two.

Good bye my darling. I live to see you again. I love you better than anything on Earth, & long to see you more than I ever longed for anything in my life before.

Your Own Loving Wife

Excuse my writing with a pencil but it is so much trouble to get the ink. Give my kindest regards to the family, & kiss Jennie for me.

New Orleans, May 13th/66

My Darling Bess,

I went to the P.O. this morning & was delighted to get a letter from you. It was so sweet & pretty & kind & in a word filled my heart with joy. I always knew Sam Kirkman had a kind & tender heart & I shall not forget him for his kindness to you. You are the best & sweetest & most considerate woman in the world & the longer I am away from you the more I am crazy to see you. I am glad that you have made up your mind not to leave me again for I get on badly without you and am not at all happy I feel as Mr. Bryan expresses it, like a "stray dog." You would have done just as well as at Glencoe for the nights have always been cool & you could do very well if you stayed in the house in the hot part of the day, but you had an idea in your sweet dear head that if you stayed here that this climate was so debilitating that you would never get strong & you know what an effect the imagination has on you, and so do I and I was willing for you to try it. You would not have had those slight chills if you had not gone up into a colder & rawer climate & when you reached the damp & humid valleys of Glencoe the disease developed itself. I was a little unwell for the first two or three days of last week but did not give way to it & got over it entirely. I am writing this in my room before dinner for I have just returned from church. It was raining & none of the family went but me. Dr. P. exerted himself on the 9th Verse of the 15th John. It was a gorgeous sermon & fuller of those startling passages of inspired eloquence than any sermon I ever heard from him. He preached about one hour & a half. He is a wonderful man the last end of his sermon always seems as if he was cutting his sermon short, for his sermons never flag in the beginning or the end. It seems to me that each sermon I hear is stronger & more powerful than its predecessor.

I was at Uncle Henry's a little while this morning, and Anna looks right badly. She says she is going up the river about the first of June. Mrs. Fee talks vaguely of going to New York some of these days. Miss Sally did not go as she expected. She is a very good woman & it is a pity she is so ugly in her face & form. Her waist & Mrs. Fee's are about the same size. Sister Fee does not run around half so much as she used to do & seems to take care of her self.

I saw Joe Scott down at the St. Charles last night. All were well at his house but Mr. Ping who hasn't been able to go out yet. They have opened an office on Camp Street, and if I get sick I would patronize them but old Jones or "thingamy" as you call him is so kind & polite that as I have him I will stick to him, but from present indications I will not need the services of any Dr. I haven't been to see the Terry's yet but will do myself the honor in a few days. I haven't looked at any woman with the slightest notice of whether she were fair or ugly and don't care for any ones appearance but yours, & I want you to get well & pretty for when you are well you are always pretty, but if you don't I will love you just as well & be just as tender & kind as possible. You know I always love you more or seem to when you are sick & oh how often have I groaned in the spirit that I was away from you when you were sick & suffering. I have added to my wardrobe & will complete my summer outfit before I come up. I have added Flag Shirts and got another beautiful pair of pants white linen, and a coat & pants of what is called "seer sucker" a striped Chinese goods, very nice & cool & two white vests one linen & one Marseilles, and some cravats & I intend to get me some more summer vests & another coat & these with what I have will serve me very well. I don't spend any money foolishly, for I need everything I get. You know I had no summer clothing at all & needed it badly. If I have good luck I will bring you up something pretty & if you scold I will not tell you what it is. I will give your message to old Elisa, & I know it will make her grin for she adores you. It is strange why every one you are intimately associated with is so devoted to you, so it isn't for you are so secret & lovely. While you are riding about over the country you must remember me & the drives we used to take & how you used to tease me about those girls, in Augusta—you know now that I didn't care for any of them and that if I had a little fun, it was not because I didn't love you. Bess you ought to love me very very much for if you didn't I would be badly paid for the perfect devotion I bear to you. I will stop now & rest a while & gather my thoughts for I find I am making love to you too fast.

Monday 14th.

Dear Bess I did not mail the letter I wrote yesterday, because I went to church last night & did not go to the Post Office, and I will enclose all in one letter. I am well, and today I have a case to try in which I am opposed by the ablest lawyers at the bar, but I will do my best for my client & that is all that I can do. My rest was very much broken last night by Mr. Fee groaning. He had a severe attack of something like cholera morbus, and Mrs. Fee awaked me to get some brandy, & he was vomiting & groaning for nearly the whole night. He is much better this morning. I have just received a short note from you dated the 7th and you say you did not get a letter from me, but Bess I write to you every day, & if you don't get the letters it is not my fault. I have nothing new to tell. Give my love to all.

> Your loving Husband,
> G.

> *Glencoe*
> *May 13th 1866*
> *Sunday 4 oc.*

My Darling Own Husband,

I wrote you a very short & hurried little note & sent it in yesterday evening by Lizzie H. I was sorry to send such a short one but I was tired & I know you would like it better than nothing & rather do without any than have me get tired, you dear precious kind thing. When Father came out yesterday evening he brought me your letter of the 8th the day you went to ride with Annie Given, so affectionate & showing such true sure enough love & longing for your little wife that it made me as happy as any queen, so happy that my heart couldn't quite hold it all & some of it, but only a very little chere' had to overflow some where in the neighborhood of my eyes. It was not all joy either but partly sorrow that I had to be so far away from my own dearest. Father also brought out your dispatch of the 11th which was a morsel of comfort to me to know that you were safe & well the very day before, but I was so sorry to think you had been made uneasy & unhappy. I was afraid you would as soon as you heard of my being sick, but then I suppose as Father replied immediately you are entirely relieved by this time. If I had the fortune of George Peabody I would hire a telegraph office & talk to you all day. Wouldn't it be nice. They had it reported in St. Louis that I was dying & all sorts of things. It is the most gossiping place I have ever seen. Mr. Whittaker came out last evening & will be here till tomorrow morning. No one else came much to everybody's relief. Mrs. K. is still here. This morning she & Mother Annie & myself took a drive in the carriage as far as Mrs. McCollach's, & when I returned I took a toddy & a nap, got up & ate a hearty dinner & feel quite well this afternoon. The weather is perfection. Everything a bright spring green, flowers blooming the sky a most perfect azure birds singing & everything lovely. All I need to make the surroundings perfect is your own precious self, your own black eyes to look in to, your own perfect hand to squezze just as hard as I could. I am glad you thought of me last Sunday when taking the communion of our blessed Saviour. You said we had never taken it together but you forget chere' don't you, remember in Paducah we took it together from your Father.

You said in your letter that you sat on the gallery wondering if I was asleep, who I slept with &c. I have slept with half a dozen different people the first three nights. I slept in a bed alone in Mother's room then Annie Ewing came & I slept with her two nights then one night with Mrs. K. & then Lizzie Hunt came & staid with me three nights & last night I had Mrs. Kennedy again & will I suppose until she goes in but I never put my head on my pillow that I do not long & long for you to lay my head on your shoulder & go to sleep. It seems to me would be the greatest bliss on this side of heaven. Father says your dispatch ought to have reached him at 3 oclock of the 11 & he could have had the answer back to you the same day whereas he didn't get it until the 12th. I have written you every single day since I have been at home but up to last Tuesday you had received no letter from me later than the one mailed at Cairo. The two Mr. Yeatmans Neppir Allan & Miss Pope have just called but as I have on my wrapper I will not see them. Chere' when you come please look in my trunk & bring me that bright striped blanket shawl of mine. You will find it in the bottom of the trunk pinned up in a towel & the name written on it. I hope you will go to church tonight. I imagine you now taking a walk or sitting in the gallery at Annie G's. Everybody sends much love to you. Read your chapter every night darling & never forget to say your prayers & pray for your little Bess. Oh chere' wont we be happy when we get together again. Love me. Take care of yourself. Be good.

Your own own wife

15th May 1866

PRIVATE AT HOME

My Darling Wife I wrote to you a letter this morning, under a strong feeling, and I will drop you this line now after dinner to give you some advice. You know that I have a clear head & good judgment, & I know that your lungs are as strong as any woman's in the world, and you must not let them dose & doctor you up for any such thing. All you need is my shoulder to rest your head on & my arms around you to make your lungs as well as anybody's & I think it extremely foolish to be having your lungs sounded every time you have a cough. Why suppose some ignorant doctor should say that your lungs were diseased. What would be the effect? Even if they were sound as a dollar it would cause you great unhappiness if you believed him, & even if you did not believe him, it would make you dissatisfied & uncertain. But Dr. Johnson says that they are sound. Now be satisfied with that & never repeat it, for the constant attrition of the imagination will wear away the most robust health, more than one has died because it has been ding-donged into them that they came of an unhealthy family & were obliged to die. You must remember what you have passed through this winter. Why no woman could have gone thro all this & be as strong as ever in a few weeks after. Look at Anna Given. She is almost masculine in her person, yet she still looks pale & thin & feeble & she had not half so hard a time as you. Don't you go to doctoring yourself, and let the everlastg. cod liver oil alone. If you want anything use something to keep you regular in your habits, say Blue Lick water. All you need is to be regular & you will be sure to keep well. There is nothing new the matter with you in any organic way than with me. If you have caught cold, why take care of yourself & you will soon get over it. Just as you did here. But for the love of God Bess dont dose yourself! I am almost afraid to stay away from you any longer yet I am obliged to stay a while longer or I will lose my business. I know how easy you are led to do things in your anxiety to be well & your experience with Mrs. Fee ought to satisfy you with womens doctoring. If you are sick enough to Doctor, send for a Doctor, & let him prescribe for you without any suggestions made by anyone else.

I sent you a nice bunch of red bananas, the best kind & would have sent you some Pine apples but they were all too ripe to last. They are on the Magenta under care of C.F. Vanderford. I am well & feel a little better, yet I feel like going to see you & neglecting everything else.

Now darling Good Bye. I love you so much. You know that I love you & you must believe & act upon all I say for it is my unclouded conviction. Write me just how you are & no concealments.

Your own Husband,
Given

Glencoe May 15th 1866 Tuesday

My Dear Darling Husband,

I sent you in a letter this morning but I take very little pleasure in writing now, & have very little encouragement to do so, as I feel you are never going to get the letters. Up to last Saturday you had no letter from me, & I have written every day. I am more fortunate in getting your letters as I have one every evening of the world. It is my daily comfort & joy, but oh! chere' I am getting so impatient to see you. You say law business is at a stand still. Then why need you stay any longer. I think you might as well start up by the last of this month & this is the 15th & that isn't very long but still even two weeks longer seems an eternity. I am so sorry you have been sick or at least did'n feel well. You must take good care of your self darling. You are so imprudent. I think Dr. Jones' bill was quite enough, $200. would have been ample. I am sorry to hear that Annie G. has been so sick. The dear little baby. I expect she is quite fat & saucy by this time. I wrote Florence about a week ago begging her to come around immediately. Have not heard anything from her as yet. Does the Buckner bride still wear the lavender silk? & do you still have the same *lovely views* from our side window? At night I mean after the gas is lighted. I know if the landscape is still unchanged that you gaze up on it with great admiration. Now confess don't you chere'. Maggie is quite well again today. She will answer Mattie's letter very soon. Chere' how could you say that in reading my journal over, you were comforted to see that at least some bright & happy hours of my life were owed to you. You know well enough that you have been the author of all the true & perfect happiness that I have ever known. You have made me perfectly & supremely happy, & my life without you would have been a very common place affair, no more to be compared to what you have made it, than a dull copper cent can be compared to a bright shining gold piece. Now you darling thing please don't say another word about "dark ages." I wish you were here to drive me about. We went up on the Melrose Road this morning. Up that rocky Hill where you got out & walked up, because you didn't like what I was talking about. Do you remember that day darling? There is no news at all. I am overwhelmed with invitations to go in town & pay a visit, at least not overwelmed but I have had some four or five very polite & urgent ones but I do not intend to go, at all, as I think I am much better out here. I have been reading Tennyson to day out on the gallery among the humming birds & so of course feel very romantic. But really I do enjoy some parts of Tennyson so much. Good Bye Chere'. I will finish this after tea.

After supper 9 o'clock.

I am just going to bed chere'. I got your letter of the 10th tonight, & Mother yours of the 11th. Mrs. K. is undressing. She is so pretty & fat. Good night darling.

Your own Wife—Bess

Glencoe Heights
May 16th, 1866 Wednesday

My Dear Husband,

We are quite lonesome to day. This morning Mrs. K. went in—Mr. Kirkman went in to start to Memphis & Father to start to Oceola. They both go on the same boat. Annie Low has been frolicking too much & has been taken with a little cold which has laid her up in bed for to day. Maggie is also sick to day & much sicker than she was day before yesterday. She really has the chills but pray don't insinuate in your letters that I have written this to you. Her fevers are high, head ache very severe & she is quite flighty-her stomach is very much disordered & mother is a little afraid of a return of the gastric fever she had last spring. So she sent Neal in by the 12 o'clock freight with a note to Father to tell him of Maggie's condition & beg him if his business was not urgent to put off his trip a few days-but I think it was only a chill & now that the fever has subsided she is much better & I hope Father will not come, tho' he will, unless his business is very imperative. It has been *raining raining* all day long—such a dismal day. I have missed my rides but stick faithfully to the toddies. I have been reading your journal a good deal. Oh! Cheri some of it is so funny. When I commenced "our mutual friend" & I find it very interesting. I have crocheted nearly a mat, talked a great deal of nonsense to Mother & A.L. taken a long nap & eaten a hearty dinner—& it is now nearly time to send this down to the train to go in this evening. Father has made arrangements with Darby to bring out my letters every night while he is gone so I look for my regular letter to night whether Father comes out or not. I am gaining in health every day I think—& I feel very well to day. We have had green peas here once & strawberries not at all—but will have them tomorrow. Maggie received the most amusing letter from Mamie Waterman last evening. It seems that Mattie T. has told Mamie that Maggie she said (Mamie) paid her too many visits & writes to know if it is so. Cheri please be sure & bring me a bottle of cinchonine when you come up. Maggie is so good & patient it is almost painful to see her sick.

Darling you dont know how happy it makes me to know that you read your bible so faithfully & never forget your prayers. God will bless you for it & if any thing could make me love you any more it would be that. Oh! I want to see you so much to day. I keep your picture & letters in my pocket & when I get very home sick to see you I draw them out & look at the picture & read the two last letters & feel a little better—haven't you got a foolish wife? Good Bye dearest thing—I would give any thing I have even my precious gold to hear you say "All a board &c." I can see you strutting about the room in your shirt sleeves saying it over & over—Do you project with the student's lamp now? I think it would be a very good idea for you to bring it with you. Have you got your straw hat yet?

>   Good Bye—Your own
>   "little Bess"

New Orleans May 16th 1866

My Dearest Wife,

I see by your letter that you have the blues & are low spirited. They have frightened my little dove & I am away & cannot reassure you.

Bess, darling, cheer up! I don't believe that anything at all is the matter with you, in any unnatural way. Your mother has made herself believe that you are irregular because you are weak & in bad health, & has had your lungs sounded. I am astonished that any woman who has her reputation for wise would do so, in order to relieve your mind from an apprehension that you are in the family way, she induces you to believe that your irregularity comes from an inherent weakness of your constitution, and is always talking about the "Woods Constitution." Look at your Father & Grandfather & compare them with her family & it would seem more reasonable to talk about the "Berry Constitution." Many a person has been frightened to death & if your Father had not had as much luck as he has he might have been talked & dosed into weak lungs. You dismiss all such illusions. I don't want to be a Job's comforter, but Bess my honest conviction is that in less than 9 months from this time you will have ocular knowledge of the cause of your irregularity in a beautiful blackeyed baby. I know it is very bad for this to be so, but still it is best to relieve your mind from any such hideous delusions as are attempted to be foisted upon you. All you need now to be well & strong is to take regular exercises & increase it by slow degrees commensurate with your increase in strength, and if you are in that delicate condition might it not be well not to take so much brandy? I ask this as a question only.

Keep your courage up my wife & don't write such blue letters to me, trust in God. He is good and you will be all right soon. Keep up your spirits for I know how much your health is affected by the imagination, if you have such blue advisers & such Job's Comforters. Why Bess you must make your arrangements to go off with me in a very few days after I see you. You know you have promised me this to go away with me at any time I say, & I will take you where Dr. Campbell can have a chance to muse you & make your little body & mind both easy.

Good bye now darling. Don't you give way to the blues. Keep up a brave heart and be fat & well to welcome your Husband.

New Orleans La. May 17th (1866)

My Darling Wife,

Your letter postmarked the 12th & written the eleventh is at hand, and the brighter & more hopeful tone of this letter relieves me very much for there is nothing at all the matter with you, except the weakness induced by such serious & frequent attacks of sickness. Why all that astonishes me is that you have recovrd. so fast. I would have been no doubt a longer time getting well myself strong & well as I am naturally. I got a letter from your father the 12th & it was a comfort to me indeed. He is a man of sense. Who had your lungs sounded? Oh Bess I miss you so much more & more every day, and yesterday as I was walking up Prytania Street I met Mrs. Gregory & it struck me all at once that I could pass away a part of my time walking around showing the old lady the city. So, I took her & we went to Canal & there got in the Levee & Barracks Cars & rode down to Jackson Square & she thought that the horse Jackson is on was rearing up too high. We went over to the Cathedral and heard some fine music & when we went to come out the doors were all locked & it was almost dark & the old lady flew around at a great rate & looked for an exit, but I knew of a side door & we made our escape in that way & then we wnt up Royal & she went into a store to see the huge wax candles they have in some of the windows to be used for burials & high mass &c. and she greatly admired the false hair in the windows of the *coiffeurs*, and then I persuaded her to go into a gift store & try her luck & she did so & got a breastpiece. I laughed at her impolitely & told her I was going to write to you & tell you she had become demoralized & had been caught gambling. But enough of this. She afforded amusement to me for an hour. I am very well darling and miss you so much. I shall get away from here & hope to see you in four weeks from today—it is seems an awful long time but I must close up some business here & make some money to get away from here on. I don't like to draw on Father. It is humiliating for a man to have to depend on any but God & himself. I must close now. Give my love to Maggie & tell her I was delighted with her letter & will answer it soon.

Your Husband

Glencoe May 17th, 1866 Thursday

My Dear Husband,

I did not get any letter from you last night, & you can not imagine how disappointed I felt & how perfectly lost without it. I suppose the horrid old mails have gotten out of order, & if they don't get in order very soon you will have to come yourself for I can not & will not stand it being separated from you & not hearing from you either is a little too much. Father expected to leave for Oceola yesterday but Maggie was not very well & Mother sent a note in by Neal to recall him, & so he came out but expected to go in today. But afterwards concluded as he had no especial business he would stay out & so he had made no arrangements to have the letters sent out & so I will not get any tonight either, & tomorrow will be three days. But I think I will get two tomorrow evening but it seems so long since I have heard from you. The 11th is the last date. My chill made me a desperate effort to come on today but I was well fortified with quinine, & missed it. My health is very good now but I am not gaining any flesh. The large dose of calomil that I took immediately after I reached home took about 10 or 12 pounds off & you know I hadn't that much to spare. But so long as I feel well I don't care for the flesh except for your sake. The weather cleared off beautifully about 12 oclock & after dinner Mother & I took a long drive. We first went to see poor Kate McGibbon. You remember the girl who served for me last Fall. The poor thing is dying of consumption will not live through the Summer. So we left her a little basket of strawberries, & then went up to old Mrs. Graham's to get some spring chickens. We have just returned, & are sitting on the front porch. Father & R.K. went fishing but caught no fish & have just gotten back. It is a most lovely evening, & everything looks so fresh & lovely after the rain. It is just 6 oclock, & the train from town has just stopped at the depot. I have been reading "Ten Thusand a Year" to day. It is a very amusing book. Of chere' I get to thinking about such unpleasant things some times, & I do long so earnestly for your living presence & faithful love to dispel all such miserable haunting ghosts of the past. The tea bell is ringing & I will finish before I go to bed, 9 oclock.

After tea we all walked up in the garden & staid a few minutes, & after talking an hour or so in my room we had prayers & are now about to retire. A.L. sleeps with me, & I make Bede sleep on the lounge as there is no one else on this side of the house. Good night darling. I read the last chapter of Romans last night & tonight I go on with Corinthians. I pray so earnestly for you every night.

What a comfort religion is. Good bye my own darling husband

Your wife

New Orleans, May 18, 1866

My Darling Wife,

The time is passing away surely but very slowly, when I shall see you & clasp you in my arms again. You do not know how much & how often I think of you. But Bess I do miss you so much I hardly see how I can stay here long enough to wind up the business I have already on hand.

I got your letter directed to Mrs. Fee out of the office. It was postmarked the 14th & came very quickly, but I got none myself, and will have to content myself with hearing from Mrs. F. how you are &c. It is very cool here today & was so yesterday, and I have a little sore throat but if it is not well tonight I will take a little chlorate of potash & cure it. My general health is very good, better a great deal than it was last week.

You must not be mad at me for writing scolding letters to you, for you know all of my warmth grew out of my love & anxiety for you. I have been doing pretty well since you left in the way of getting cases, but have made very little ready money, but all of these cases will bring the money when they are decided. I forgot to tell you the news around home. Mrs. Tarlton, Dr. Jones says, will probably lose her baby. It has something the matter with its head, and has convulsions & is sinking fast. Mrs. Clark & her child look finely. Annie Given has been getting well & is going about again tho' little Henry is not at all well. The Dr. says he has intermittent fever, but I believe that he is sick because they allow him to stuff so. I have devoted two afternoons to Mrs. Gregory, and she expressed herself rightly gratified & pleased with what she saw. I took her aboard of a ship, & you know she is great on ships but she bored me the last time & I am not going to take her out any more.

I suppose by the time you get this you will have recd. the bananas I sent by Vander & in this connection, I will tell you but don't say anything to your Mother or anyone about it. Vanderford has a power of attorney to collect these claims your Uncle Jimmie sent to me, & in that he agreed to give Vanderford one half of all he can make. He wished to assist me & give me some thing to do &c. & offered me ¼ of all I could make, I paying all expenses. His kindness is overpowering. He was much more generous to Vanderford. His name instead of James M. ought to have been James Liberal Hamilton. I must now close. Good Bye darling,

Your Own Loving Husband

> *Glencoe*
> *May 19th, 1866 Saturday*

My Darling Husband,

I am getting more & more anxious to see you each day that passes & if you dont start by the first June I can not stand it. But I know you will Cheri. It is three weeks to day since I left N.O. & oh what an age it seems. That morning of the day I left when I was so cross to you & behaved so unreasonably & wickedly seems like some thing that happened a year ago. How patient & forgiving you were with me that day you darling thing. I shall never forget it. You say in your last letter that, that I would have been just as well in N. O. & you wish I had not left. That is rather a good joke. When you were the moving spirit in the whole matter the first one to propose my leaving the very one who hurried the matter up, & finally packed me at a few hours notice. A great deal sooner than I wanted to come—but I think it has really done me good. Oh! I got such a delicious long letter from you on yesterday evening written last Sunday (13th) & Monday. I have read it over five or six times. Having my lungs examined was entirely my own notion neither Mother nor Mr. K. knew any thing about it until I spoke to the Dr. myself. We took a long ride this morning up to the chicken woman's on the Melrose Road. I lay back in the buggy & think of you on these roads where we used to go together.

Good Bye dearest. I am very much hurried this evening as I have to send this in by the evening train & it is much later than I thought. Mr. Jarret went in this morning, says he will come out again & bring Dr. Hendricks. I suppose all the conservative Southern members will be sent away, isn't it outrageous.

Good Bye, Your own own loving wife

New Orleans, La. May 19th (1866)

My Most Prescious Wife,

This morning your letter written on Sunday the 13th is received and it was so sweet, so satisfactory, & filled my idea exactly of what a wife should write to her Husband. It made me feel so happy to get another letter from you full from shadows & vague fears for yourself. At the same time I had a letter from Mary & one from Florence, but all my relations & friends seem as nothing in comparison with you. I did not believe 15 months ago that I could ever be so entirely in love with any woman.

I was a little disappointed that I did not hear from you yesterday, but Mrs. Fee sent me the letter written to her, and that was some consolation. I would be glad to have a letter from you every day & a long one two, but I don't want you to write if it tires you and don't you waste the strength that ought to be devoted to me in writing to your female correspondents. Last night after tea I went down town & dropped a card on Genl. Wheeler & his wife. They were not at home and I also called to see a gentleman from Paducah at the St. Charles, and stayed there till about half past eight & came home & read the third chapter of Corinthians. Last night was the 19th night since I left you & it seems to me a much longer time. Uncle Henry was suffering a little yesterday from a hammering in the head. You know he is sometimes threatened with apoplexy. I did not see Annie Given, but I talked with Mrs. Gregory a little while I was waiting for the Baronne Street Cars. The weather is a good deal warmer today than it has been for two or three days past. have come to prefer these bright sunny days with a lively breeze, for I always feel better on such days. I feel the heavy musky weather more than most people. It has a corresponding influence on my spirits.

My eyes are a great deal better and stronger than they were when you left me. I will bear in mind your request about the shawl &c. If I can find any nice Pine Apples today I will send you some on the Olive Branch. The health of the city as far as I can hear is very good.

Now Bess don't you ever get low spirited again while you are away from me for it almost runs me mad for you to be unhappy away from me.

Your Own Loving Husband

New Orleans, May 20th, 1866

My Darling Wife,

    Your letter of the 15th is received & it is low spirited & blue. You must not get low spirited for it is not conducive to health to have your spirits below zero. You see if you are not right well very soon after having been sick. You must not be surprised at it, and what if you are dark under the eyes, were you not just as dark under the eyes here as you are now, and didn't you get over it? I know you have an absurd idea that you are ugly & all that, and I have seen you whirl away from the glass saying, "I am so ugly," when I didn't at all agree with you. Don't let your appearance distress you as long as you are improving in health every day. You wish to see me almost as much as I do you, and I intend to get away from here in about fifteen or 20 days, and hurry to my own darling precious little Bess. I groaned in the spirit this morning when I thought it would be yet so long before I would see you. I will telegraph you tomorrow to let you know how I am & that there is no cholera here or anything like it. The health of the city is excellent, and all the doctors say that there is no danger of cholera here during "the hot weather." I will let you know how the case that you speak of turns out.

    Bess I would give almost anything in the world to see you this bright pleasant Sunday morning. Sunday is getting to be a blessed day to me, for its own sake. I feel that I am becoming a better man every day, & every night I pray for your restoration to health & strength. I have read a chapter every night & am in Corinthians now. I feel that God will preserve you & make you right again, but darling don't let the irregularity of your courses trouble you, for if there is no natural reason for its stoppage, you will soon be all right again, and if there is a reason for it, you will know it before long. I think that there is great probability that there is a good natural reason for it. I have stopped at my office before church to write this to you, and will go to the P.O. & mail it & this afternoon I will write more to you. I sent you 8 nice Pine apples by the porter of the Olive Branch, and he promised to deliver them to Bess, Woods Christy & Co. Now Bess Good Bye,

                     Your Own Loving Husband
                     Given

Glencoe
May 20th 1866
Sunday

My Own Darling Husband,

All day yesterday I enjoyed the idea of getting a letter from you in the evening, & when finally the cars arrived I sent John down post haste. Father left yesterday for Osceola, & consequently did not come out but sent a bundle out which I opened in great haste found a newspaper enclosing two letters for Mother, one for me from Carrie, a Presbyterian Index forwarded by you but no letter. Oh! I was so much disappointed. I would even open the paper, & didn't half read Carrie's letter & could have cried if I hadn't been ashamed. Oh I felt disconsolate, & at last the tea bell rang. At first I felt no appetite until I got to laughing so immoderately at a ludicrous mistake Mr. Graham made through his deafness, poor old man, that I finally got over my disappointment & finally dispatched two or three biscuits, a soft boiled egg, a slice of ham, a cup of coffee & finally ended with a glass of fresh buttermilk & a heaping saucer of strawberries & cream, after which we adjourned to the front porch & soon afterwards Mr. G. took his departure (he brought me several spring chickens) leaving Mother the children &myself alone. We had some music & I read the papers to Mother & finally at half past nine, we retired feeling a little bit lonesome. Annie Lou is in town & we miss her very much. This morning just as we finished breakfast Dave Clarkson came. He is just at home for a day &returns tomorrow to Tenn. where he has a hope of striking oil. He is very much improved in personal appearance—is really quite handsome—he staid an hour or two, & finally we all went to ride, Neal driving Mother & myself & the children in the carriage & Mr. C. riding on horseback. We took quite a long drive, parted from him in the road, he returning home. We stopped & saw some of Mr. Hutchingson's fine horses. Angeline & Revellie. The first was beaten in the races just over last week. As we were coming home we met Jim Yeatman in his dog cart with his fine new mares, driving Hillis Sorkin & Willie McCree. We did not get home until 2 oclock & I took a toddy & had a good appetite for spring chickens, lamb & green peas & strawberries. Since dinner I have been reading the Bible, your old love letters, & the Presbyterian Index. But chere' it makes me *so mad* to think I have to be kept out of your letters when I know you have written them just through the carelessness of those provoking mail agents. Mother says I am very unreasonable, but I can not help it. I wont stay here away from you if the mails are going to get irregular this way for I cant stand the suspense. I wonder what you are doing this Sabbath day. I know you want me dreadfully & miss me more on Sunday than any other day. Maybe you are writing to your little Bess now like you were this time last Sunday. Darling I am so glad you went to church last Sunday morning & evening. Has Mrs. Fee received my letter yet? I am glad you have gotten your self a good supply of summer clothes for you didn't get a thing pretty last summer & you are so handsome & sweet when you get dressed up. It is worth while to take the trouble to do it & then you will have to do the dressing up & beautifying for both of us this summer for I am so ugly & thin now. I never feel like dressing in any thing but a wrapper. I had a very nice letter from Carrie which I will enclose as it has some little items of news that may interest you. We are having the most lovely weather but oh chere' I want to see you so much. This is the 20th & now it is only ten days will the First of June & then I look every day for you & if you dont come then— but oh darling I cannot bear to think of any longer separation from you my own dearest Husband. I am so dependent on you. It may be foolish but it is so & cant be helped now.

Good Bye Chere'.

I hope you are keeping this Sabbath day holy & God will bless you if you serve him.

Your own loving wife
Bess

Paducah, May 21/66

My Dear Bettie,

I have a few moments to spare before taking the Rail Road for Maryfield and feel that I could not use the time more pleasantly than in writing to you if only a short letter. You have had a hard time at N. Orleans my dear child but I ardently hope in your native climate of St. Louis you will soon recover your former good health. We expect Given to leave N. Orleans by first July and after a short stay there you & him must come over to Paducah. We have renovating our house & repairing the dilapidations of four years war. We have not any soldiers here & every thing is quiet & peaceful. I want Given in July to go to Virginia & see after my land there & I have an idea of going with him & taking my wife along & spending some days at a watering place. We look for our daughter Mary about first July and then with Given & you we will have all our children together under the family mansion a blessing vouchsafed to few. All the family write in sending their best love & with my best wishes to your father & mother & family I am truly yours

Very affectionately
J. Campbell

Paducah May 21/66

My Dear Son,

   I write only a few lines to let you know we are all well. There is nothing new. Our town is clear of soldiers & every thing is peaceable. Business here is like every where very dull. I have just written to Bettie that I look for you about first July. I intend to take your Mother on a trip some where in July. We have been a good deal troubled about servants & she has had a hard time & needs rest and recreation. Florence is spending a week at Turners, where she can riot in strawberries.

   We are all well. I have been busy in repairing the delapidations of four years war. We are all in fine health.

                                    Your Affectionate Father
                                    J. Campbell

Glencoe
May 21st, 1866
Monday

My Darling Husband,

I sent you in a letter by Hugh yesterday evening & have very little left to add today. One day here is very much like another. They all pass pleasantly but monotonously along—breakfast, a ride, a nap, dinner, a little talking reading, & writing then dressing, car time, a stroll in the garden, tea, music prayers, bed—This evening I am going down for Annie Lou who is the only person expected out this evening & it is now past 5 & I will have to write rather a short letter. I got interested in Little Bat's Adventures, & did not know it was so late.

I hope very earnestly for a letter from you this evening as I have not had one for two days but I will not be too sure of it as I might be disappointed again. I know that you write chere' but the mails are so irregular. Oh! aren't you most through with that tiresome law business. I do want to see you so much but you never say one word about when you are coming. I enclosed you a letter from Carrie yesterday. There is no news in the world to tell chere' at least I know none. I love you more & more every day & the more I see of other men the more entirely I see your superiority in every way.

Good bye my own dearest with a heart brimming full of love I will say Good Bye.

Your own Bess

Glencoe May 22nd, 1866 Tuesday

My Dearest Husband,

I have just finished reading over for the fourth or fifth time your letters received last evening by which I plainly perceive chere' that you are worrying your precious self very unnecessarily. I am acting only under the orders of a sensible cautious & experienced Dr., am improving every day & have never been doctored or dosed by Mother or any one else. But I trust are this those tiresome tardy mails have carried you some of my late letters, by which you will see that I am doing very well, & am as cheerful & happy as I can ever be away from my own old chere'. I was not conscious that I had ever written you a single line that could be called "blue low spirited & disconsolate." Please bring my letters with you for I want to see which one it is. I wrote a note to Cal. Christy last night requesting him to answer your dispatch which I received yesterday, & also to attend to the bananas. I hope they will get out here safely, & I am so much obliged to you for sending them chere'. We miss Father & Mr. Kirkman very much. It is quite dismal having no gentlemen about the house. We look for Father back the last of this week & Mr. Kirkman Sue & the children the first of June. Aunt Loulie has written for one to come on right away to join them & Nashville & go to the Buinanster Springs in Ky. Of course I do not think of going. I went in the buggy this morning with John & R.K. to Baldwin & bought a plough. Am I not getting to be a great business woman? I enjoyed the ride exceedingly. The morning was perfectly smooth & even. Now darling I am going to give you a regular scolding before I close my letter. Why do you sit down & write me two letters one six the other 4 pages & say *not one* word about your self. That is all I care about hearing of but not one word have you said in your last three letter relative to your dear self. I want you to tell me how you are, what you do, where you go, how you spend your time after dinner, when you are coming, about your business & in short all about your self. It is nearly car time & I believe I will drive down for Annie Lou & I hope to get a letter from you dearest with something else in it besides my own health. Oh! Darling I want & long to see you so much. Come just as soon as your business will allow it but do not neglect that for I do not really need you except for my own happiness, which is not quite so important as our living & your reputation, but I look for you the first week in June. Mother wrote you this morning.

Your Own Little Bess.

Give my love to all at Mrs. Fee's, & be sure & kiss Charlie for me.

After tea.

Good night Darling. I got your two precious letters 14th & 18th this evening. I will write you a long letter tomorrow.

Your Loving Devoted Wife

After Supper.

I drove down for Annie Lou darling, & also to take my letter to the mail train but got there too late for it, & so had to bring them back & wait until morning, so I will add a few lines. A.L. brought out two letters from you 15 & 16, & also a dispatch of today saying you were well. It made my heart jump for I thought it must either be to say you were sick or on the way, & so I was both relieved & disappointed, but both feelings subsided into great delight at knowing that *this very day* you are safe & well. I am surprised at your letters chere'. I can not understand why you make such a fuss because I had my lungs examined. It cannot possibly do me any harm, & was entirely my own idea, not suggested by a human being, as to the cod liver oil I have never once thought of taking it, nor do I remember that any body has ever spoken of it to me since I have been at home. The toddies I will stop as you seem to disapprove of them so much, but they were advised by Dr. Johnson & I think one a day does me good. Mother has never proposed *one single thing* for me to take or do, & every thing I have done has been by Dr. J's orders. I am sorry you have taken up such very wrong impressions chere' but you will find out better when you come but in one thing you are exactly right, for I do want your shoulder & your arm more than any medicine or anything else for some times when I wake up in the night, or early in the morning, oh darling I do want to get into your arms & be hugged up close to you so much oh so much. I will write a note to Cal. Christy & get him to attend to answering your dispatch tomorrow & also to getting the bunch of bananas which you have sent. My mouth fairly waters for them now. Mother is just wearing her self in to the grave, altho. she has a full complement of excellent servants, it is really ridiculous & distressing to see the way she does. Chere' please keep my letters & bring them with you for I want to see what you call *the blues*. I have taken particular pains to write you cheerful letters & think I have done so. The Dr. says I don't need the Blue Lick while I am regular which I now am. I wish you would write me when you think of coming.

Good Night Darling
Your Own Loving Wife

These last letters are 5 & 6 days on the way.

N. Orleans, May 22nd 1866

My Dearest Darling Wife,

   I didn't get a letter from you today, but I got an answer to my dispatch on yesterday. I received two letters from you one the 15 and one the 16th. I will bear in mind all you say and answer some of your questions. I have not seen a very pretty woman since I saw you, but today when I got in the car there were sevl. gentlemen standing up, and after I had put the ticket in the box, a young lady very well dressed drew in her skirts and made room for me. I was so grateful I thought her right pretty.

   Mrs. Fee laughs at me for telegraphing you, but I don't care. Whenever I get uneasy I would give the pitiful some of five dollars to be satisfied you are well. You ask me if I still had those views from the side windows. No they are cut off, but last night I went on the gallery & could look into the brides window & saw her sit down in her husbands lap & kiss him & caress him, and hug him & he took it very patiently. She made a great deal more love to him than he to her, and to see it reminded me so much of when I used to have you in my lap, but then I always did the petting. I came in my room & did not continue to look. It made me mad to think that another man could have his wife &c. & I be deprived of my own Bess. I was up at Uncle Henrys yesterday for a little while & Annie G. & the family were all well. Mrs. Fee does not look like she would be sick for a long time. I saw Harry Courtenay. He asked after you & told me his wife had come down & invited me to come & see her. I am keeping a diary but I declare it is so foolish I don't believe I will show it to you. I came mighty near losing my dinner today for I had to attend to some steam boat cases for a man & it took me till late. I am getting new business every day. Bess I am going to write to you with a pencil here after, so that my letters will soon rub out, for you haven't written but one or two to me in ink, and I have them all in an envelope & keep them in my top drawer of the bureau. I will be sure & bring you the cinchonine & if I have good luck something else. I hope you have the bananas by this time, & you will get the Pine Apples on the "Olive Branch." Good Bye precious.

   Your Husband

May 23 (1866)

Bess I am going to scold you a little while the offence is fresh in my mind and will enclose this in my letter to you tomorrow. In your letter you get the blues and get to thinking about my past misdeeds &c., and in your darling little prescious mind the spectre of doubt shakes his wings. All this is very wrong darling. If you would consult the true heart in you, you would never doubt your Husband that loves you more & more as each day passes over his head and expects that that love will go on increasing this life & during the countless ages of eternity. You are the *solitary* occupant of my heart, and that tenement has been thoroughly cleaned out for you, and when you were given up the later possession of it, you were privileged to furnish it as best suited your pleasure, and my darling wife I don't think that you have hung up any portraits on its walls but images of your own sweet self. I am as truly & entirely yours as you are mine, and since you left I have never in my waking moments nor in the hours of my sleep thought a single time of any woman but you, and I tell you plainly, if the prettiest & nicest woman in the world (saving yourself) were to come into my room at night & desire to occupy my bed with me I would drive her away. My heart, my body & I would almost say my soul, is yours, & yours alone, and I think it is right unjust to your absent Husband to entertain any doubts of mine. Don't you know that I am obliged to tell you all I do, and don't you know I will now make it necessary to do anything to you that wd. make you at all unhappy. Cast your eye back over my conduct & treatment of you since we were in New Orleans and tell me wherein I have fail'd to try to make you happy, & if you will tell me I will amend my conduct in the future. Now Bess with the assurance of my perfect love & truth, you ought to be satisfied & if you are not then pray for wisdom from God, & he will enable you to see that you are wronging me.

I will write more tomorrow.

New Orleans, May 23rd 1866

My Darling Bess,

   I wrote a letter to you yesterday & intended to mail it but did not do so & today I will write another & enclose the two to you. It is nearly four weeks since you were wafted away from me, and I am beginning to get thinner and want to see you so badly. The fact is I need your presence to cheer me & comfort me for sometimes I have the blues and if I had you rub my head & tell me that I ought not to have them that I had nothing to give me the blues &c. I would soon very soon get over all such feelings. But thank Heaven it will not be a great while longer that I will live this lonely sort of a life for I shall make my arrangements to leave here by the 10th of June & will be in St. Louis about the Fifteenth. I am very much rejoiced to get the dispatch so emphatically announcing your improved state of health for I know you well enough to know you would not deceive me in that respect. Keep your courage up & try & get well & strong so that you can pet me when I come up, for I will take any quantity of petting & caressing. I feel now that if I was with you I would not leave you day or night for a month. I expect you will want to go off & shut yourself up with Susie in her room but you had as well make up your mind to the fact that when I come I claim your entire time & attention & if I find others intrenching on my rights I will take you off some where. I had a long talk with old Eliza in my room last night. All the family were out & she brought me tea up to my room on a waiter. She says she don't believe that Mrs. Fee is going away from home at all, and she talked a great deal about you. She said she liked your ways &c. Really she seems to be very much attached to you. She said she didn't want to see you the day you went away &c.

   I will be right busy till I leave here for I have a good many cases to try, and they all come on along about the 26th 28th 31 &c. I am doing quite well in law business, but my cases though all of them important are generally severely contested—I must close now Bess—you write some to me every day. I have not been to look for a letter yet at the office.

                                    Your devoted Husband

Glencoe May 23rd 1866
Wednesday

My Own Darling Husband,

I enjoyed your two letters that I received last evening so much because you told me all about your self, & your adventures with Mrs. G. at which I was highly amused. Tell her that I am afraid she is leading you terribly astray. Of course if such a good Methodist or Baptist (which ever she is) goes to gambling you will feel privileged to do so too. When I read that part of the letter where you said you would be with me in four weeks from that day (17) I laid the letter down & cried heartily-*four weeks* when I looked for you in two. Oh it seemed so long. I felt perfectly desolate & as always the minute I begin to feel unhappy I thought I would give every thing I had on earth to lay my head on your shoulder & cry out all my trouble chere', when suddenly it occurred to me that if I could put my head there I would not be in any trouble nor have any occassion to cry. I counted up the time & found that four weeks from the 17 would bring it to the 15 of June before you would reach here, & the 15 of June is just three weeks from Friday & from Friday week only two week, & then you will soon be on the way & after you are once started then I count it the same as if you were here so it is not so frightful as it seemed at first. I have to argue with my self this way all the time & by doing this way I feel reconciled but I wish I could go to sleep & not wake up until you come. My heart swelled with real pride when I read what you said about the humiliation of depending on any thing but God & your own strength. There is an independent manliness & a spirit of honest & noble pride about that feeling. That is perfectly charming to me, & makes me love you if it is possible more devotedly than ever. It is this feeling that reconciles me to this separation. When I think of this, I feel that it must be bourn. Life has stern duties as well as sweet pleasures & God has so ordained it that we can not fully enjoy the one unless we perform the other. I have left you now & it would be foolish to go back, but, hereafter, *I stay with you come what may*!!!!

I was perfectly disgusted with our lovely Uncle James. Has he written to you yet? I always knew he was intensely selfish but did not think him guilty of actual meanness. I am writing by my bed room window. It is the most peculiar kind of day, rather cloudy, & still bright, quite warm & yet a little too cool. The sky is neither blue nor gray & a soft low wind sighs unceasingly through the trees making the pink clover blossoms bow to each other with solemn dignity. Mother is in here with me reading. She has neither stirred nor spoken for two hours, marvelous! So absorbed is she in her book. The children have gone in town to spend the day with there dear man & Annie Lou to school. So we are all alone except the servants. I have just been looking at your ambrotype, the one you gave me just before you went to the war & I have come to the conclusion that it is as handsome a fellow as ever a fastidious young damsel fell headlong, desperately & irretrievably in love with. I am very sorry to hear about poor Mrs. Tarleton's little baby. I hope you have received the answer to the dispatch. You ought to have done so yesterday as Cal Christy wrote me he had sent it. It is very strange that you did not get a letter from me the same day that Mrs. Fee did as I wrote you at the same time & the letters must have gone in the same mail. Hugh has just brought me in the most beautiful bunch of roses I ever saw. They are blooming now in profusion. Your lovely & accomplished friend Mr. George Allen is in Nashville. I believe or was to be there to see to the setting up of Mr. Greenfield's estate—lovely creature: I suppose if I were to die he would be kindly providing you with another wife immediately. We took a short ride this morning & I am now as soon as I finish this going down for Annie Lou in the buggy. I have just been reading the 108 Psalm. Read it as soon as you this darling. The same night I mean. It is so beautiful every word of it. I wish I was there to go to church with you tonight. I have not heard from Florence yet but am still in hopes she will come. Good bye my heart's dearest love.

Your wife

Maggie was delighted with her letter.

New Orleans La. May 24, 66

My Darling Wife,

Your letter of the 18 came this morning, and it made my heart glad to see that you are again regaining your lost spirits & health. What were you writing to Dr. Johnson about? I am very busy today for a man has been in to see me to get me to defend 8 suits for him tomorrow & it will take a good deal of my time today to get ready and I have a case also for Saturday & two for Monday. So you see I am right much pressed for time today & can't write you much of a letter today. I miss you more & more every day & though I would make a great deal more by staying here till the first of July I have made up my mind to leave here by the tenth day of June. I cannot stand it away from you any longer. You must eat rich & healthy food & get a bloom in your cheeks & all that. I am very glad to hear that you have no cold or cough, but still you don't tell me why you had your lungs sounded. I believe that I know how that came to be done & at whose direction it was done. Miss Sally Fee left us last evening on the Henry Ames. I was right sorry to see the good servt. go. She seemed to think a great deal of you & I liked her for that though she was mortal ugly. I took a long ride yesterday down town & out Esplanade & over the Bayou Bridge & by the City Park & the Halfway House & back by Washington Avenue & I have felt fine all day today. You think no doubt I am very silly & extravagant sending dispatches when I get uneasy about you, but I would pay five dollars at any time to know you are well my darling. I will close now. Give my love to all.

Your loving Husband

Glencoe
May 24th 1866

My Dear Mr. Campbell,

I now sit down by my window to have my usual afternoon chat with you which I believe is the pleasantest part of the day to me. I did not get any letter from you last night which was a great disappointment although I know you wrote chere' & the letter will doubtless be here tonight. Cal Christy is very good about sending them out since Father is away. Annie Lou was left to day so we have had her company. My health is still improving, slowly however but of course I can not expect it to be otherwise & I am truly thankful to God that I am as well as I am. I enclose you a picture for you to see how much you think I have improved. I do so earnestly hope it is not warm in New Orleans. You must be careful darling to change your clothes with the weather and if you get the least bit sick chere' give up your business & come right to me, to your own little wife & I will muse you, & cure you right away.

After supper. I got your letter of the 19th this evening—a sweet precious letter—I am tired tonight but darling but I will write you a long letter tomorrow. I hope you wont send the pine apples as I have never gotten the bananas.

Good night my own darling

Yours lovingly Bess

Glencoe May 25th, 1866 Friday

My Precious Husband,

I sent you a letter this morning in by Annie Lou, but if you do not get your letters regularly now you must not think I do not write darling for I have no one to trust my letters to but Annie Lou, & she is so extremely careless & giddy that I don't feel at all sure she ever attends to their going. I have written you *every day* without missing a *single one* (except the day Mother wrote when I first arrived & I added a post script) & by rights you ought to have received a letter *every day.* I have not written to any one else excepting a very short letter to Charlie Berry, one to Mrs. Fee which I really felt that politeness & good feeling required, one to Florence & this morning one to Sister Mary, which I will have to endorse to you as I do not know her address, & now my correspondence is finished, except with you which I hope will soon be ended too by your veritable presence. It is two weeks & five days from to day before you will be here according to what you said in your letter of the 17th. I think I was more home sick to see you this morning than I ever was before since I have been away from you. I had such a vivid dream about you, saw you just as plainly as I ever did heard the sound of your voice saw your eyes so plainly felt the touch of your hand on mine, & then woke up, to know that you were more than a thousand miles away. Oh it was dreadful for a while but I didn't cry, but just got up & dressed myself, & felt very disconsolate all the morning, almost as if I had just parted from you. In my last letter I enclosed you my picture to let you see how you think I have improved you must write me what you think. I have just gotten to the 10 Chapter of First Corinthians. I mean that is the Chapter for tonight & it is so pleasant to me when I read it to feel that you will read the same one the same night.

Chere' be sure & don't forget your promise to me about smoking only three cigars a day. I am so glad. Your eyes are so much stronger now. Take good care of them chere'.

There is some talk about Charlotte Erwin being engaged & very soon to be married to a young Mr. Cline, but I think it very doubtful if the wedding ever comes off. Christie is getting so wild with standing in the stable & eating corn that I am afraid of him. I take very little pleasure in riding. Yesterday the shaft broke as we were coming up the hill, but Walter Sled was fortunately with us, & so no necks were broken, & after a few minutes Isaac came along with the cart & we got in. I clasped a rooster in my arms & we drove up in triumph. Good Bye dearest. Mother & Maggie both send love to you.

Your Own Loving Wife,
Bess

New Orleans May 25th (1866)

My Darling Wife,

Your letter written the 20th is received. It is too bad that the mails go so irregularly, & keep you from receiving the letters I have written to you. Why don't you write & tell me how you feel and all your little ailments if you have any. Have you any backache. or headaches, or darling are you free from all your aches. I will come up by the 10th that is I will leave here by that time and as I will go as soon as I can. Will reach you by the 15th. I am almost crazy to see you and if I could would leave here tomorrow. I think from the accounts you give me of yourself you ought to be regaining your lost flesh, for if you feel well & have a fine appetite there is nothing to prevent you from growing more fleshy unless you worry too much about your old goodfornothing Husband.

I had a visit from a charmg. & fascinating female yesterday. She called after dinner to see me, and she was very warm in her salutations & looked at me like she admired me, but told me she thought I had grown thinner since she saw me last. She is a widow and an old acquaintance. She asked me where my wife was & when I told her, & that you were well she smiled very pleasantly and asked me to come & see her. Now you jealous little thing don't you imagine that I intend to fall in love with her for I am faithful & true to you. Guess who it was? It was Mrs. McLaughlin, your old nurse who came to inquire how you were, & get me to try & find her a place to go up the river with some family to take care of the children. After she left I had a visit from Mr. Kennard, his wife has left him desolate too & he called to see me to sympathize with me. He made a proposition to me to go into partnership with him and though I haven't concluded, I have an idea of doing so for it will be advantageous when I have to leave here to go North to have some one to leave my business with. I have known him a long time and have always regarded him as a gentleman & you like his wife. If we unite in professional partnership the firm will be "Campbell & Kennard." He stayed till 9½ & then I read my chapter & prayed for you & went to bed and slept well and woke up with a good appetite.

I must close now Bess for it is almost time to go to the trial of some cases I have. I think of you my darling more & more every day. Just make up your mind to try & forget all the time between now & the 15 of June & about that time you will see what is left of me, for I have grown some what less fleshy & Mrs. Fee says it is because I grieve for you so much. I am getting your letters very regularly now & it is such a comfort to go to the P.O. & find a letter every morning.

Good Bye. Love to all.
Your Own
Given

New Orleans, La. May 26th, 1866

My Precious Wife,

Your letter of the 19th & marked Glencoe Station 21st is received. I think that if letters are held at the Glencoe Post Office for two days, it would be better to mail them at St. Louis.

This is a very warm day & I feel very well. Warm weather agrees with me. It brings out a free perspiration & that is always beneficial. Yesterday I was busy and missed getting my dinner, & I tell you I had a very hearty appetite, though at lunch I had devoured a whole sheephead fish & plate of soup. I would love to be with you now Bess, driving you about, & so you think that you have been benefitted by going up to Chillville. I hope Maggie has recovd. from there, & Anna Low too. I am almost afraid to go out there either in the morning or evening, and if I arrive in the morning I think I shall take the noon freight train so as to avoid the malasious air of the morning & evening. I sat and talked to Sister Fee till nearly nine o'clock & then went up & talked business to Uncle Henry a while and came back & took tea & went up & read my chapter &c. & went to bed to lie & think of you & wish for you till I went to sleep.

I haven't been out at all anywhere for some time & don't have any desire to. I sit & think of you, & it is singular how much absorbed I am in you. I hardly ever think of any one else. I will close now for a while.

Later.

Mrs. Gregory is going to leave this evening & take the lovely Miss Mary Frances with her. I will try & see her off.

We have watermelons. There were some on the fruit stands yesterday, and we have fresh ripe figs. Oh how I wish you were here to eat them with me. The fruit market is crowded with tropical fruits of all sorts. Bananas, plantain, pine apples, limes & lemons & oranges &c. coconuts &c. The weather has turned warmer again in earnest. I don't see how I can stay away from you till the 10th & if I can possibly get away before that time I intend to do so. I want to see you more today than at any time since you left & it is my chief pleasure to sit when I am alone & think of you & it almost makes me sick to feel that you are so far away from me. There was more truth in Mrs. Fee's jest than she thought there was, about my falling off grieving about you, when I get you back again I don't intend to leave you at all, and all day long you shall sit in my lap & kiss me & tell me that you love me & all night long you shall sleep in my arms. But Bess I am making this letter ridiculous, and you must not show it or read it to anyone. I am afraid the fruit I sent to you will spoil. The boats are making such slow trips.

I have no consolation now but to smoke & read my bible & it would amuse you to see how I economize a cigar. You know I promised you that I would not smoke but three a day and I tell you I always lay away one if it is only half smoked up to get the benefit of my three.

I gave Maggies letter to Mattie & she was perfectly delighted to get it. It is sad to see Mrs. Tarlton with her little sick baby. It has spasms every day & the Dr. has little or no hope of its recovery, but she nurses it all the time & won't allow any one else. I have not seen Uncle Henry or his family for two or three days. Carrie speaks in high praise of her son. I had a letter from Mary. She says she is very well and fatter than she has been since she was a girl. Dr. Pine says his wife is very delicate. I will stop now and write some more after a while. I haven't any more to write now for I have sevl. cases to try today.

Good Bye Love to all.

Your Own Husband,
G.

Glencoe May 26th 1866 Saturday

My Darling Husband,

Yesterday evening Mother & I drove down to the cars to get our papers & letters & were pleasantly surprised to find Father there. Jim Yeatman joined us, & came up to tea, & staid all night. I was charmed to get your two letters of the 20 &21, both written on Sunday, & the last mailed Monday. I also received a very nice letter from your Father which I shall answer very soon. He says he wants you to go to Virginia to see about those lands the middle of July but I give you fair warning now Chere' that if you go you might as well make up your mind to take me, for the idea of giving you again so soon for another six weeks is perfectly out of the question. I might as well not have any of your time at all. I have had enough of separation. Your Father reported all well in Paducah. This morning the Misses Whittaker & then brother Frank came out to spend the day. Also a large pic nic party of young ladies & gentlemen came out to Jim Yeatman, & when the train drew up at the depot the most furious storm was raging that I ever experienced. It blew, thundered lightened & poured in torrents. Our carriage brought up the Misses W. but the unfortunate pic nicers were at the mercy of the storm until Neal returned & took them over to Jimmie's by installments. The Misses W. seem to be very nice well bred good hearted girls, a little over dressed, but on the whole I liked them. They go in this evening, & I will get young Whittaker to take this letter.

The time as you say is passing surly but oh *so slowly* away until we meet again. I count every day with joy, & my last thought at night is that one more day has passed. I am so sorry to hear that I have written you another blue letter. I really was not conscious of it at the time, & still think you must have given your own coloring to my words, but I am so entirely in the habit of opening my whole heart to you & telling you every foolish little thing that I may have let out some little fears that happened to be troubling me at the moment & now you see what it is to spoil your wife. It is now 5 oclock. The storm has passed off, & left as lovely a May day as you can well imagine. Oh! how I long for you this evening to take a ride. It seems to me that I did not half appreciate the happiness of having you with me every day when it was so. Just one glimpse of you now I would consider the most precious boon. I wonder what you are doing just *right now,* try & remember chere' when you get this & let me know. I have a peculiar feeling about it. Do you still keep your journal? Good bye darling, my own precious Husband. I trust you under the shadow of God's wings. If it were not for that I would be always thinking something was happening to you. They are drinking coffee on the porch & I must go & get some.

Good bye, Your Own Loving Bess

May 27th (1866)
Sunday After Church

My Dearest Wife,

I received your letter of the 21st and was glad to hear that you were well &c. and sorry & glad too that you miss me so much. I don't want you to worry about me & then if you did not always want me I would not like it much either, for you do not know how much *I do* want you. There is communion at the church opposite & the servers are all come out & have left the communicants to remain till it is over. I did not go to Dr. Palmer's church today. It was so hot. But I went to the Josephine Street Church & heard a very very dull sermon & a prayer that would rival Dr. Whites longest ones. It has cured me from going to hear any one else when I can hear Palmer. It is a great treat to a finely educated mind and edifying to a Christian no matter how simple.

This is a beautiful day & everything looks peaceful & sweet & quiet up here. There are Va. trellises of flowers that you have never seen, and right under our window that looks towards Mrs. Tarltons is a beautiful crape myrtle tree in full bloom. It reminds me of that tree at the end of our room at Columbus, Miss. at Col. Longs, but that was a mimosa. Mrs. Tarltons little child after struggling a long time for life was finally given up to its God last night. This was the first child she ever lost & it goes hard with her.

I have seen Leigh Wickham from Saint Louis, and he gave me the St. Louis news. His account of the Washington & Sonlard trouble was much worse than I had heard. From his accounts the man must be a *cowardly devil.* Suppose Bess you had such a husband as that? Wouldn't you be afraid to get into a pet? And be cross & perverse? You sweetest thing don't you know that I love your very faults? And I don't care if you do get a little cross, it only gives me a chance to be good to you & not to get mad at you, but to make you pleased & love me more at the end of the little storm. You are the most lovable & lovely woman I ever saw & as you are away from me, I look at you more in the perspective, and can see the tout ensemble of your beauties & graces more distinctly. But you must get well & strong so that I won't have to be scared about you when I want you to go with me, and though you say you give up the toddies because I am so desperately opposed to them yet if you will remember I only threw out a suggestion, & if they do you good & the Dr. prescribes them why then you do as he says. He ought to know better than I. If I am unjust to any one I am sorry for it?

I never forget to do anything for you and on yesterday, just as I had got through some troublesome business with my head all rumpled & no vest in I went into a photographic gallery & asked the man if he could take my picture right away. He said he could, and he told me to go into the dressing room & fix up. I told him I had none to do & to be quick. He took it on porcelain as you wished & he said it was excellent, and I showed it to old Eliza & she said it is just as much like me as anything can be. I think it is too but may be a shade too serious, but it was just as I looked & you wanted one just as I was. The eyes are very well taken. I will bring it up to you. I had a letter from your Father on business from Osceola, Arks. I will attend to it. I argued a case yesterday in the 3d. Dist. Court & was busy till 8 o'clock at night trying cases before a Justice of the Peace, and I came home hot & worried & had a head ache, and as I sat out on the gallery rubbing my head I thought how nice it would be to lie down & put my head in your lap & let you mesmerise all its ache by the touch of your fingers. You can tell Susan that she had better come over & get her satisfaction of you before I come up for I tell her and everybody else I will claim my unimpeached & unalienable rights to my wifes exclusive society whener I wish it. I don't intend to stand on any ceremony about it at all. If they were not prepared for it, they ought not to have allowed you to fall in love with me & marry me. Some people I know of didn't want it to take place *very much*. But they couldn't help it could they Bess. It is time, "Man proposes, but God disposes," and you & I were intended for each other, and I hope in Gods good providence we may live together for 50 years to come— whilst I am writing I am sitting by the table by the front window with my ink before me & a pitcher of ice water before me also. Old Eliza always has ice water for me when I come home—she attends to me very well & quarrels with Margerite if my clothes are not washed in nice order. Little Mattie Tarlton came over this morning after flowers to put on her little brother's grave, and she looked so sad. Mr. Fee has been very kind to Mrs. Tarlton. She is a good hearted woman. Mrs. Bruff has a daughter 10 pounder. Mrs. "Weeler" & her interesting family have just left the house. I will close this for the present as I smell dinner very strong.

As I was going down Canal St. yesterday a man came whizzing by me as fast as he could run, and behind him came a heavy fat lubberly looking fellow hollowing in unmistakable tones "Stop that Thief." I would not have recognized the heavy going craft if I hadn't heard the voice. It was "Amos" of the mocking bird celebrity. He was bareheaded & had a pair of pants under his arm, & the last I saw of them he was still bellowing stop thief & the thief wasn't stopping. It is 2 ¼ o'clock & Beckwiths Church is just out. He ought not to keep church so late these hot days. If Maggie was here she would be washing, but the hot weather agrees with me & I always feel better on hot days. I am I think getting thinner & when I come up I am sure that you will say I am just right. I think after dinner I will go up & see Uncle Henry & his fair wife for a little while. I have not been there for two or three days. I expect she is very lonesome now, for her Mother & sister have left her. It was amusing to look at some of Mrs. Gregory's baggage. She had some plaster of Paris images and a couple of plaster of Paris vases she was going to take up to some of her numerous progeny. It may have been to "Tho's Uncle, Dr. Stone" the gentleman who has his photograph taken with his hand up to his head. Business has been dull with me for a few days. The thermometer was near 100. Yesterday & last night it was very warm till about 10. & then the breeze sprang up fresh from the gulf, and it was delightful. We have had a fine breeze all day. The Drs. all say that we can't have cholera here in the summers. I don't know the reason why but they announce it as a fact & you may rest easy on that point. You are the sweetest darling in this world, ain't you? Now the dinner bell is ringing & I will cut off this long letter. I hope it won't bore you. I am going to church tonight if nothing prevents. I am very well today & hunger.

So good bye my darling.

> Your loving Husband
> Given

Glencoe
May 27th, 1866
Sunday Morning

My Darling Husband,

We woke up this morning to find ourselves in the midst of Winter. It is really a black day. The sky is dark & lowering & the wind whistles through the trees & then dies off in the most profound sights & groans. We have fires all over the house & it is hard to believe it is a May day. I sent you in four pages by Frank Whittaker yesterday evening & when the carriage returned from the depot after taking the young ladies & brought no letter from you I was, as usual, sorry, furious, ready to cry & fight both. Father didn't come out & there was no one here for tea but Mr. Graham. This morning Father came & with him Mr. Whittaker, young Mr. Jim Whittaker & horrible to relate "old George Moore" who is as thin, smiling & prosy as ever. Father brought me out your two previous letters of the 22 & 23 both enclosed in the same envelope which he got out of the office last night. The idea of your saying I am almost as anxious to see you as you are to see me. You could not *possibly* want to see me as much as I do you. You are not as dependent on me as I am on you & you have your business to absorb & interest you which I have not. You may just measure your desire to see me & then *treble* it, & you have mine to see you. It is now 1 oclock, just four weeks since we parted from each other to the very *hour*, & oh doesn't it seem like as many months. I would not go over the misery I endured that day for a great deal. I told you in my last letter about receiving a letter from your Father & his saying he wanted you to start the first of July to Virginia but I tell you now chere' that if you go, I am going too, sick or well, for I cannot stand another long separation from you again so soon. I have been reading in Ruth this morning & she exactly & exquisitely expresses my own fixed resolution "whither thru grist I will go, & where thou lodgest I will lodge." I write you every day of my life without fail, generally four pages but it seems to me you dont get half my letters which would not be much of a loss to any body else, but I know it is to you, & it is quite provoking. I wrote & enclosed you a letter from Carrie & at another time my picture. Did you get those? I also enclosed you a letter for Sister Mary the other day as I dont know her address, & then some time ago (a week or two), I enclosed you a letter sent to you about some land in Jefferson City. Did you get those? The bananas have never been heard from. I have been eating those delicious pink & white cherries this morning. We have such quantities of them. The picnicers all went in last evening tipsy. The gentlemen I mean of course, & the girls had no married lady with them. Wasn't it disgraceful? Jim insisted up Mother & I going over & then wrote up another note in the middle of the day but of course we did not go. Next Friday is the first June & then in two days you start. Oh! isn't it delightful to think that this dreadful time is almost over. You need not fear about not getting enough petting. I will be only too thankful for the chance to put my arms around your neck & kiss your precious rough cheek & rub your head to miss one single opportunity. I will now go out in the hall as dinner is very nearly ready & finish after dinner.

After dinner
4 oclock

Well darling after going through with an endless dinner, any amount of drinking sherry mediera & claret any amount of anecdotes & any amount of laughter, we adjourned & then came a long prosy talk with George Moore, who informed me in a tone of deep compassion that I was looking very badly. At last he concluded to follow the rest of the gentlemen on to the porch & I retreated in haste to my room, & to a renewal of my pleasant talk with you. Mr. Moore & I drank your health at the table & to your speedy arrival which made him a little endurable for the moment. They say those young men at the picnic behaved shamefully on the cars going in town, threw water all over the passengers & the young ladies, took the water boy & his can & put him out of the window, &c. & now another bit of gossip, Lizzie Giles (is said) to have separated from her husband & is now here at Mrs. Bridell's, though keeping very quiet. When they were here last winter living in such style at the Lindell, he paid none of his bills & when they left Mr. Bridell & one or two other friends of Mrs. Giles had to unite & pay their hotel bill to keep him from being sued. The last part of the story is positively true but I dont know about the separation.

Well chere' I do wonder how you are spending this Sabbath afternoon. I hope you will read a good deal in the Bible & then write a long letter to me. It is very cosy & smug in here, a warm fire in the stove. I am sitting by the window in my rocking chair with my feet on the bed & oh would'nt it be nice if you were in here with me, & instead of writing to you I could be talking & listening to you & probably you would be in the rocking chair & I in your lap. I am surprised to hear you say that Mrs. Fee will not be sick for so long but I think you are mistaken but I suppose you think your self very learned in such matters now. Chere' hasn't God been good to us to keep you safe & well & to let me get better. Oh! I feel that I am so unworthy of such benefits & such mercy. I have to pray all the time for strength to love Him more. It made me so happy to hear you say that Sunday is becoming such a pleasant day to you for its own sake. I think that is one of the truest signs of a genuine Christian & I thank God every night that you are so good & so true to the principles which Christ taught. I think I will try & take a walk this afternoon after I am done writing altho it looks so unpromising. I feel very well indeed to day but still I am gaining no flesh rather it seems to me losing. My face looks *so* sharp & peaked & my eyes have such blue rings under them. But still I feel well & am well & it is only for your sake that I care about looking so badly. Now dont callthis being blue for I am not at all uneasy about my self but you know chere' I tell everything to you. I am glad to hear you are getting more business but now chere' please dont take any cases that will keep you chere' after the 10 of June because my heart is fixed up on your coming then. Blow's large drug store, on Maine St. opposite to Father's office burned up last night but fortunately none of the other buildings in the street. They were fully insured. We look for Sue & Mr. K. on Tuesday or Wednesday. Sue has gotten pretty well again. But I must close this long letter; though I feel as though I could write on until dark. Did the lovely Mrs. Dreau offer to kiss you last Sunday when you dined at your Uncle Henry's? But I suppose she had Captain Bradford to kiss & was satisfied. Be sure & keep your journal every day & bring it to me. Has Miss Sallie gone yet? If not give her my best love.

Good Bye darling. I will only have to pass two more Sundays without you, God willing.

Your own loving wife

You see I took your hint about writing with a pencil. Have any of the letters been rubbed out before you got them?

Good night chere'. It is 9 oclock & I am just going to bed. It is very cold tonight.

Good Bye
Your Own Bess

New Orleans, La. May 28th (1866)

My Prescious Darling Wife,

   I have been so busy all day today that I have had no time till now to write you a line. While I am now writing it is raining heavily and has been blowing still harder. It is a very bad night to be on the sea. This has been a very hot day & it is now so cool since this weather arose that I have to close the windows. I haven't been at court all day. This morning I went into the 3d. Dist. Court & the clerk told me that the judge had decided my case in my favor which I argued on Saturday. Then in the 4th Court came up the case of the Bk. of Ky. vs. Goodale in which I was opposed by Rozelius Phillips & Hunt. I argued the case before the judge for more than an hour & I think made a favourable impression though the judge at the beginning intimated that we had not a good case. But I think I turned him & we shall see when he gives his opinion. Then I had another case to come up, but after a while not being ready fortunately we had it continued. And after I came to my office. I was making out a brief of authorities in a case for the judge. I was delighted to get yours & your Mothers letters, in both of which I find assurances of your health & improvement. I think of you more than I ought and sometimes am really afraid that something will happen to you. Last night I went to hear the Dr. preach & in the cars saw Judge Lackland. He has just returned from Texas and doesn't look much better. He said to me, "My career as a lawyer is ended." I felt so sorry for him. He asked about you and if you had gone up &c. I told him, & also told him why you hadn't called to see Mrs. Singleton & he said he would explain it to her. It is getting late now Bess & I must go down & mail this to you so that it will go out tomorrow.

   Good bye my dearest wife & love to all. I had a letter from Father today.

Your Husband, G.

Glencoe
May 28th 1866
Monday

My Dear Given,

  I wrote you a long letter yesterday which went in this morning & to day I have nothing in the world left to tell you except that I love you, I love you, I love you & that darling I am sure you must know but oh we have had such a dismal day. I can not describe it. The gentlemen all went in this morning & it has been steadily raining a cold, penetrating drizzle so that I have not dared to poke my nose out. I had nothing to read, & ransacked every corner & bookshelf in vain. So I fell back on the Sunday Republican which had a very funny letter from "Bill Arp." I then ripped up an old dress in sheer desperation & finally took a nap till dinner. It is now time to dress for the evening. It is 5 oclock & the sun has come out gloriously, so I will drive down to the depot in the carriage to get a little air. I do hope that we will have no more of this gloomy weather.

  Oh darling I want to see you so dreadfully. I think I will be better satisfied & more patient after this month is out, for then I will have only ten days to wait. Now chere' please dont put it off any longer than that. There is literally no news to tell you that I know of & you must excuse such dull letters. Oh! Yes there is one delightful piece of news. George Leighton has been slapped in the face & otherwise grossly insulted by Tom Ratcliff, one of the men he had with any cause imprisoned for six months during his provost marshal days here. Leighton said not a word. Ratcliff told him he was a nonentity, had done nothing but marry a rich man's daughter & many other much worse things which I don't remember & then ended by saying he would give him a whipping every time he met him. The next day Leighton wrote a note of apology to Ratcliff for having him imprisoned, said he regretted it, & begged the matter might be allowed to drop. Leighton is a man of spirit. I do hope I will get a letter tonight from you. I will finish this after tea. Good Bye.

Just before tea.

  Well chere' I went to the depot, met Father & drove right back. Father brought me out the pine apples —one had to be thrown away and two or three of these are decayed. The rest smell delicious. But I got no letter at which I was disappointed but I will get one surely tomorrow.

      Good Bye
      My Darling
      Your Bess

New Orleans, May 29th 1866

My Darling Wife,

I am very tired, having just returned from the Court House. I argued the case in which Rozelius & Phillips & Hunt were employed against me on yesterday and the court after taking all night to consider it, gave a judgement in favor of my client for the full amount claimed. This was a gratification to me more particularly because the judge, when the argument of the case was begun, was against me in opinion & said so, but after he heard my argument & read the brief I presented to him, he changed his mind. I was also successful in another case when success looked remote. I am working very hard for a reputation here & think that I am succeeding. I got another law client today a large Mercantile House here.

I will leave here certainly & surely on or before the 10th day of June, and you may look for me about the 15th. Your letter of the 23rd is received. I am sorry you did not get the bananas, for Vanderford told me he would see them delivered. They were fine ones & the fruit man said they would keep 9 days. I am proud of you too my darling wife that you have sense enough to appreciate the stern duties of life. If I could conscientiously do so I would never leave you at all, and I am glad to hear you say you do not intend to leave me any more. I want to see you all the time, day & night, and it is very slow rolling away of time. Now it is twelve days before I will leave here not counting today.

You must take good care of yourself until I can come & see you, and take care of you. I took tea at "Aunt Annas" last night. She kicks up at having tea, but Uncle Henry insists on it.

I believe that she is very fond of him and the baby is growing to be right pretty. I will close now Bess. Give my love to all the family, and remember me in your prayers.

> Your loving Husband
> Given Campbell

Glencoe, May 29th 1866 Tuesday

My Darling Husband,

Another day & still no letter. Well chere' I just can not stand this any longer. If the mails continue in this condition of irregularity you will have to come to me or I must go to you, & that is just the amount of it. It is painful & terrible enough to be separated from you, even when I hear every day, but it is now nearly a week, & not a word or line from you. I am tortured with fears & anxiety for you. I can see pictures of you lying ill & alone, & oh darling it wrings my very soul with anguish for a moment, & then I think of my dear Father in heaven, & put all my trust in him. He is always with you, & has promised to take care of you, & then I feel happy again. I have been busy all day, & this evening it came time to go to ride before I had written you & we did not get back until tea time, & thus I am writing after supper so can not write you a very long letter. Sue Mr. K. & the children all arrived this evening. Sue looks only pretty well. Uncle Jim Hamilton will be here day after tomorrow. I will not be at all glad to see him, & intend to treat his lordship very coolly. Mother is playing & all the children are dancing, & making a great racket. Neither of the gentlemen, not Annie Lou go in tomorrow, so I shall go in myself, to get your letter if there is one, as I am afraid to trust to the young men at the office, & on the cars, when it has to pass through so many hands it might get lost. Charlotte is to be married in the Fall to John Cline.

Good night my own dearest darling. Lou has come in to bed. I will pray for you tonight with all my soul. I am so thankful I have a Power, higher, than any on Earth to trust, you to, it is such a comfort to rest on Him.

Your Own Loving Wife.

P.S. I forgot to tell you that I am very well indeed. *Thin as a rail* but I feel very well.

Your Bess

I wrote you 4 pages yesterday.

New Orleans, May 30th, 1866

My Darling Bess,

  I will write you a short letter today, and make amends some other time. It is now very cool & I have on my woolen clothes & am sitting by a good fire in my office, blowing my nose every half minute on the silk handkerchief you gave me. It was stormy & rainy day before yesterday after dinner & the thermometer fell from 95° to about 70° and I was very thinly clad & caught cold & as usual it fell into my head, being the weak part, and I would not be surprised when you see me if my nose is not as much disfigured as at any former time. The condition of it is very promising for a bill. But I will be very gentle with it. I am very well indeed except for this cold in my head. I have had no letter from you today, & I have been getting them so regularly that I am spoilt. I will answer your mothers letter very soon. I was quite busy all day yesterday, but today I will be more at leisure having only to take some depositions. Your deposit fund has accumulated rapidly & now I find that the little envelope has $32.00 dollars in it, quite enough to buy you something nice isn't it, and beside the photograph is paid for out of it too.

  It is raining now, a cold bleak November rain, and it is just such weather as this that give's me the blues, so dreadfully, but I don't intend to have them at all. Just think Bess it is now only 11 days till I leave here to meet you, and I hope they will pass swiftly away. I have no local news at all. I will close now. Give my love to all, & remember your loving Husband,

      Given

Glencoe
May 30th, 1866 Wednesday

My Dear Darling Husband,

I wrote you yesterday & as neither Father nor Mr. K. went in, sent it by A.L. I intended to go in myself & get your letter myself to day in case there should be one, but A.L. changed her mind, & said she would go & then there was no need for me. I have had no letter from you for three days, & I am quite miserable about it. If A.L. doesn't bring or send me one this evening I shall get Father to telegraph you tomorrow for Oh! Cheri I can not bear this suspense. I wish it was time for you to come & darling please dont ever take it in to your head to send me away from you again. But thank goodness this is the last day of this interminable month & then in one more week & three days you will start and then I think I see myself ever losing sight of my old cheri again. It is very nice to have Sue here but she is such a slave to the children that it is perfectly provoking. Mr. K. thinks she does not need a nurse so she has none & has to do every thing for them herself & they are very expecting. Little Susie is as much of a baby as she was last summer. Sue sleeps with me, & little Sue on the lounge; last night we talked till 1 o'clock. Father took me a nice long ride this morning. It is a lovely day right cold but still bright, which is a great relief after the gloom & rain of the last few days.

Lilly Greenfield will be here next week, & then I will see her in person about my wedding dress. I believe she does not want me to have it the way it has been represented to her but I will manage it without any trouble. Oh I think about you so much & so often & long for you every hour. Father, Mother, Mr. K. Sue & myself are all in my room & such a chattering I can hardly tell what I am writing.

Good Bye darling. I am afraid you are tired of getting so many letters. Oh how I hope to know something from you this evening & how much I want to see you, nobody knows but you & you know, because you know how entirely you have taught your little Bess to depend upon you for comfort & happiness.

Good Bye
Your Loving Wife

After Supper.

Sue & I drove down this evening to get the letters & got quite a mail & among the budget were three from you, (24,25,26). Oh Cheri I can not pretend to tell you how charmed I was after not hearing for so long & they were such delightful letters. I have read each one three times & will take another reading in the morning. I did not read or tell what you said about the chills, for that is a subject upon which Mother cannot bear jesting. You know cheri every body has a weakness & that is hers. I grant you it is a weakness but we must conciliate some in this life, & if you had a tender spot you would think it unkind in her to continually be probing it, so darling please for my sake dont say any thing about it when you come. Who did you get to ride with on the 23rd? I hope you did not go alone. That long drive it would have been so stupid. They all say I write to you all the time & so I must stop until tomorrow but I had rather write to you than do any thing else. Good night my own dearest,

Your Bess

New Orleans May 31st, 66

My Darling Wife,

Your letter enclosing a photograph & the one written the same date was received. I am much obliged to you for the beautiful picture, and if you have improved as much as that picture represents, you have done admirably. But Bess you sweetest thing, I am hard to fool, especially about you, for I know every picture that I have ever seen of you, and though you rubbed out Bordertown on the back of it I knew it & recognized it. You have sent this to me now & it is mine & I will resist any body's claim to it here after. My cold in the head is much better, and this morning when I got up my nose bled a little, which is almost a certain sign with me that the cold is broken. I feel first rate every other way, but I sit with my mouth open about half the time, because my "doze" is stopped up.

I sent your letter to Mary yesterday. The cold weather is passing away and it is much more mild today. I am sorry that you did not get those bananas for they were very fine ones & a large bunch of them. But I am certain you will get the Pine Apples. I want you all the more & am delighted when morning comes for generally I get a letter from you. Last night I went to Dr. Palmers to prayer meeting, and wore my winter overcoat, but it was rather warm in church, but not at all uncomfortable outside. Went to bed after reading my Chap. & saying my prayers & slept well.

The bride at Mr. Tarltons has the intermittent fever, & Mrs. Tarlton is sick from long vigils over her little baby. Mr. Logan's house was sold & bought by Mr. Kearney, Mr. Bruff's Father in Law for $25,000. I have not paid a visit for a long time, and will do better when my cold improves. I believe that I will have my lungs sounded to see if I haven't consumption. Wouldn't it be nice to have some Dr. tell me that they were sound. I haven't the slightest symptom of a cough or pain in them but then my head feels full & stopped up & is running like a sugar tree in February and as there is a strong sympathy between the head & the lungs. Don't you think that I had better have them sounded?

I am beginning to need some Camphor pills, but as you object to my taking them I will not do so till I see you which will be in about two weeks from today.

Take care of yourself & be well & strong when I come home for you must muse me well when I come.

Your loving Husband
G.

May 31, 1866

    You ask me to tell you what I was doing at 5 o'clock on the 26th, that you have a peculiar feeling about it &c. Well I was at the 2nd Justices Court at that particular time & remained in the same place till nearly 8 ½ o'clock at night, trying some suits brought against a steamboat called the Spy. Are you satisfied you prescious thing that I was out of mischief? I am now writing this after I came home this the 31st of May, for when I wrote you this morning I had not recd. your letter of the 26th. I am very sorry that you didn't get the bananas. I went on board the Magenta today, & Vanderford did not go up on her as he told me. I placed a card on the bunch to you "Politeness Mr. Vanderford" and the steward or porter said that Vanderford did not go up & that he tried to find out where you went & could not succeed & brought them all the way back here & that they had rotted. You ought to have told Cal Christy to send aboard the boat & get them, then you would not have missed them. You ought to have had the pine apples by the 26th. I am wanting you awfully and do not know how I can do without you two weeks. I will now wash my hands for dinner. The weather has cleared off bright & beautiful & I am in hope the cold weather is over.

After dinner (June 1st yesterday).

    I went up to Uncle Henry's and took tea and staid till near nine o'clock. All the family were well. Came home & went to my room & went to bed & after I had been to bed for about fifteen minutes, Harrison came & knocked & waked me & asked me if I wanted tea. I told him no & went to sleep, and waked up about 2 with a night mare. I dreamed that I had a struggle with a man who was on me & after violent exertions I succeeded in throwing him off me. I lay awake a while & went to sleep & slept till the bell. We eat about 7 ½ now & this morning Mr. Fee was not well enough to be down stairs. Charley was in despair all day yesterday. His father made him go up into the attic & stay all day till 10'P.M. at night for chunking a horse who is now occupying the stalls of Mr. Fee. Seaver has been away for sevl. days. Mrs. Bruffs baby has had a severe spell, spasms. There is nothing of interest in our locality. I have not seen the Buckner bride for a long time. They have gone to Vermont. Mr. Tarlton bride has not yet recovered from her intermittent attack poor thing. She has been sick & lying around for some time & I suppose will not be well for sevl. months to come.

June 1st.

    I am rapidly winding up all my business now, and when Kennard returns will go & see him thru over all the unfinished business I may have & then ho for St. Louis. You are exactly right about my going to Va. and leaving you. I don't intend to do so.

If I go we will take it easy & stop on the way & look at the Battle Grounds, &c., and then you can stay at the Hotel at Abingdon Va. until I get back, or you may go with me if you wish. You are the sweetest thing in this world & I love you more than I do everything else put together in the world. I will close now. Give my love to all.

Your devoted Husband
G.

Glencoe June 1st 1866 Friday

My Dear Husband,

I did not write you yesterday the very first day I have missed since I have been at home, which is four weeks to day. But I did not feel at all well, & I knew you would prefer to go with out a letter to have one when it would have cost such an effort. I feel very well to day, so do not be thinking I am sick. It was only a little fit of indigestion. I think that caused me to feel a little lazy. You can not think what a relief it is to me, & what a pleasure, to put June instead of May at the top of my letters. In ten days you will start. Why do you come up on the boat? I should think you would so much prefer the cars. It is so much less tedious in warm weather, though I can not realize that it is warm weather, time for it is uncomfortably cool here. We have fires, & wear Winter clothes, & a few days ago, there was a heavy frost in the valley; but I suppose it is very warm down in N.O. & I should think you would find it more comfortable on the cars. It is safer too, but chere' is not much to be gained in point of time as it takes the cars four days & the boats five. I did not get any letter from you yesterday but received one from Florence. There was no news in hers particular. I hope very much for a letter from you this evening. Florence said she could not come around to St. Louis just now, but might pay me a visit some time during the Summer. She spoke in raptures of Carrie's baby which from all accounts must be a splendid little fellow. Chere' if our baby was living it would be four months old today. Just think what a great big son we would have had.

The children & Sue & Mr. K. are all going in to the "Olympic" tomorrow. Poor Susan I pitty her, with such an undertaking on hand. It is reported that Mary Sonlarde is living with her husband again. Oh frailty &c. Do you know I was beginning to get quite excited when I read your account of your visitor. The charming widow who enquired for me, & when told I had gone away smiled so sweetly, &c. I thought at once of Mrs. Drewy, & then I read on all eagerness & when I found it was the old nurse, I was amused at my self, & a good deal relieved too. Sue & Annie Lou are making cake in the kitchen. Mother is circulating around among her chickens & ducks, & so I am sole occupant of the house, but as it is nearly car time I must take a bath & dress so I will bid you good bye. I was hunting around in odd corners the other day for some books, & came across a package of old love *notes* carefully put away, from an old Dr. friend & I put them away for you to look at this is a shocking pen, & I am too lazy to get another one, & you have vetoed the pencil. So you will have to accept a *scratchy* letter.

Good Bye Darling
Your Own Bess

After supper.

I received your precious long letter of the 27th tonight & oh you dearest thing I am so much obliged. I am charmed that you have had your picture taken just as you were. You don't say anything about coming in this letter but if you don't start by the 10th of this month I will cry my eyes out, & you know the Dr. says I must not be distressed about anything. There is an account in this evenings paper of two frightful accidents by steam boats which almost makes me tremble for you but I will pray & where ever you are God will watch over you.

You can come in two days instead of four as I said by cars. It was too dro. about "Amos" the nightingale. Good night.

Your own loving wife.

Glencoe June 2nd 1866

My Dear Husband,

This is a capital morning for writing letters. The rain is pouring in torrents & the wind occassionally dashes it as it were in great hand fulls, against the window panes, where it trickles down in dreary tears, as if it felt itself much abused & insulted by such treatment. Oh it is an *awful* day. The poor roses are nearly dismantled of their bright leaves, by the combined forces of rain & wind. It is quite cold. We have good big fires all over the house, which makes it quite bright & cheery indoors but the outward prospect is dismal. This was the day for the children to have gone in to the "Olympic" but the rain prevented, & now they are all shut up tight & fast in the nursery keeping themselves very quiet for a wonder. It is 9 oclock & we have just finished breakfast. Sue Annie Lou & Mother are setting in the hall with their sewing, & Mr. K. is trying to define his position on some point in his usual *soft tones,* but the three ladies are down up on him, & I think he is nearly overpowered. I expect he would like to have you here to help him out. Father went in town to business but will be back this evening & I hope will bring me a letter from you my darling. Sue has just come in & says "Well Sue Bettie! You are certainly not writing *another* letter to Given Campbell." They say I don't do anything but scribble off letters to you, but I know it isn't so, & I don't mind it. I am so sorry for poor Mrs. Tarleton. It must have been very dreadful to see that little helpless baby suffer so long & so much. Well just as I had proceeded thus far, I had to stop Sue & Mother abused me so much. It is now afternoon & I will finish, but I have not time to write a very long letter as I want to answer your Father's letter this afternoon. I am glad to hear you are getting a little thinner. I think you both look & feel better. I am so delighted that you have had your picture taken, just as you were without any primping. You could not bring me anything that I would be half as much charmed with. I have counted up on your starting a week from tomorrow, you can come on the cars, in very little over two days, & there are so many fearful accidents on the river now, that I am so afraid to have you come that way, but I know how much you prefer it, & I also feel that in God's hand you are safe everywhere.

I am sorry I have made such a mistake with my paper but I confess I am too lazy to write it all over again, so you will have to take it as it is. I wish I could have been with you the day you came home so tired with the headache. I would have seated myself on the lounge & made you lie down on it with your head in my lap, & then I would have cooled it off with ice water & lavender, & then rubbed all the pain out of it, & then when you had fallen asleep (which you always do on the slightest provocation) I might possibly have taken my pay. I suppose Gus Given is in N.O. by this time wife daughter & all. I am glad to see you go so often to your Uncle Henry's. I hope Mrs. G. is more agreeable than of yore. I am going to send this in by the mail train this evening so must close. All send love to you. Somebody always does but I never take the trouble to put it in. Good Bye. You are the most precious thing in this world, & I am always

Your Own Loving & Devoted Wife.

New Orleans, La. June 2nd 66

My Darling Wife,

    Your letter of the 27th came today, and it was doubly welcome for it was a double letter, and I had not heard from you yesterday. If I hadn't heard today I was going to telegraph you, for I don't believe in being in the dark about how you are. You urge me to come up by the 10th, and here let me tell you all the inducements that will be offered by business no matter how important can keep me here after the 10th. I am too anxious to see you to let anything detain me. You don't know how much I do want to see you. I have half a mind not to let you see the diary I have kept, for it is so love sick silly that it would amuse you more than it would interest you, but all you need now is to *laugh & grow fat,* & when I come up I will make you laugh & grow fat. If the climate of Glencoe dont bring you out perhaps the climate & water of Paducah would do better, & if I have to go to Va., why it would be very nice for you to go with me & stop at Chattanooga & see the battle grounds & then go to East Tennessee & I will show you some of the fields where I fought, bled & died, and then you could go with me to the Montgomery White Springs & stay awhile & then I would go to see about the lands in Russell Co. and come back in a week or 10 days and we would take our time coming home. I don't intend to leave you, & if you are weak why we can stop at nights & rest &c. But I am going to try to get out of going at all. It would be nice if Father & Mother would go along, wouldn't it, & he wrote me he intended taking her on a trip this summer. I will write to him & propose the trip, & then we would come back by Richmond & Augusta & you could see the famous Augusta? Don't I gild a bitter pill? I am not surprised that you have fires at Glencoe on the 27th for I will enclose to you a slip from the times & you will see how we have been faring here for weather.

    Oh Bess I could write to you all day, but I haven't time. I am in first rate health. My cold has left me with the cold weather. It is very warm now.

                    Good Bye Sweetest
                    Your Husband
                    Given

June 2nd
New Orleans La. ~~May~~ 6/3

My Darling Wife

Your letter of the 27th
came today, and it was doubly
welcome for it was a double
letter, and I had not heard
from you yesterday, if I
had'nt heard today, I was
going to telegraph you. for I
dont believe in being in the
dark about how you are.
You urge me to come up by
the 10th, and here let me
tell you all the induce-
ments that will be offered
by business to make how
important case keep
me here after the 10th. I
am too anxious to see you

to be anything dearer to me —
You dont know how much I
do want to see you — I have
half a mind not to let you
see the diary I have kept,
fur it is so long sick silly that
it would amuse you
more than it would inter-
-est you, but all you need
now is to laugh & grow fat. &
When I come up I will make
you laugh & grow fat — If the
Climate of Greece dont bring
you out, perhaps the climate & water of Paducah
would do better, & if I have
to go too, Why it would be
very nice for you to go with
me & stop at Chattanooga
& see the battle grounds &
then go to East Tennessee
& I will show you some of
the fields where I fought

bled &died, and then you
Come &c with me to the Montgom
=ery White Springs &Stay, awhile
&then I would go to See about
The lands in Russell Co. and
Come back in a week or 10 days
and we would take our time
Coming home— I dont intend
to leave you, if you are
weak why we can Stop at
nights & rest &c.— But I am
going to try to get out if going
at all —

It would be nice if Father &
Mother would go along. wouldn't
it. She wrote me he intended
taking her on a trip this
Summer. I will write to him
& propose the trip. then we
would Come back by Rich
mond & Augusta & you
Could See The Armory,
Augusta? Don't I fill

a little pill? — I am not
surprised that you was
furs at Gleuco on the
27' for I will enclose
to you a slip from the
trees & you will see
how we have been faring
here for weather —
Oh Bess I came a write to
you all day, but I
havint been — I am
in just nice health —
my cold has left me with
the cold weather it is
very warm now
Good Bye Sweetest
            Your Husband
                 Geo—

New Orleans, La. June 3rd 66

My Dearest Bess,

Your letter of the 28th is received, acknowledging the receipt of the pine apples. In it & in the several preceding ones, you urge me not to put off coming up any later than the 10th, for you have set your heart on it &c. Now don't you be at all uneasy about my putting it off, for I don't know anything that could induce me to put it off an hour after the 10th. I am almost crazy to see you, and yesterday I declined taking a $50.00 cash fee & 50 more in a few days because it would keep me here longer than that time. I was awful home sick, or wife sick, I should say yesterday after dinner, and did not know how to put my time in, and I stayed at home & thought of you. I will try & see you by the 14th of this month, Providence permitting. That is 11 days from now, & if I could annihilate those 11 days I would do so.

Our house has been very quiet for sevl. days as Brother Seaver has been away, & Mrs. Fee has almost stagnated for news. She is getting to be quite robust in her figure. Old Eliza was talking to me last night & she said that she told Mrs. Fee that she was going to leave her, that she didn't think she was going away. Mrs. Fee told her she must stay until she was sick & got up. Anna Given is very gracious & polite to me, and I have taken tea three times there & had an elegant bowl of cobbler each time, but she did not put any cream on it. I wish I could forget some things, but I can't forget her meanness to you about the cream when you were sick. Her baby is getting to be very pretty & sweet looking. If our little boy had lived, he would have been a fine fellow by this time. But may be God in his mercy will give you another some of these days when you are strong enough to bear it.

Yesterday I was asked by a gentleman of very high standg. to be his adviser. He had been challenged by a judge of one of the courts. I acted for him & have his reply & succeeded in amicably adjusting the affair without bloodshed. I will tell you about it when I come up. I am afraid that the society of St. Louis is sadly demoralized. I never heard of such a piece of scandalous conduct as the picnicers were guilty of.

I will close & mail this now before church & write more this afternoon.

Your Husband, faithful & true

G.C.

June 3rd (1866)
Sunday after Church

My Darling,

I wrote & mailed a letter to you this morning & now I intend to do a little gossipping with you on paper. I have been to church and heard another of those wonderful discourses of Dr. Palmer. His text was from the 13th verse of 17th chapter of John. His sermon today was magnificent. I walked up home & watched the ladies defile away from the P_____ Church just opposite. It is beautiful weather, warm but a fine breeze, and we have now a good many beautiful roses. I have on my mantle piece a bouquet, and it is placed right between two photographs of you—stuck in the glass. If I can't offer my gifts to you I can to your images. I hope their is no idolatry in that. The fire bells are ringing again. This is the third alarm since this morning at two o'clock this morning Mr. & Mrs. Fee sprung up & rushed out, a watchman sprung his rattle, right in front of our house & roared fire most vociferously, and they thought the house was on fire, but it was on St. Andrew Street. You need not write to me after you receive this letter, for I will not be here to get your reply. Oh you hafe no idea how I long to fly to you. Everything here annoys me now when I get to thinking how long it will take me to reach you after I start up. I shall go from here to Memphis by rail, and take a packet from there to St. Louis. It will be about a day longer than going all the way by rail. I would go all the way by rail but it is so fatiguing, and I don't want to get to St. Louis broken down & tired. I may change my mind and go to Mobile & from there to Columbus, which would be a quicker route & not much more rail roading. I wish I had Fortunates Cap. I would put it on & wish myself at St. Louis and in a few moments you & I would be in each others arms. I never see a pretty woman, but I draw a comparison & always turn away complacently saying to myself, "Pretty but not half so pretty as my wife." You have completely filled up the ideal of my life & I am for you & you are for me, aren't you Bess? But I wont make love to you any more, and will look around for an idea. These trees on the pavement or "Banquette" are all now loaded with a graceful feathery bloom, and as they hang down from the ends of the twigs they remind me of nodding plumes.

This is a beautiful place. It is a pity it is so wicked. No wonder these people have been scourged, and that the high water has swept away the last vestiges of many a princely fortune. They haven't an idea above a muckrake, & money is their eternal anthem.

I am delighted that you did receive the pine apples, but it seems to me they were a long time getting to you. I sent them on the Olive Branch the 19th & you got them the 28th. Eliza has been in & says send her "best 'spects" to you. She is full of the idea of waiting on you when you come back, and I think it would be an excellent idea, don't you? She has asked me to give her one of the photographs of you. Margaret brings in my clothes all right I believe. Eliza says so. Tho' she says she has got a pair of socks. I must try & go to see Mrs. Newman before I go away. She met me at Popes Drug Store and was very cordial in her invitations to come over socially. Mollie Dreux is *very friendly* with Capt. Bradford. He sits with his arm around her in the parlor & holds her hand and Anna Given says that he sat on the porch with his arm around her & she told them to quit it. That it didn't look right. I think they had better get married as soon as possible, for if a slip should occur & they did not marry it would damage the fair widows prospects very much. She continues to call me "Cousin Given," & "Given," & to be very sweet, but she hasn't offered to kiss me yet. I kiss no lips but yours & would not give a cent to kiss anybody elses in this world. It is singular how I am coming to love you so exclusively. I have seen the day since we have been married. Before I left you the first time at Tuscaloosa, that I could not have conscientiously told you that I loved you better than anyone else, for I loved Mother the best then. But now I hardly love anybody else but you. I am afraid I am losing my natural affection for my parents in the intensity of my love for you. But here I am making love again! A boy has just passed crying out ice cream. I wish I had some nice ice cream & strawberries & that we could eat them together out of the same dish this evening.

The Tarltons dinner bell has just rung, & it is generally the *avant courier* of ours, but I will finish this page before dinner anyhow. Don't you get tired of my stupid letters. I feel that letter writing is not my forte. If we were lying down on the lounge & your head on my shoulder, I could then tell you in eloquent terms how much I love you & may be interest you, but I will close now for the present & prepare for dinner.

New Orleans, La. June 5th 66

My Darling Bess,

Your letter of the 30th is received. I am very glad that you have at last got some of my letters. So Susan is with you, and now you are happy, but I am afraid you won't gain much flesh if you talk till 7 o'clock every night. It is very uncomfortable now. There is that continuation of heat & moisture wh: is the quintessence of sultry. I went into your trunk today & amid your things & got out the two shawls that you spoke of, and I will get you your cinchonine & your porcelain type & some other little present & start home in the course of five days. I have a good deal to do in that time and will not have time to write you very long letters. But I have written you so many & so often that you are no doubt tired reading them. I am very well indeed & have fully recovered from my cold and am picking up some of my lost flesh. I will have my hair cut short all over my head today if we don't have another storm.

Business is getting very dull indeed in every department and after the 10th I will not have another case to try. Isn't that nice. You must take good care of yourself and be ready to go to Paducah with me as soon as I feel like going which will be pretty soon after I get up. Anna Given told me that your Mother told her that Mr. Woods was opposed to you marrying me. I was very sorry to hear of this. Don't you say anything about this to your Mother or any one. I must close now. I long & earnestly hope to see you very soon.

Good Bye sweetest thing in this world.

Your true & loving
Husbd. Given

New Orleans, June 6th 1866

My Darling Wife,

I have had no letter from you today, though I have haunted the post office. I feel very well today, tho' it is very warm & the dew is standing in drops on my forehead while I am writing this to you. It was delightful on our gallery last night & I spent the evening at home and was entertained by the conversation of Jennie & Charley. I amazed & surprised him several times. Mrs. Fee is visibly increasing in breadth, and does not look so well, as she did when you were here nor is she half as gay & frisky & I notice she doesn't go out "gadding." Circumstances alter cases. She was always taking you out gadding last winter, but now as the story goes it is her "bull," and the thing is quite different. Anna Given was well at last accounts & she seems to be very fond of Uncle Henry. It seems to me as if she is getting to be a better woman. She speaks in the highest praise of you, and said that she thought you were the kind of woman any man would want for a wife &c. All this sounds very sweet, but I can't forget some things. Mrs. Fee said she was going to write that I had got an attachment for a young lady. If she does I will explain for I know how jealous you are. I have a suit, and the defendant in the case has a sister who is an important witness for my client and I want her to come to the Court House & give her testimony and Mr. Fee said may be she would not come. I told him if she didn't I would get out an attachment & have her brought by the sheriff. I will leave here for St. Louis now very soon. It is only four days till the 10th.

Give my love to all the family. Your own loving & faithful

Given

New Orleans June 7th (1866)

My Dear Bess,

I have time to write only a line or two to you to let you know that I am in the land of the living. I must hurry & get away from here or I will soon be so thin & yellow that I can't leave, or if I have strength enough, I will be taken for an American citizen of African descent. But joking aside I am falling off distressingly fast tho' Fee says it is the best thing for me in this climate. I saw Annie G. yesterday. She was rigged out very gaily—white Grenadine dress & white lace shawl & an abundance of diamonds, necklace, bracelets, breastpin & earrings. She is looking better & better every day, & I believe that this climate would have agreed with you as well if you had staid here you would not have been so thin. I saw Dr. Jones & he asked if I had heard from you & how you were, &c. & said send you his regards. I had no letter from you yesterday & today I have not one though the mail is not fully distributed yet. I will pack up some of my things today. The weather is very warm & close & splendid weather for intermittent fevers. I will not say anything about the chills at Glencoe, unless I catch them myself, and then you know if I am overtaken & conquered by the miasma of Glencoe I will have to complain. I am writing this in my room, and Jamie is pulling at the door to come in. She has taken a great fancy to me lately. My business in court is all concluded for this year but one case set for the 11th. But I won't stay till the 11th to try it & will make arrangements to have it go over till next time. Now Good Bye prescious thing. This letter won't beat me many days.

Your Husband

New Orleans, La. June 8 (1866)

My Darling Wife,

I have been busy for two hours packing up everything so that I may be ready to start tomorrow afternoon on the Olive Branch, *deo volente*. I would go on the cars but it is such a miserable road & the comforts are so few, and the difference in the time is only about a day or a day & a half. I can go to Cairo in about four days ½ & take the cars to St. Louis & make it about five days trip. The weather is awful hot here & I have pulled off one set of under clothing which were as if they had come out of the wash tub. Jennie is at my elbow with complaints against Charley for his meanness. She runs in & out of my room now at a great rate & seems to appreciate the privilege very much. Whilst I was writing this a *marchand* is creaming "Black berries." We have them in great abundance and I do wish you were here to enjoy the figs & water melon & cantalopes.

I had a letter from Florence & she says that they have had very cold weather there for sevl. days. All were well. Eric Casey is going upon the Olive Branch & wants me to go with him. I saw the widow Dreaux & her fiancee and they were very doves cooing &c.

Little Henry Given has had the chills again, but is running about the house. I hope to find you well, very well when I come up & if I don't I will though there is no virtue in the famous atmosphere of Glencoe.

You are right let them talk as much as they please about your writing to me, for as long as you are well & strong it is not going to hurt you to write a letter a day to me whenever I leave you. "But if the count knows herself & she think she do" I never intend for you to stay from me long enough to have to write to me. I will bring some bananas up with me when I come & I know you will get them safely for I will have a persl. supervision of them.

Good Bye my Own

Your Husband
Given

June 9th (18) 66

My Darling Bess.

    I wrote you yesterday but forgot to mail the letter & I will add a line to let you know that I am well & leave here on the Ohio Branch this P.M.

    I am very busy indeed & have a great deal to attend to to day. No news of consequence. Good Bye Darling sweetest thing. I will see you in about five days.

                   Your devoted Husband
                   Given

June 9th 86

My darling Wife I want you yet
many times for you to have the
letter & I will add a line to
let you know that I am well
& have her on the Ohio
March this Pm—

I am very busy indeed &
have a great deal to attend
to today—

No news of consequence—
Goodbye darling devoted truly
I will see you in about six
days—

Your devoted Husband
Gwin

Paducah Dec. 26/66

Dear Given,

Your welcome letter telling of you being the father of a fine living boy, and that Bettie was getting on so well, gave all us much pleasure, and we hope that Bettie will soon be up. I shall begin to realize that I am old when dear little grand children are comming up around me. Gittle Campbell is running all about the house & begins to talk. The family are all well. Christmas has passed very quietly. Every thing here is very dull & money remarkably scarce in town & country. The banks have none & there is not money to handle the produce I am off of all paper & intend to remain so. The deps. in Johnsons case were taken yesterday & I think satisfactory. Give our best love to dear Bettie & to our kin & believe me.

                              Your affectionate Father
                              J. Campbell

Given Campbell
Atty. at Law
N. Orleans

Paducah Dec 26/66

Dr Givin

Your welcome letter telling
of your being the father of a fine living
boy, and that Bettie was getting on
so well. gave all us much pleasure.
and we hope that Bettie will soon be
up. I shall begin to realize that I am
old. when dear little grandchildren
are comming up around me.
little Campbell is running all about
the house & begins to talk. the family
are all well. Christmas has passed
very quietly. every thing here is very
dull & money remarkably scarce in
town & country. the Banks have none
& there is not money to handle the produce.
I am off of all paper, & intend to remain so.
The depo in Johsons case were taken
yesterday & I think satisfactory

Give our best love to dear Bettie & to our
Kin   & believe me   Your affectionate
Givin Campbell   Father
atto at Law   Campbell
N orleans

Part Three

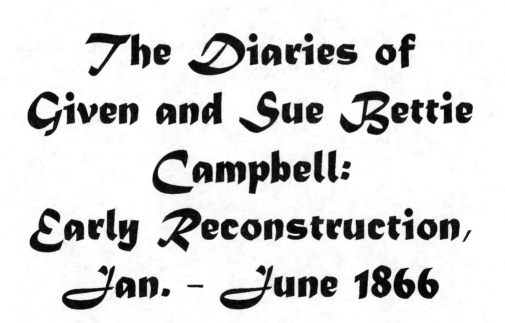

The Diaries of Given and Sue Bettie Campbell:
Early Reconstruction, Jan. - June 1866

PRIVATE JOURNAL

S.B.W. Campbell, New Orleans
Jan. 1866

Any one reading this book will be regarded, will forfeit all claims to honour,
from others & respect from self.   B.W.

The Journal of Sue Bettie Woods (Campbell) of St. Louis

Jan. 1st, 1866

Today, a sad one to me. Dark & gloomy out of doors. I sat in my room all the morning mending, also wrote a letter home. Mrs. Fee sat with me part of the time. Mr. Campbell down town until about 2. At 3 he went to Mrs. Given's & spent an hour. While we were dining Dr. Scott, Dr. Pine, & John J. Anderson called to see me, made a very pleasant little New Year's visit. At 6 I came to my room & not feeling at all well I undressed, being physically out of sorts. I was nervous & depressed & my husband who wanted to see me well & cheerful & could imagine no reason why I should be otherwise was discouraged, & out of patience with me & was not quite as tender & kind as usual, & I like a foolish woman had a severe nervous crying spell over it, & when he saw this, his darling old self came back again, & then when I had my cry (about nothing) out, I felt better & went to bed. Mr. Given called in the evening to see me & also Mr. Terry. I did not see them of course. After they left Mr. C. & Mr. Fee went to pay a few visits & Mrs. Fee sat with me. They came home at 9 or 10.

Jan. 2nd.

Today I did not get up until 1 o'clock, not having slept well. Mr. Campbell came up at 1 to bring me some letters two from Mother 21 & 22, & one from Mollie Curtis, very saucy. He ate lunch with me, & I dressed & walked down Prytania with him to the picture framers. He then put me in the cars, & I rode up & paid a visit & Mrs. Given's saw Mrs. Gregory & Miss Haines. The others came just as I was leaving. Came home & took a nap. Mr. C. did not come up until 5 o'clock while we were sitting at dinner. Got Ida's wedding cards today.

Jan. 3rd, 1866

Today has been bright & lovely but quite cold, mercury at 40 at breakfast time. At 10 o'clock, Mrs. Fee, & I went down to Canal St. I went to the dress makers & then went & bought some corsetts, & after got through shopping I went to call on Mrs. Dr. Pine, found her out. Saw the Dr. Got home about 2 o'clock. Laid down until nearly dinner time. While we were at dinner Mrs. Given called. She staid until about 7. & then I undressed. Mr. C. sat in the parlor until 8, & then came up & we spent a pleasant evening together. Mrs. Bowling came today & I engaged her for Feb. 15th.

Jan. 4th.

Still bright & clear, but very cold. At 11 o'clock I went to Mrs. Given's for a few minutes to tell her about & girl & then I went to Mrs. Kinnard's. Found her at home & very agreeable. I then went to Canal St. changed my corsets, got some sewing silk for Mrs. Fee, pins for self & came home at 1 o'clock, when I took a delicious cup of tea & a nice lunch in the rocking chair by the fire. After tea Willie Matthews & Capt. Woods called & spent the evening. Mr. Given also called to bring me 4 letters three from Mother (25th 27th 27th) & one from Susie.

Jan. 5th.

Not well. On the bed all day. Mr. C. & I had a cosy evening, took tea in our own room, & I worked on the slippers by the reading lamp. Dr. & Mrs. Pine called in the morning. Did not see them.

Jan. 6th.

Bright & cold. Feel much relieved of back ache but otherwise not very well. Mercury at 32 at breakfast time. G. complaining a little of pain in his eye, & not feeling well. I was in pain & rather restless part of the night which disturbed him. He was crabbed to Mr. Fee at breakfast which mortified me deeply. The little Fees greeted me this morning with the remark that they thought I was dead. As my husband had so reported. This shocked me & made me nervous all breakfast time. Several times the tears came into my eyes, & I was terribly afraid somebody would see me. I know it was the very extreme of nonsense, & yet I could not overcome it for a while. He was evidently not right well. I wish I could see him now, poor fellow. Fixed my balmoral. Sat in my room till dinner time & came up about 9. Spent quite a pleasant evening.

Jan. 7th.

Today the happiest & most peaceful I have spent in N.O. Mr. C. went for the Dr. after breakfast & the rest of the rest of the day we spent alone together, excepting the half hour in the morning that Dr. Jones' visit lasted & about an hour after dinner that Mrs. Given & Mrs. Gregory were here. I was not well enough to go to church & he staid with me. It is needless to say I was happy. I felt very well too all day.

Jan. 8th.

Also a happy day to me. Given came home at 1 o'clock & staid all the rest of the day with me. He brought me 4 letters 2 from Mother 1 from Father & 1 from Jennifer. After dinner we took a little walk & sat in the parlour until 9.

Jan. 9th.

Don't feel at all well. Weather bright & pleasant. Given not very well this morning but went down town early. Wrote a letter to Mother before luncheon. Afterwards served a while. At 2 Dr. Jones came. He sat about half an hour. He is a nice old man, talks freely rather, but means nothing. At 3 Mrs. Archie Woods called & while she was here Miss Elisa Dean, the same old "lies" as ever. Given did not come home until nearly 5 o'clock. From 9 till 5 I think it is barbarous. Had quite a hot discussion at the dinner table about Southern people. Came to our room early. Given still not very well tonight.

Jan 10th.

Very pleasant. Mrs. Scott & Mrs. Newman called very early. About 12 Dr. Palmer called to see Mrs. Fee, & I went down to see him. He does not compare with Mr. Brookes socially but is a very agreeable gentleman while he was. Mr. Campbell came home & sat with me until 3 o'clock when he had an engagement to drive with Mr. Kennard, & he afterwards dined with him & did not get back until 8 o'clock which made the evening extremely stupid. He came home quite sick from indigestion. I was also feeling wretchedly so we both came to our room grunting. He was the kindest & best nurse to me tho. Bathed my feet then rubbed them, helped me to undress as skillfully & tenderly as a woman, & then gave me a dose of valerian & we both went to bed. He got a letter from Paducah saying that Dave Flournay has the varioloid.

Jan. 11th.

Did not get up until 1 o'clock then felt much better. As soon as I was up had an exquisite little lunch of quail, hot rolls & tea, enlivened with Mrs. F's chat. Mended & darned then until 4 when G. came home, & then I held my hands & talked & looked & listened the happy little goose I always am with him. Pain & blues vanish in his presence like snow before the sun shines. After dinner sat in the parlor until 8 & then came up to our room & spent the evening together. Had a letter today from Mr. Kirkman & G. one from Jim, reporting all well at Paducah. Today warm & cloudy.

Jan 12th.

Felt miserably all day. Went to breakfast however & sat in Mrs. Fee's room till after luncheon. From that till 4 o'clock I felt equal to nothing more than lounging & reading today. At 4 my husband came bringing with him as always joy & comfort. We spent a sweet long evening together. I did not go down to dinner, but at 8 o'clock slipped on my dress & went to the parlor for a cup of tea. Afterwards in our own room I worked by the student's lamp, & G busied himself in various ways, one among others fixing my flaxseed tea & bath.

Jan. 13th.

Today warm & murky & horrid. I feel decidedly better tho. of my most miserable ailment. Spent the morning pleasantly sewing, reading, talking &c., showering all day. G. did not come till nearly 5. Brought me a letter from Father.

Jan. 14th.

Weather lovely, but unreasonably warm. Given went to church, & while he was gone I talked to Mrs. F. Took a bath, read the Bible & finally took a nap from which I awoke to find him returned. I am afraid I love him too much, because I hail Sunday now with more pleasure than ever before in my life & I fear yes I know it is just because I can have my husband with me all day. If this is wrong & sinful which I am almost sure it is, I pray God to forgive me & enable me to conquer the extent of love that amounts to sinful weakness. After he came home from church, while I was dressing, we were talking & the conversation fell upon Hettie Casey, & I was teasing him all in fun but he declared that if I didn't stop he would go off & leave me, so I told him to go & stay as long as he pleased, & not to stop short of Augusta if he preferred to go there. So off he went & was gone about three hours, which was a very lonesome & dreary time to me, but I managed to read the Bible, loll in the rocking chair & build Spanish castles until dinner time. Just as we were finishing soup Given came in, said he had dined but sat down at the table. He went to take a swallow of water & choked, & I thought it was going to be a spell like the one he had at Mr. Given's & I yielded to the very foolish impulses & rushed from the table to my room. When I arrived was weak, dizzy & feint, could scarcely breathe from the effort of running so rapidly up stairs. G. soon followed, gave me some valerian. I had a crying and laughing spell & then suddenly remembered that I had intended to be very cold & dignified with him but it was too late to assume that role so I laughed it off, & we had a very happy reconciliation. About dusk Mr. Garachi called to see us, & immediately after he left, tea was ready, after which we came to our room, & spent the evening by the student's lamp reading the Bible & a sermon of Cummings'. And so the day that was to be all sunshine has had its clouds. For the sake of a girl who I never saw, & my husband does not care a fig for now I am sure. Three or four hours (a large slice out of a short winter's day) have been entirely lost that might have been so happily spent. I received a letter today from Aunt Addie Berry. Dr. Jones called this morning but I was in the bathroom & did not see him.

Jan. 15th.

Very soon after breakfast to my surprise & delight Anne Green & Mr. Matthews called, the former just from St. Louis. After they left I went out to walk, stopped & paid a visit at Mrs. Given's got home at two, laid down an hour & then worked & read until Given came at 5. He brought me a nice long letter from Mother. I received today from Annie Ewing a beautiful little shawl, for the little black-eyed baby that God grant will soon be nestling in my arms.

Jan. 16th.

Today much colder but very bright & pleasant. Went down to see Mrs. Sire, had a pleasant visit, but when I got down in the St. began to feel sick, & came very near fainting. Had to call a carriage & drive home. Felt sick all day. Dr. Jones came about 4 & advised me not to go down to dinner so I did not. Given came home at 4. brought me a letter from Sister Carrie & one from Sister Mary announcing the birth of Carrie's son, born Jan. 6th.

Jan 17th.

Felt much better after getting up this morning & going to breakfast. At 9 o'clock took a short walk with my husband after which he went down town, & I sat down to write letters. Wrote one to Father & one to Mr. Kirkman, fixed my writing desk & just then Mrs. Singleton called to see me, & after she left I laid down until G. came at little past 4. Dr. Jones called just after & paid a short visit. Mrs. Fisher dined here. I came to my room immediately after dinner & did not go down again. Do not feel well tonight. Mrs. Fee sat with us a little while during the evening. These are monotonous days old friend.

Jan. 18th.

Today dull enough within but bright & beautiful out. I did not feel well enough to go out except for a little walk after breakfast. Mr. Chiles came to see me for a little while, but with that exception I dragged through a lonesome dreary day. Only saw Mrs. Fee for a few minutes once or twice. Oh! What would I give for some girl to talk to for an hour. I am very happy with my dear darling husband, but still I some-times long for the olden days. Being married has its drawbacks. Every rose has a thorn. At 3 came the hair dresser & combed me for the Opera, to which Mr. & Mrs. Fee, Mr. C. & I went. It was Faust, poor opera, poor troupe, had a nice time. Came home very happy as I always am with G.

Jan. 19th.

Lovely weather, warm & sickening. Went to the dressmaker's with Mrs. Fee. Came home lunched took a long nap. At 5 Given came & we dined. After dinner he went down town to see Gov. Lubbick. George Allen & wife. He returned at 8. o'clock, & wasn't I glad to see him for I had not expected him till 10 o'clock. Feel very well today & very happy.

Author's Note: At this point the diary shifts to Given Campbell with all further entries in his hand.

April 30th, 1866. Monday, New Orleans.

Arrived at New Orleans on the St. Louis d'Or about 5 ½ A.M., dressed and went out in town, mailed a letter to my wife, got out of my box sevl. letters for self & sevl. for my wife. Came up to Mr. Fees, and went into our old room & oh it looked so bare, dressed & put on clean clothes and then looked around, saw that my wife's rocking chair had been taken out, and that the little lunch table had been removed and the room looked so lacking in everything to make it comfortable & sweet, but after all it was the same only the tenants who had but so many charms & attractions to it had gone. I went to breakfast. Mr. & Mrs. Fee were so much surprised to see me back so soon. Did not remain at all after breakfast. Went to my office & was out a good deal during the day on business & thought of my poor little wife so often. Came to dinner, and after dinner got very lonesome & went up to Uncle Henry's, and found all out but Mrs. Gregory talked a while with her & was not satisfied—restless—came back home and saw Miss Sally Fee sitting on the porch, our gallery, was right glad to see her, to see any woman on that gallery was a comfort. Sat a while & talked with her. The mosquitoes bad & Bess was the theme of my conversation but this did not satisfy my heart at all. Came in & old Eliza was turning down the cover & it did me good to talk to her. I commenced this Journal & hear the bell rings for tea. Charley has been very noisy on my gallery, and is a very bad boy. At tea had a confab with Mr. Fee. Mrs. Fee did not come down. Paid Mr. Fee 50 for May & 30 for Bess & Fee owes me $6.65.

Oh it is so dreary without those we love. I shall be very anxious to hear from my wife that she is well. I am afraid she will make herself sick crying about me. I will close this for tonight, and go out. Smoke a cigar on the gallery. This morning I got out my wife's pictures & put one photograph in the glass & two amrotypes on the mantle, & carried a photograph to my office. I would give anything to see my poor little Bess for one half hour.

May 1st.

Arose. Was late for breakfast. After breakfast went down to my office & smoked a cigar, and wrote two letters one to my own precious wife. Oh how I miss her. Attended to a good deal of business & bought 5 pr. linen drawers. At night went to Annie Givens, but she was out & I went down town at the St. Charles found two Miss Flournoys cousins of David and paid them a call, & at 8 o'clock came home & sat out on my gallery thinking of my wife, until I got the blues & went down stairs to tea & after went to a wedding & was amused at the action of the groom who when the ceremony was over kissed his wife audibly & instantly took out a handkerchief & wiped his mouth. Sat on the porch with Fee & Mrs. Fee & Miss Sally till 4 o'clock & then came up read 2 Chap. of Romans & went to my solitary bed.

May 2nd.

Slept well last night, but waked not feeling so well. First thing I think of was my poor sweet little Bess, and how much I missed her. I shave after breakfast & Eliza looked in the washstand, & found an enema. I took it & wrapped it up & send to B. by express. Went down town. Not very busy today at court. Wrote to my wife. My eyes troubled me a little, took one Claret punch. The day dragged out weary & I had nothing to look forward to as I have had before the society of a sweet & charming wife. Came home. Had a pretty good dinner. After dinner went to see George Langstaff & wife from Paducah, & had a pleasant visit. Came home at 8 to tea, sat & talked with the Fees till 9. Read a chapter in Romans and Eliza having prepared some hot water for me I went to bed, & after having said my prayers went to sleep.

May 3rd.

Awoke early this morning & had a good long time to think before breakfast, and it was devoted to those most dear to me. After breakfast went to my office & wrote to my wife. Remained in my office & then went to P.O. and looked for a letter from my wife a little. Went to office & saw a man on business. Went out to Capt. Woods to see if he had any news. He had a letter from his Mother at Natchez, where the boat had to lay by in a storm. Oh I wish I had gone to N. with my wife. It would have lightened her burdens so much. I look for a dispatch tomorrow afternoon, to tell of her arrival. I went on the Atlantic & gave him the paper box for my wife, & directed him how to deliver it. Read a letter written by Bess's mother telling of the sad & miserable action of Ned Washington to his wife. Went to dinner & after dinner went to Uncle Henry's a little while & Annie G. was going to a party. Went to Dr. Scotts. Saw Mrs. S. & Mrs. Dean & Dr. Pine & Scott. Mrs. P. was too unwell to see company. I really envied Joe Scott his happiness with his family, his wife & children. Came home late to tea & Miss Sally Fee served my tea to me. I talked to her about my wife, and my resolution is breaking down fast I don't see how I can stay away from her till the middle of June. Oh I never knew her worth or how much I loved her. I must stop this now & go out & smoke a little to drive away the mosquitoes. Have read 4th Chap. of Romans.

May 4th.

After breakfast lit a cigar & went down to the post office, had a letter from my dear wife. It was overflowing with love for me & was most precious to me. Wrote a reply & attended to some business when about 12 o'clock a dispatch came for me from R.K. Woods telling me of the safe arrival of Bettie & Maggie. It made my heart glad & made me feel easy & happy. Today have had long consultations with E. Levy

& A. Levy in relation to the attempt of traders to swindle the Crs. in N.Y. A gent H.F.G. came into my office & disclosed an attempt to levy black mail of him & asked my advice. I went out & had lunch, and passed the day away engaged in business. Came home to dinner & made a glass of lemonade. Everything makes me think of the kindness & goodness of my darling little Bess. Went to Annie G. & stayed talking with Uncle Henry till 8 and when I went to leave Mrs. G. invited me to come to her house & stay (a while). I told her that I was very comfortably fixed and it would not be worth while moving for so short a time. Came home to tea & after fighting mosquitoes returned, read in the 5th Chapt. Romans. It almost makes me mad to think of my dear wife away so far.

5th of May.

Arose had a good breakfast. Went down town & to the Post Office the first place hoping to get a letter from my wife, but recd. none. One came from her mother enclosing one from her Aunt. I wrote to Bess & was happy in writing to her. I love her as truly & purely as ever man loved woman & miss her oh so much. Was right busy had two new cases. After dinner went awhile to Uncle Henry's and was so awfully homesick that I couldn't stay but went down town and went to the Clay monument to see the speakers of Natn'l Democrats who are to have candidates for Parish offices tomorrow & from there went to a Catholic fair & spent some money & from there to meeting of the working men at Lafayette Square. Did not stay long. Came home too late for tea & went out on my gallery & Mrs. Fee & Miss Sally were there. Talked till after 10 and then retired.

6th May.

Communion Sunday at Dr. Palmers Church. Breakfast at 9, shaved & went to my office. Wrote a letter to wife & went to office & got sevl. letters one from my wife. It was a sweet & affectionate letter & breathed love every line of it. Went to the church and heard a very powerful sermon and we had the sacrament. Came home and washed my hands & went to Annie Givens to excuse myself from dining with her. Ate dinner & wrote a letter to Mother, and thought of Bess till I had to go out. Went to Uncle Henry's a few minutes & then went to see Mrs. Langstaff and after to Kennards, where I took tea, had rather a pleasant visit left & came by Uncle Henry's & he was setting on the porch. Talked with him till 9 and came home. Went out on my gallery and and sat there thinking of her far away & imagined what she was doing & where she was. Smoked a cigar to keep off the mosquitos, came in & read a Chap. in Romans & said my prayers & went to bed, but it is as hot & sultry & it was long before I slept.

May 7th.

Was late to breakfast. Went down town and wrote a short letter to my wife. Did not have time to write a long one. It was very hot this morning, and I had sevl. letters to write, and then had a long talk with Rozier on business, then I went to Court, & filed a petition asking for a jury trial in case of R.L.Woods vs. Bostock & others. I miss my wife so much & would be glad to see her if only for a minute. Took depositions during the afternoon, and then at dinner, just as I finished I was sent for by Uncle Henry to take a ride & we took the same ride my darling own sweet wife used to go. The River Road, and by the Sedgewick Hospital, came home, had tea & am now sitting in my room with Jimmie, sitting by my side asking questions & Charly standing at the door. I won't let him come in. He is too bad. There is a concert tonight but I don't care for amusements while Bess is not here to enjoy them with me. This is election day & all the courts are adjourned but the Sup. Court. I don't know who is elected. I will go out & smoke a cigar on the gallery & after read my chapter in Romans & go to my solitary bed for I do miss my darling every hour of the day.

May 8th.

Slept well & waked & find breakfast ready. Went down town. Expected a letter from my wife but got none, was much disappointed. Was right busy during the day. Came home & ate a hearty dinner. Wrote to Bess. After dinner went to Uncle H's & his wife had been threatened with cholera, so Mrs. Givens said. I felt badly. Came home & asked Dr. Jo Scott to come up & take a cigar. Gave him a drink of brandy & cigar. I felt better, but when I went to bed felt cold & slept very badly. Had a nightmare.

May 9th.

Arose feeling badly. Ate a slight breakfast & went town. Stopped at Dr. Jones office. His charges were 3 per visit & from 50 to 75 for confinement, and at those prices his bill was 275, but of his own accord he made it 250, having paid my wife 70 odd visits. Poor dear creature she was sick so long & so much. Then went to P.O. but found no letter from my wife. This made me sick almost. When I got to office had to lie down but towards 1 o'clock I took a plate of soup & felt better. Wrote to my wife. Came home and ate dinner & sat out on the steps till dark. Went to Uncle Henry's, and afterwards came home & talked to the Fees till bed time. Came up & read my chapter & my prayers & went to sleep.

10." May 1866 – Five years ago today, I
was field in arms against the U.S. Gov't
so they said, and taken at Camp
Jackson Mo. by the U.S. forces under
Gen'l Lyon & carried with Joo others to
the U.S. Arsenal as prisoners of war
& what has passed since then it
requires long to tell – I have fought
& seen many strange things &
I have married. & I have seen the
dissolution of grand armies &
the majestic disappearance of
a strong Gov't. But on the 10th of May 65
I took my course westward to my
young wife. Jefferson Davis having
been captured that day, which
released me from my oath as a
soldier. I have thought of my wife
much this day. for during
these last five years she has
been dethroned from
my reach –

35

This morning went down town feeling much better, but night languid
& weak, went to the P.O. & received
Out letters from St Louis & one from
my dear Bes. written on the Boat,
with a postscript after reach _
St Louis, but I had hoped to
hear from her after she had
got home — was pretty dreary
home, at noon went with Julia
to the Oddfellows Hall & an
Orphans fair & got much
for two $4.00 Came back to my
office, it rained hard this
afternoon, see by the evening
papers that Neefounga Swa
has given way Came down
Town — had very little appetite, after dinner laid down to take a
nap which was almost a failure on
acct of the noise made by Jennie
& Charlie on the Gallery in front of
my window, I got up sending them
away

10th May 1866.

Five years ago today, I was first in arms against the U.S. Govt. so they said, and taken at Camp Jackson, Mo. by the U.S. Forces under Genl. Lyon & carried with 700 others to the U.S. Arsenal as prisoners of war & what has passed since then it requires long to tell. I have fought & seen many strange things & I have married & I have seen the dissolution of grand armies & the magical disappearance of a strong Govt. But on the 10th of May 65 I took my course westward to my young wife Jefferson Davis having been captured that day, which released me from my oath as a soldier. I have thought of my wife much this day, for during these last five years she has never been dethroned from my heart. This morning went down town feeling much better, but right languid & weak. Went to the P.O. & found sevl. letters from St. Louis & one from my Dear Bess, written on the boat with a post script after reachg. St. Louis, but I had hoped to hear from her after she had got home. Was pretty dull day to me. At noon went with Gautier to the Oddfellows Hall to an Orphans Fair & got lunch for two $4.00. Came back to my office. It rained hard this afternoon. See by the evening papers Great Mesgauga Levee has given way. Came home to dinner. Had very little appetite. After dinner laid down to take a nap which was almost a failure on acct. of the noise made by Jimmie & Charlie on the gallery in front of my window. I got up & ordered them away and then slept & arose feeling rested & refreshed. Went down town. Did not meet any of my friends & concluded to go to the Academy of Music did so & was well entertained. Got home about 11. Read in Romans & went to bed.

May 11th.

Went down town this morning & went to the P.O. & took out two letters & on one I thought that I recognized the hand writing of my wife & I was certain I had a letter from her but when I opened it found it was a letter from Lizzie Hunt to my wife. Oh I was so much disappointed, and it made me almost mad at Miss Hunt. I went to my office & wrote a letter to my wife & I thought she must be sick or she would have written to me. I went to the office again & sure enough a letter from Mr. Woods told me that she was sick of the chills & that she had had those on the boat. It almost made me crazy to hear this & I telegraphed to know how she is & expect an answer tomorrow. It does seem very hard for her to get well again & it is a misfortune for me now to have so much sickness in my family. I am poor & my poor dear wife is so little able to bear such protracted sickness. Oh I wish I could releave her & oh be with her. I believe it would have been better for her to have remd. here than to have gone away from me to be sick away when I can't nurse her. Dinner bell rings & I cease this. After dinner go down town & walk up Canal Street lookg. for Genl.

Wheelers house. Did not find it. Came back by Bellanger's and took a glass soda & got on the Baronne cars & came home. Took tea & went out on the gallery to smoke, read a chapter, sd. my prayers & went to sleep.

12th May.

It is two weeks today since Bess left me, and it seems a great deal longer time. I went down town today to Post Office, but recd. no letter at all, and was so much disappointed. But at 12 o'clock recd. a dispatch from Mr. Woods saying she was well going about, riding out every day & has a good appetite. This filled me with joy for I feel that she is as happy as she can be without me. The magnolias look very sweetly. There are sevl. such fine blooms on the tree at the right of the gallery. There is a fine breeze blowing this afternoon, and the air is delightful rather warm in the house. Wrote to Bess this evening. Went down town after dinner & bought coat Pants & vest, for 17.50 and a shirt *.00 & pd. washing 5.00. Came home, had tea & went up stairs. Read chapter in Romans & went to bed.

May 13th, Sunday.

Arose to a breakfast at 8½, came up to my room & sat down & shaved & then walked up to the Cor. of Jackson & St. Chas. Talked a while to Uncle Henry & his wife & then I got on the cars. It was raining & went down Baronne St. to a place where I had left my umbrella & went to St. Charles Hotel, & saw Jo Scott, & Genl. Loring. Came from there to the P. Office & got a letter from Bess & went to my office & got paper & put it in my pocket to answer it. Read the letter & it was so sweet just what I wanted. Went to Church & heard Dr. Palmer. He preached from the 15th Chap. of John 9 verse & it was a most powerful & eloquent discourse lasting about an hour & a half. Came home & wrote a long letter to my wife, & then took a lonesome & solitary walk out Jackson & every step reminded me of Bess, for we walked there just before she was taken sick. Came back & out Prytania to First & across to Camp & to cor. of Secd. & Camp to see Lucius Lorry & his wife. Had rather a pleasant visit. Came home & finished my letter to my wife & wrote this in my diary on the gallery on my backgammon box, with my ink stand in a chair & the magnolia blooms thick around me, & the oleanders rosy & red, & the mocking birds making music in the trees. I will go to hear Dr. Palmer after tea. It is getting too dark to write so I stop. At night went to church and heard an excellent sermon at Dr. P's church. Came home & went to bed.

May 14th.

Went down town & went to P.O., but before this I will state I slept badly last night for Mr. Fee had cholera morbus & Mrs. Fee came to my door for camphor or brandy. I volunteered my services but she would not accept them. He was very sick purging & vomiting. This morning he was better. I went to the P.O. & got two letters from Bess the last of the 8th. I went to office & wrote letters & then went to Ct. & tried to get at the trial of a case of the Bk. of Ky. v. Goodale in the 4th Dist. Court, but it was laid over by preference to the 28th. Came to my office. C.S. Bandeford was there, and saw Leach Hillman, and came home & remd. at home all day & evening & then I went to bed & had read chap. in Romans. Bought a hat today & paid old Dr. Jones his bill of $200.00. Mrs. Campbell called to see my wife.

May 15th.

Went down to the P.O. & got a letter from my wife & in it she said her Mother & Sam Kirkman had been dosing her on brandy & had had Dr. Johnson out to see her if her lungs were affected & he said they were not now. I suppose the inference he left was that she was to die with consumption in a few years or perhaps months. Oh it almost made me crazy. I am not surprised that all the Woods have died of consumption since Mrs. RKW came into the family for she would induce a cast iron statue to believe that it was destined to die if it had a Woods constitution, & oh it makes me regret sending my wife away so much. I am so much afraid they will fix this belief in her mind so firmly that if she has a cough it may make her sick from the imagination itself. If I were with her it would be different for I have more influence over her than all the rest & my assurances would increase her strength. Oh how I regret sending her away. I will pray for her oh devotedly. I must hurry away from here as fast as I can, & get her away from the baleful influence of croaking. But enough of this. If she does oh what will I do. I love her & long for her this minute, more than I ever did in my life. After this I went down town to try & get away from my own sad self. Went down town & mailed the letter & then got on the Levee & Barracks cars and rode to the Mint & back to Jackson Square. Got out & walked thro' the square & went to the Cathedral to vespers. Came by perfumery store, bought a cake of Monpelas soap, & came home. Took tea. I sent a bunch of bananas to Bess on the steamboat Magenta. Will smoke a "Figaro" & go to bed after reading Romans.

May 16th.

Another letter today from Bess, & the same melancholy sadness & alarm pervaded it. I answd. it & gave her ssome advice & wrote a warm loving letter. Oh I am so anxious to see her. Was busy today, filed two suits in U.S. Courts one in Circt. &

one in Dist. Took to whiskey toddies, and am sorry I did so. Drew up papers in a case in the 2nd Dist. Court. Saw old man Allard. He is just from Paducah, Ky. He said all were well. Saw Mat. Joyce & he staid a long time in my office. Came home. There was a hard rain about 3 & 3½ P.M. I do not feel so blue today. After dinner took Mrs. Gregory sight seeing to Jackson Square & the Cathedral & gift store. Came home. Read 1 Chap. Corinthians & went to bed.

May 17th.

Got a letter from my wife & also one from her Father which greatly reassured me. She is evidently improving at the dates heard from the 12th. Was not very busy today. Brought two suits on claims. Have nothing particularly new. I want to see my wife more & more every day. I wrote to Bess & her Father. I have no doubt that I have made some of her family mad, but I don't care if it has a good effect. Came up on the car with a man who had the largest & finest pineapple I ever saw. I will go down tomorrow or Saturday & get some for Bess, & send to her, and I will not forget my Mother when the Virginia returns. Went & took Mrs. Gregory out again, but she bored me this time & I won't do it again. Came home at 8. Will take tea, read Chap. & go to bed after praying for Bess.

May 18th.

Nothing new transpired today except that I didn't get a letter from my wife, but one came post marked the 14th to Mrs. Fee, which I suppose Bess thought wd. be communicated to me. I will bet if I ever get her again she will not get away from me soon. I have done some business today & am much encouraged. I will now sharpen my razor & prepare to shave for I have an idea of going to see Genl. Wheeler & his wife as I have long promised to do so. After dinner went to Genl. Wheelers but did not find him at home, left a card for him & his lady, also left a card at the St. Charles for L.M. Flournoy. Saw sevl. acquaintances, & came home & read a chapter & finished this page in my diary. Read Bess letter to Mrs. Fee & went to bed.

May 19th.

I had very little appetite for my breakfast. Went to the Post Office & got a remarkably sweet & well written letter from my wife, and one from Mary & one short courtly note from Florence. I sat down & wrote out a petition against Mr. F. Goodrich & also wrote a letter to my own sweetest one. Went to the Fruit Market & bought eight nice pine apples & had them done up in a package & gave them in charge of the porter of the Ohio Branch to take to my wife. Went to court & had some business & then I went to my office & then paid a visit to R.H. Marr. Came home and now will eat dinner & then finish this. After dinner came up & got a cigar. Walked up & chatted with Mrs. Gregory & an old Mr. Huey. Went down town & talked with L.M. Flournoy will 10. Came home & read & went to bed.

May 20th Sunday.

I received a letter of the 14th from Bess & it was not at all satisfactory as to her health, But overflowed with love for her husband. I shall telegraph her tomorrow, for I cannot endure this suspense, & I wish to relieve her mind of all anxiety about me. I heard a splendid sermon from Dr. Palmer from Psalms. "Mercy & truth have met together, righteousness & peace have kissed each other." Came home & felt hungry. It is cloudy & threatening rain, but a good deal warmer than it has been for some days. Oh how I wish that my wife were well. Went to Uncle Henry's to dine & found Fayette Flournoy, Mattie Deney, Jesse Bryan & Fanny & Capt. Bradford & Anna, & Uncle H & A. Had a good dinner. Came home & had something like a chill but feel better at dusk but am warm and feverish though perspiring. Will tell how I feel at bedtime—I had a fever & felt sick. Think I have a chill. Took a dose of calomel & went to bed.

May 21st.

I slept very badly last night. Did hardly sleep at all till after 2. Had a fever & a headache till 2. My Medicine commenced to operate & continued at intervals till near day break. It operated several times, though I was not much weakened. This morning was clear of fever & went to breakfast. Ate a piece of toast & drank a cup of coffee. Went down town & went by telegraph office. Telegraphed my wife, & then went to office, & then on my wat to court went to the P.O. & got a large number of letters among them two from my wife. She wrote in better spirits. Went to court & case contd. to Saturday. Took quinine all day. Came home to dine. Took a lunch to day with Shackleford. Nothing else before dinner. Ate a light dinner. Have a slight head-ache, or eye ache. Went to bed early.

May 22nd.

No letter today from Bess. After a refreshing sleep I waked, dressed & went to breakfast. Afterwards went to my office & Mr. Allard called to see me on business. I went to see the Live Oak sold. She was bid in by W.M. surl. for $8300. Came to my office and then went out & attended to some business and ate a plate of Creole gumbo which lay heavy on my stomach & took 10 grains quinine today & missed my chill. Was busy till 5½. Came home & ate a light dinner. Went down town and took a walk out Canal Street & stopped in at the new Ice Cream Garden. Did not eat any.

Came home after taking a glass of Blue Lick water. Feel very much swelled up. Had no letter from Bess. Weather fine. I am looking very sallow & am bilious & have very little appetite. Will read a Chap. in Corinthians & go to bed. Had a dispatch from my darling wife. She was well.

May 23rd.

Nothing of much interest today of news. Except news of a great money panic in England & a rapid rise in gold. Got a letter from Bess today, bless her jealous little heart. She is a little doubtful of me & God knows how little cause she has. She says she was very well, had not much to do today. Came home at 3 o'ck. as we had an early dinner. Miss Sally Fee is going away on the Henry Ames. I have been suffering a good deal from indigestion & took some cream a tatar which operated on my bowels in about two or three hours. After dinner I took Anna G. & little Henry out riding, out Esplanade Street over Bayou Bridge & by city park & half way hour & back by Washington Avenue here. Came home, read Chap. & went to bed. The ride reminded me of Bess.

May 24th.

I was busy today. Went to the Post, & got a letter from Bess a sweet nice letter & one that did me good. I answered it. Went to Court House & then we went to the office & I had a long talk to old man Allard and attended to other business. I have to attend to 8 cases tomorrow. Came home & lay down on my bed & thought about Bess & how much I wanted her. The bell rang & I went to dinner, tolerable fair dinner, but we don't live as well as we used to. Mrs. McLaughlin called to see me. Kennard came & proposed a partnership. I paid Capt. L.S. Allard for his son $80.00. Read my chapter & wished for my wife & went to bed.

May 25th.

Went down town after breakfast & was greeted at the Post with a nice sweet letter from Bess. I read the letter over & it made me love her if possibly more than I do. There was also a letter from Carrie, giving the Paducah news. I went out but little today, took a bowl of soup & a broiled "sheep head" for lunch & it did not disagree with me at all. It was very warm today but warm weather seems toagree with me better than the sort we have had lately. Was detained will near six by business. Came home & ate heartily with a relish. After dinner sat out on the porch, & talked with Mrs. Fee till near 9. Mr. Tarlton's baby is said to be dying. At nine went up & talked a while to Uncle Henry & his wife & took a glass of milk & a piece of bread. Came back home & took a cup of tea & came up to go to bed. Wrote to Bess today.

May 26th.

Went down early & got a letter from Bess but written before the one I had yesterday. Went to the 3rd Dist. Court & argued the case of Allen vs. Shepherd on exception and came up home & got a lunch. Went to office and at 5 P.M. the Justice Peaces cases of the "spy" came up & after a long & tiresome trial we then submitted them to the Justice & I then came home & got something to eat. About 8 ½ o'clock lit a cigar & took a walk out St. Charles & back Prytania. I wanted to see my darling wife so much & thought of the walks we used to take. Got a letter from Mr. Woods on business. I will close. It is very warm no breeze. Read my Chapter &c. & go to bed. Had my picture taken for my wife today.

May 27th Sunday.

Went to hear a minister in the Josephine St. Church in the morning, and he was very dull & uninteresting. Came home & wrote about 11 pages of note paper to Bess. After dinner went out to Uncle Henry's & took little Henry riding on the cars. After tea, Leigh Wickham came to see me, but I had gone down to hear Dr. Palmer. In the cars saw Judge Lackland of St. Louis. He was on his way home from Texas. Heard a fine sermon. Came home & read a chapter & went to bed to think of Bess, and wish she were here.

May 28th.

A month today since Bess left me. Went down this morning & took two letters out of the office, one from Bess & one from her mother. In both they told me of my wifes improvement, and the letter of Mrs. Woods was very kind. Went to my office & prepared for trial of case of Bk. of Ky. and think that I will gain it. Continued the case of Hall vs. Mitchell. I came to my office & wrote out a brief for the Judge. Came home wrote a letter to Bess. It was stormy & rainy & is cloudy at bed time. Will read chapter & retire.

May 29th.

Arose & took a gin toddy before breakfast, and then went to breakfast. Ate a pretty hearty breakfast & felt pretty well, but the weather is really cool & has been all day reminding me of an October day in Ky. Went to my office & then got a letter from Bess & one from Carrie & one from Mrs. Callen. It was a sweet letter from Bess & made me proud of her. I then had to attend to those horrid cases before Justice 2nd Dist. Then went down to the 4th Court & gave my brief of authority to the court & then after a while the Judge delivered his opinion for my client, giving him a judgement in full. I was gratified for the court was evidently against me at the beginning of my argument. Came to my office wrote to Bess &c. Came home will read chapter & then go to bed, & dream of Bess.

May 30th.

I slept well, till just before day and then I was waked coughing & my nose dripping all the time clear hot water, so that I could not sleep. I have an awful cold in the head, and keep two Hdk's in requisition all the time. Went to office & it being quite cold & raining I had a good fire made and sat down & wrote to Bess. After I had finished writing to her & some other letters I got two letters out of the office, & from her & in one was a photograph of her taken at Bordertown which she tried to make me believe was a recent one. I then attended to some business and went shopping looking at blue silk dresses. She wants a blue silk & I will get it for her. Went to prayer meeting, wore my over coat, but it was rather warm in the church. Read & went to bed at 9½.

May 31st.

Slept much better last night than I did the night before. Rose early and find my cold much better than it was. I am always delighted for morning to come for I am almost sure of getting a letter from my wife, and sure enough there was a sweet nice one of the 26th her father had arrived. I was tolerably busy down town today, bought a trashy novel & glanced thro. it & threw it away. I ate fresh figs for the first time this season. They are not much good. It rained & cleared off & rained & has at last cleared off beautifully. I have just been writing to my own darling Bess & Annie is now about ready, & I must close. I read the chapter & thought of my absent dear ones & at last the thought combined in one.

1886

June 1st The first day of June 1886
I was in old Tuscaloosa this day
one year ago enjoying a delightful
Honey Moon, & today here I am
disgusted with a horrid bachelor
Mood — ~~or that~~ It is mightily hard to
be away from the wife of my bosom,
I don't intend this shall happen
again if I can help it — I want
to see my wife more & more as the
slow days crawl by. and today
I got no letter from her the Boat
was closed at 11. am on acct of
the death of Genl Scott. The weather
has moderated very much & so
has my cold — I was not very busy
to day. Came home at 4½ & wrote
a letter to Mrs Woods, If I don't get
a letter tomorrow I will telegraph
again — I will be in St Louis by
the 12" if I have luck — for I don't
intend Staying here any longer than
the 6th if I can get away, will
go on own —

3
6⁵

it rained or rather poured today
about 3. P.m — but now it looks
like it had cleared off.
Eliza has just come in to put
my kitchen to fit me some ice
water, and it is pretty pleasant
& warm again. Just the kind
of weather I would like to have
Bess with me. I had a nightmare
last night, and it is the second I
ever had in my life, and if I
had had my own precious
little beauty by my side &
in my arms I would not
have had it — But it will
only be a little while now till
I see her — After dinner went down
town, and bought a very handsome
plum silk dress 15 yds at 4⁵⁰ per
yard for Bess. It was what I
had intended to put in a coat
for myself & I would much prefer
to see my wife with that on than

June 1st, 1866.

    The first day of June 1866 I was in old Tuscaloosa this day one year ago enjoying a delightful honeymoon, & today here I am disgusted with a horrid bachelor moon. It is mighty hard to be away from the wife of your heart. I don't intend this shall happen again if I can help it. I want to see my wife more & more as the slow days crawl by, and today I got no letter from her. The Post was closed at 11 A.M. on acct. of the death of Genl. Scott. The weather has moderated very much & so has my cold. I was not very busy today. Came home at 4½ & wrote a letter to Mrs. Woods. If I don't get a letter tomorrow I will telegraph again. I will be in St. Louis by the 12th if I have luck, for I don't intend staying here any longer than the 6th if I can get away, will go on my own. It rained or rather poured today about 3 P.M., but now it looks like it had cleared off. Eliza has just come in to get my pitcher to get me some ice water, and it is getting pleasantly warm again. Just the kind of weather I would like to have Bess with me. I had a nightmare last night, and it is the second I ever had in my life, and if I had had my own precious little beauty by my side & in my arms I would not have had it. But it will only be a little while now till I see her. After dinner went down town and bought a very handsome blue silk dress 153.00 at 4.50 per yard for Bess. It was what I had intended to put in a coat for myself & I would much prefer to see my wife with that on that to buy a coat I didn't need. I know she will scold me for my extravagance, but I don't think it is extravagance. I bought blue because she said a day or two before she left that she had a very pretty blue silk once & that it was very becoming & she would prefer a blue to another color. Came home & took tea & now after tea am writing this. Will read a while & then read the first chapter of 2nd Corinthians & go to bed to dream of Bess. I feel much better tonight than I have since my cold was contracted. Saw Mrs. Bolling today & she asked how my wife was, & asked me if she was in the family way. I told her I did not know that she had never hinted at the subject in any letter to me. Good night Bess.

June 2, 1866.

    Went down town & then went to the Post & got a letter from Bess a long one written the 27th. It was sweet & nice & all that, but she does not hold out much encouragement as far as her appearance is concerned. I am very much afraid she is not so well as usual. Then I bought two boxes of cigars from a man who was steward on a steamship, & he I suppose did not pay much duty on them from the price. Went to court & then to Parish prison to see two men who were charged with receiving stolen papers & books, but they did not pay well enough & I would not take there case. Then I came back & dropped into Roziers office & he showed me a note from Robt. B. James, very pointed & by my advice he answered it and I bore his answer. I was the party to blame, but they did not try to bluff me, for they were particularly polite. It was all amicably adjusted. Came home & felt awful homesick or wife sick & here I am writing away at this diary. I now think that I shall leave the 7th or the morning of the 8th. Margerite has just come with my clothes, & tea bell has rung. Was at Uncle Henrys tonight & Bradford & Mrs. Dreux came & I left. Will go to bed & then read & go to bed to wish for Bess. It is very warm, but a good breeze is blowing. I am so lonesome tonight, and I want my little wife so much. After tea, sister F. did not look so well tonight. She had been to the Kearney's. Jim was very hard on Jennie & sent her away from the tea table. I will close. They are practicing at the church.

June 3rd. Sunday. Blessed Day.

I got up late for breakfast. Went down to the Post & got a letter from Bess 28th. Answered & mailed the answer. Heard a sermon from Dr. Palmer on the 13th V. of 17th John. It was magnificent. Came home. Wrote a long letter to Bess and took a nap & then dined & pulled off my coat & pants & lay down on the bed till about 5½ & then went to see Uncle Henry a little while, & came home to tea & then went to church. It was very warm in church. The text was from 2nd V. of 2nd Ephesn. It was a very good sermon. Came home at 10 o'clock & drank a tall ice water & wrote this & now I will finish the day by readg. chap. & say my prayers & go to bed. I am better today than usual. Good night.

June 4th 1866.

Went down town. Fine morning. Got a letter of my wife the 29th. She was very much provoked because she had not heard from me for sevl. days, and it is provoking to think I write every day & she does not get them. I then went to a Justices Court to attend to a bill filed about a bond & listened to two long winded & stupid speeches from the Ajax & Achilles of a Justices Court. Went to the 4th Court & had a motion to answer & then had atta: issued for witnesses in the 3rd Court but the case went over till next term. Went to my office in the morning about 10. It rained & stormed. It is now only about 8 days at farthest till I shall have her in my arms. After dinner went & sat a while with Uncle Henry and went down town & returned at 9:45. Read chapter & went to bed.

June 5th 1866.

Another day has passed, & I am here far away from all that I love best. I have been busy today & have taken a little cold, for I have a cold & pain in my back & limbs, but I am better since dinner. The dinner was one of those interminable stupid kinds that make me fidgetty. I had my hair shingled off & it is much more comfortable. The handsome Charles is out on the gallery looking in & smiling. I think I shall send to Popes for some Blue Lick water & drink a quantity. I think I will stay at home tonight & rest my tired bones. This night one yr. ago I was at the first stopping place from Tuscaloosa, with Susan & Bess, and tomorrow night one year, was the "Atterberry" night. Good night. I have read the chapters.

June 6th 1866.

Went down town after breakfast feeling pretty well, but after going to court & attending to a good deal of business, came to office & went out & as soon as I went out I felt chilly & cold the day was very warm. Came home to get a paper. Went back with a chill on me & at my office was taken very sick. Came home with a raging fever. Mrs. Fee was very kind, took a hot foot bath & sent for Dr. Jones. The foot bath made me have a profuse perspiration, & this relieved the height of my fever. I was quite sick till 10 o'clock when I commenced taking quinine under Jones direction. Slept tolerable well. Took quinine during the night every three hours, said my prayers in the night, did not read the chapters.

June 7th 1866.

I am in my room at 10½ this morning feeling much better, but remaining in until after my chill hour. Anna G. was in to see me last night & Mt. Singleton & this morning Uncle Henry called. I am perspiring profusely & think that the quinine will keep the chill off. This chill has delayed my departure. I intended leaving this P.M. for Mobile, but will not leave till tomorrow or next day, until I feel better. Wrote to Bess today. Didn't say anything about my being sick. The Dr. came & said I was better &c. I missed my chill & went down town, staid a little while, but did not feel well & came home, and remained till after dinner on the bed. Then took a short walk. Came home, & Mrs. Fee read to me for two hours till bed time.

June 8th 1866.

Went down town after breakfast for I felt right well having slept sweetly & soundly till 3 o'clock when I got up & took a dose of quinine, and waked about 6 o'clock. Ate a very light breakfast, went to my office, & transacted some business & then went to Post, but got no letter from anyone & I was considerably disappointed.

Came home at 11 o'clock but I lay down & felt better. Then ate a lunch & drank cup of tea & Eliza packed my trunk & I read the Black Dwarf. After dinner went down town & felt so much better. Returned early, and am writing this. I wrote but forgot to mail a letter to Bess. I will go to bed early. It is very warm. We had a shower this P.M. I will read chapter tonight.

Author's Note. The last diary entry coincides with Given's leaving for Mobile where he is reunited with Bess.

Epilogue

The following funeral sermon was preached by Dr. John Cannon over the remains of Given Campbell on November 22, 1906, at the Grand Avenue Presybterian Church, St. Louis, Mo.

In one of the oldest books of the Bible the Patriarch Job asks two great questions concerning death. First, he says, (Job 14:10) "Man dieth and is laid low; yea, man giveth up the ghost, and where is he?" That is a question concerning the immortality of the soul, and the condition of the dead. When the body perishes, does the real man still live, and if so in what state? Next he asks (14:14), "If a man die, shall he live again?" That is a question concerning the resurrection of the body. When the union between body and spirit has been dissolved by death, is the dissolution final? Or will the union be restored? In that age these questions had not received their full answer. This Old Testament saint was gropping after an answer through the dim light of nature, and a partial revelation. The full and satisfying answer is siven by our Lord Jesus Christ when he says, "I am the Resurrection and the Life." He is the resurrection of the body, and the life of the undying spirit. Not only does he reveal the facts of a future resurrection and a life beyond the grave; but He is Himself their Author and Source. In Him resides the power by which the dead will be raised, and He is the Source of a life which is spiritual and eternal in its nature. To all who are joined to Him by a living faith there is sure promise of a glorious resurrection and a blessed immortality. Because he lives, we shall live also. The life of the Head ensures the life of the members. He has achieved victory over death, not only for Himself, but also for His people. So that for such, "There is no death; what seems so is transition." It is but the gateway to life eternal. The soul released from its earthly tabernacle goes to be "Forever with the Lord;" the body sleeps in the grave until the resurrection morning.

These are the truths which give us comfort as we lay away our dead, and I would that the present occasion might impress them deeply upon the hearts of all who are here.

The character of this assembly gives evidence that our friend who has fallen asleep filled no small place in the life and activity of this Community. His natural gifts, his culture, his public spirit and forcefulness of character made him a strong factor in many departments of our City's life. For this reason his name will be honored among us, and his memory will not be allowed to die. Many of us knew and valued him as a friend. He had a rare faculty for friendship. His genial and generous disposition, his chivalrous bearing, his strength and trueness of character invited friendships and securely held them. As a friend we shall ever hold him in loving remembrance.

But that of which we think with most satisfaction today is the fact that he met death in the confidence of a certain faith, and in the comfort of a sure and reasonable religious hope. He was a God-fearing man. He believed in "God the Father Almighty, and in Jesus Christ His only Son our Lord." The great verities of the Christian religion he held with a firm and unwavering faith. The doubts with which so many dally, the winds of doctrine by which so many are tossed about had no effect on him. He found that in the Gospel of Jesus Christ which satisfied the demands of his intellect as well as the craving of his heart. His piety was not of a demonstrative kind. Too much, we sometimes thought, he shrank from any public part in religious worship or work. But whenever his Christian faith was challenged it answered with a true ring.

In the relation which for some years I was permitted to sustain toward him, I discovered that the simplest presentation of Gospel truth was that which most appealed to him. When the great Dr. Guthrie lay on his death-bed, he said to those about him: "Sing me one of the bairns' songs." The simple hymns through which the faith of childhood is expressed were what he wished in that hour to express his faith, and the attitude of his soul toward God. That is the right spirit for us all. "Whosoever shall not receive the kingdom of God as a little child shall in no wise enter therein." Hence it is not surprising that our friend in his last illness dwelt most frequently on that simple shepherd psalm, "The Lord is my Shepherd, I shall not want."

Mr. Campbell had long cherished a plan that, when he reached a certain age, he would retire from active business and spend the evening of his life in a quiet home in his native state. That hope was realized, but its fruition was brief. Only for a few months was he permitted to occupy that home. How sad the ending would be if he had cherished no higher or more far-reaching hope! But how small the disappointment if he could say as we are assured that he could, "For we know that if the earthly house of our tabernacle be dissolved, we have a building from God, a house not made with hands, eternal, in the heaven!" "The righteous hath hope in his death." All men have hopes in life. But too many are living without any hope that will survive the grave. Their hopes are all bounded by the life that now is. Like the lamps of the foolish virgins they go out at the very time when they are most needed—the midnight hour, when the cry is heard, "Behold, the Bridegroom cometh."

Let me then beg you all, in this solemn and impressive presence, to seek a portion of which death cannot rob you: to make sure of a hope which takes hold on that within the veil, and which, like an anchor, will be your stay amid the storms and trials of life, and your comfort in the hour of death.

Authors Note: As Dr. Cannon instructed the congregation that November 22nd, "...and his memory will not be allowed to die," we believe this book will last as a testament to Given Campbell— the soldier, the lawyer, the husband, and the friend.